Sir Richard Posnett's long and distinguished career of overseas service began as a District Officer in Uganda where he rose to head the new Foreign Service at independence and later returned as British High Commissioner. He also served at the United Nations, in the Pacific and in the West Indies, became Governor of Belize and then Bermuda.

Chairman of the Uganda Olympic Committee, student of Islamic Law, keen Mountaineer and a member of the Royal Institute of International Affairs, he was knighted in 1980.

'Most of all I owe to my wife:
few know what she has endured for her country.'

(High Commissioner in Kampala to Secretary of
State for Foreign and Commonwealth Affairs)

THE SCENT OF EUCALYPTUS

A Journal of Colonial and Foreign Service

Richard Posnett

The Radcliffe Press
London · New York

Published in 2001 by The Radcliffe Press
Reprinted in 2003
6 Salem Road, London W2 4BU
175 Fifth Avenue, New York NY 10010

In the United States and Canada
distributed by Palgrave Macmillan,
a division of St. Martin's Press
175 Fifth Avenue, New York NY 10010

ISBN 1-86064-637-9

A full CIP record for this book is available from the British Library
A full CIP record for this book is available from the Library of Congress

Library of Congress Catalog card: available

Produced digitally by Bookchase (UK) Ltd

Contents

Maps and Illustrations

Maps

Illustrations

Acronyms and Abbreviations

AAA	Amateur Athletic Association
ADC	assistant district commissioner
AO	agricultural officer
BOAC	British Overseas Airways Corporation
BPC	British Phosphate Commissioners
CBE	Commander of the Order of the British Empire
CMS	Church Missionary Society
CRO	Commonwealth Relations Office
CSI	Church of South India
CWP	Charles Walker Posnett
DC	district commissioner
DFC	Distinguished Flying Cross
DMO	district medical officer
DO	district officer
ECOSOC	Economic and Social Council of the UN
FAO	Food and Agriculture Organization
FCO	Foreign and Commonwealth Office
FO	Foreign Office
GOC	General Officer Commanding
HE	His Excellency
HMG	Her Majesty's Government
HMY	Her Majesty's Yacht

HRH	His Royal Highness
IAEA	International Atomic Energy Agency
ICAO	International Civil Aviation Organization
ILO	International Labour Organization
IMCO	Intergovernmental Maritime Consultative Organization
IOC	International Olympic Committee
KAR	King's African Rifles
MO	medical officer
NA	native administration
NCO	non-commissioned officer
OC	Officer Commanding
ODA	Overseas Development Administration
OP	observation post
Pan Am	Pan American World Airlines
RC	Roman Catholic
RM	resident magistrate
SABENA	Belgian airline
SAS	Special Air Service
SNOWI	Senior Naval Officer West Indies
SOE	Special Operations Executive
SS	steamship
SS	sleeping sickness, trypanosomiasis
SW	stern-wheeler
U-boat	German submarine
UNO	United Nations Organization
WAAF	Women's Auxiliary Air Force
WHO	World Health Organization

Glossary

askari	constable, soldier
banya	cannibal
Birigi	Belgians
boma	district commissioner's office
botlass	small black fly
choo	latrine
dirili	hornet
diwan	assembly, council (in West Africa)
duka	shop
guayabera	loose-fitting Mexican style shirt
hodi	hello
jembe	hoe
Kabaka	ruler of Buganda
Katikkiro	Prime Minister of Buganda
Khedive	Viceroy of Egypt
kuku	hen
lukiiko	assembly, council (in Buganda)
Mahdi	Sudanese spiritual leader
mailo	system of land tenure in Buganda
Mukama	ruler of Bunyoro
murram	laterite
mwalim	teacher
namaste	Indian greeting with both hands together
Nizam	ruler of Hyderabad
Omulamuzi	Chief Justice of Buganda

posho	corn meal
puja	Indian religious rite
putti	coracle made of mud-covered basketwork
rwot	prince, chief
shamba	garden, farm
salongo	father of twins
tiffin	a light meal
toto	child
toto jikoni	kitchen boy
Wakil	sub-chief

Foreword by The Rt Hon The Lord Owen

The British Empire did not end, as many believe, in 1947 with India and Pakistan becoming independent. Only in 1957 did Ghana become the first of the British colonies in Africa to gain independence. It is easy to forget that at the start of the 1960s the Commonwealth had only nine members whereas 30 years later it had over 50. We administered the transition with the Commonwealth Relations Office taking over the Colonial Office in 1966 and then itself being merged into the Foreign Office in 1967.

This is the fascinating story of how Richard Posnett began his career as assistant district commissioner in Uganda in 1941 and then transferred into being a diplomat finishing up as Governor of Bermuda in 1983. His period of service covered an amazing period in British history and there are, in his highly readable account, many insights and lessons to be learnt from an immensely varied experience.

I was fortunate as Foreign Secretary to be well advised by Richard Posnett, first on financial compensation for the Banabans from Ocean Island in the Western Pacific who had suffered from the mining of phosphate; and second when I sent him, at 36 hours' notice, back to Uganda to liaise with an old friend of his, Yusuf Lule, who was heading up a government in exile in Tanzania prior to the ousting of General Amin. For me personally his mission was of crucial importance for I had stretched my own legal authority to the absolute limit by helping Julius Nyerere finance and mount his military operation to invade Uganda on the grounds that Amin's monstrous human rights record was by far the greater evil. I needed, however, to ensure that Uganda did not become a satellite of Tanzania. Richard Posnett, as our newly established High Commissioner, played, in those first few months, a crucial role in that task.

This book will, however, resonate not for the big political picture, but for the much-needed balance it brings back to the British decolonization record. As the African continent becomes, at the turn of the twenty-first century, the despair of all those who love it, the only way forward is for Africans to rediscover the virtues of sound administration. Hopefully that will be this book's legacy.

Preface

Five thousand years ago a remote ancestor of mine was living a life of unremitting hardship. His prime concern was survival in the face of famine, cold, battle and disease. Written language was unknown to him. Maybe he scratched with a stick to make a figure in the dust. He learned from his mother and father, from his companions and from hard experience. He knew nothing of his origins beyond his immediate parents. He taught his children how to survive but had no thought of his future descendants. He knew only the small part of the world in which he lived. The excitement of the hunt may have been his only recreation but even that was a matter of subsistence. Perhaps there were moments when he was able to enjoy some simple pleasure, but he would not have known what was meant by happiness. Life, he assumed, was always like that and, if he thought about it at all, would always be so.

Now, a mere 150 generations later, there are millions of his descendants scattered about the world, bearing some of the genes that he passed on. And in that short period of human history life has changed out of recognition, not just in its physical qualities but in the power of our brains to understand the world we inhabit. We can read; we can calculate; we can travel. We can be moved listening to Beethoven or watching a sunrise. We can identify the stars. We know about our origins and we can ponder the future. We can actively seek happiness, for ourselves and for our fellow men.

All these riches have accumulated within only a brief span of time. And in the last 100 years the pace of growth of our understanding has accelerated so that what was science fiction in my boyhood is now accomplished technology.

At the same time the world has been changing its political shape and nowhere has this been more noticeable than in Africa and some other parts of the so-called 'third world'. It has been my good fortune to spend most of my life in just those countries where the upheaval of change has been most evident and to be involved in some exciting moments in the history of Britain's colonial empire and of its dismantling.

This book tells of some of the adventures that have befallen me. Whether exciting, funny or sad they have provided the spice of life. And those I have met along the way, people I have known, have worked with, have loved, it is they who have been my inspiration and my good fortune.

Acknowledgements

I owe more debts of gratitude than I can hope to repay or to mention here.

It was Anthony Kirk-Greene whose persistent encouragement, not to say pressure, persuaded me to draw together some isolated tales of overseas adventure into the form of a book about life at the sharp end of government. I thank him: it has proved a rewarding experience to summon up recollections of people and places that had sunk below the horizon of memory but fortunately not beyond recall.

I thank my son Jonathan in New York for his design of the book's jacket despite the vicissitudes of communication across the ocean.

1

The Scent of Eucalyptus

There are moments in life when a flash of inspiration may, if one is fortunate, light up the way ahead. Feeling and thought suddenly coalesce and determine with absolute certainty the course of our future. That happened to me one spring morning at school when, leaning out of the window of an empty classroom, I caught the unmistakable scent of eucalyptus. All at once I was carried back to my childhood, to the house where I was born and raised among eucalyptus trees in the Nilgiri Hills of south India. And at the same moment I knew with blinding clarity where my future life lay.

I was 14 years old. It was to India that my thoughts turned and when I told my father, who had spent his life there, he was quick to understand. Realizing that I was not cut out for the church he warned me that, by the time I was ready to embark on a career, the administration of India would be in the hands of Indians. Instead of the Indian Civil Service, he advised me to think of Africa and the Colonial Service. The die was cast: from that moment I never doubted the course I was to follow.

* * *

My great-grandfather Leonard was a Methodist minister in Yorkshire. Three of his four sons followed him into the Church. The youngest, born in 1831, was Robert, my grandfather. He became the Methodist minister in Sheffield Brightside and married Mary Walker of the leather tanning family from Cumbria. Early photographs show him with a long beard and a flat black hat and Mary as a woman of great beauty. Robert forbade his wife to use her own money so their children were brought up accustomed to straitened circumstances. Two of the older boys, Robert and William, set out to atone for this in later life by becoming millionaire tanners in their own right.

My father Charles Walker was born in 1870: the youngest of five boys, he had to wear his brothers' cast-off breeches even after he was sent away to boarding school. Kingswood, founded by John Wesley, offered places to the sons of Methodist ministers at reduced rates. My father left a watercolour of the school façade, done at the age of 16 which shows a grasp of architecture and draughtsmanship that he put to good use in later life. After studies at Richmond Theological College, he set out to become a missionary in India. He landed in Madras in 1895 and was sent up to Hyderabad in the Nizam's Dominions, now Andhra Pradesh. After a year during which he learned Telugu, the local language, he was moved to a village called Medak, 60 miles away near a prominent rocky hill on which earlier rulers had built a fort. There, in due course, he was appointed superintendent of the Methodist mission station.

Medak lay in a poverty-stricken area of subsistence farming subject to periodic drought and famine and surrounded by tiger-infested jungle through which my father made his way by bullock cart. The people were mostly from the untouchable class of outcastes. CWP, as my father widely came to be known, saw at once their need not only for food, education and medical assistance but also for spiritual solace from the degraded position assigned to them below the bottom of the Hindu caste hierarchy. He saw that their children must learn to read and write, and that a mission must offer them relief from the worst scourges of disease, notably leprosy. From these decisions there arose over the years the mission station in Medak with its schools and hospital.

In due course, he started work on the design and building of the great church, now a cathedral of the Church of South India which gave to the converted outcastes a temple of their own, larger and grander than anything the Muslims or caste Hindus enjoyed. For this immense project in the jungle, where he had only primitive transport, he enlisted his brother Robert to help find much of the finance in England. During a serious famine in 1916, he managed to import rice and offered it to local people if they would work for him on building the church. It took ten years to finish and, on Christmas Day 1924, it was formally opened.

Soon after starting work in Medak, CWP was writing to his parents about the need for a doctor at the mission. His sister Emily was at that time studying medicine at the London Hospital, where she was the first female student. Cutting short her studies to go out to India, Aunt Em arrived in Medak accompanied by a nurse, her lifelong friend Sallie Harris. These two proceeded to set up a medical centre, making up in energy and determination what they lacked in formal qualifications and proper facilities. They spent the rest of their working lives in India.

Furlough came round only every five years and my father made good use of these infrequent opportunities. In 1906, with typical enterprise, he took ship from India to Hong Kong and Japan and thence across the Pacific to San Francisco where he arrived while fires were still burning after the devastating earthquake. The long train journey to New York and an Atlantic crossing brought him home at last.

For his next furlough in 1911 he went directly to England where he met the Barker family in Cheshire and set his eyes on their daughter Phyllis. His courtship must have flustered her: walking down a street after rain he picked her up and carried her across a puddle of water. She did not immediately accept his proposal of marriage and confided in her best friend Dorothy, who tried to dissuade her:

'I would *never* marry a missionary,' she declared.

But two years later they found themselves both living in the same mission compound in India. Dorothy had married another missionary, Gordon Bennett.

My mother was quite a tearaway for her time. She had flaming red hair and, if boys teased her, they were likely to be punched by her twin brother Aubrey, who was always her close friend and protector. She had a good eye for a ball and played centre forward for the north of England in regional hockey matches. Both supporters and opponents knew of her as 'the red devil' on account of her hair.

Her father, John Lees Barker, was a Manchester stockbroker who rejoiced in having one of the first motorcars in the area, in which he used to drive with her to matches to cheer her on. If he wondered about housing for his daughter in the wilds of India, he would have been surprised to see the big two-storey house my father built at Medak with rooms 12 feet high and a spacious upstairs verandah. It became known as the Big Bungalow (which just means 'house' in Hindi.) For a young woman who had lived a sheltered life, the sudden change — marriage, a voyage to India, and having to take charge of a large house and staff in a strange land far from her own friends and family — it must have been a dazzling yet daunting experience. She had to learn Telugu with its strange script. She tried to create a garden in sandy soil in a difficult climate, and she became at once the hostess for the whole mission community. She was also relied upon for music and played the organ for services, at first a primitive harmonium but later, once the great church had been built, a substantial pipe organ. This involved learning the Telugu words to fit the tunes and the notes she made in her hymnbook survive.

Their first child, Aubrey, was born in 1913, followed three years later by a girl, Molly. The strain of child-bearing and of long years in India during wartime, when it became impossible to return to Europe, turned my mother's hair from auburn to white; but her spirit and her sense of fun never deserted her.

Medak, lying in the centre of the subcontinent, suffers extremes of climate and the temperature can rise to 120 degrees Fahrenheit in the hot weather. During those periods, my mother and the children were sent south to Kotagiri, 8000 feet up in the Nilgiri Hills, and there I was born on the morning of 19 July 1919. No sooner had I emerged, than Aunt Em, who presided at the function, was heard to observe 'Isn't nature wonderful!' — a sentiment that annoyed my mother at that particular juncture.

Childhood in India

The house in Kotagiri was set among eucalyptus blue-gum trees, and small branches from these would be laid under our beds at night to protect us from colds or possibly mosquitoes. The scent has ever since evoked for me a powerful nostalgia. Eucalyptus logs would burn in the grate during the evenings which could be cold up there. The house stood on a low ridge from which a driveway led down to the main road. It was down this driveway that, a few years later, I sped on my new tricycle only to find that the brakes were not working. I took the left-hand corner at the bottom in a flurry of gravel, but managed to stay upright. My father, who was watching from the top, observed: 'My word, Dick, I thought you'd gone to kingdom come!'

The two-day train journey from Medak to the hills was exciting for a boy. Lying in my bunk I watched the rhythmic rise and fall of the telegraph wires between their poles as the train swept along. I imagined that the driver steered the engine and puzzled over how he kept it on the rails. The train would eventually halt at Mettupalayam, from where we could see the mountains looming above us. There we changed to the narrow-gauge mountain railway that climbs 7000 feet up to Ootacamund, known as Ooty.

My brother Aubrey was sent back to school in England when I was still a child and my sister Molly was my companion for my early years. We had a governess, Mary Bartlett, and it was with Barty, as we called her, that I learned my first law of physics. Out walking one day along a dirt road near Medak, we came to a boulder a few feet high. Barty produced a piece of string, tied a stone to one end, and draped it across the boulder, giving me the other end to hold. I found that by pulling my end of the string downwards I was able to make the stone move upwards. What supplied the force that pushed the stone upwards? The more I thought about this the more it puzzled me; it was then that I first felt an interest in physical phenomena.

Barty was succeeded by Jennie Key who took over our education. With childish malice we nicknamed her Hag on account of her scrawny neck but she adopted the name with glee and so won our love and respect. While out for a walk one day, we ventured off the road and came across two tiger cubs. We withdrew rapidly, wondering how close their mother was. Another time, Molly was chasing me round some bushes when I heard Hag shout 'jump'. I jumped — right over a coiled cobra fast asleep on the ground. Hag had seen it just in time.

Hag believed in stretching a young mind. As soon as I could read and write English reasonably well, we started on French and, by the time we returned to Europe when I was seven years old, I could converse simply in that language. On the first occasion I was taken into a shop in Marseilles, I created a mild sensation by announcing to the lady behind the counter: *'Je t'aime.'*

Accompanying my father on tour involved living in tents and riding ponies through the jungle. After one trip, on which we crossed the Godaveri River in a *putti*, a coracle made of mud-covered basketwork, my sister and I wrote an account of 'Our Tour in the Jungle'. This was later printed and used to help raise funds in England for mission work in India. My father wrote that this was 'quite their own composition and spelling', but I suspect we had a modicum of help.

My father had a remarkable gift for attracting the confidence of people of other religions beside his own. He had travelled in many parts of India, including Darjeeling in the foothills of the Himalayas, where he went to work undisturbed on the translation of the New Testament into Telugu. He visited Kashmir with Gordon Bennett, who on one occasion got cramp while they were swimming in the cold waters of a lake. CWP was a strong swimmer and he managed to pull Gordon to the bank.

Decorated by the Viceroy with the Kaiser-i-Hind medal, CWP left India in 1938 after 42 years' service. When the Nizam, ruler of Hyderabad, heard of his departure, he sent a special envoy to chase after him to Bombay to present him with his own personal decoration. Retired in England, he kept up a voluminous correspondence until his death in 1950, just short of his eightieth birthday.

When I returned to India 60 years later I found in the church at Medak a simple plaque which reads

CHARLES WALKER POSNETT K-i-H
'HE SAW WITH HIS HEART RATHER THAN WITH HIS EYES'

Boyhood in England and Germany

My sister and I came back to England with my mother in 1926. Barty rejoined us and kept me interested in science. To show that the gas used for cooking was lighter than air, she let me blow up balloons from the gas tap and send them off with labels asking the finder to return them. None I think got very far.

We acquired a car, thanks to Uncle Robert, which my mother learned to drive. She once coaxed it up to 40 miles per hour, where the speedometer stuck as if to record the achievement.

When Uncle Will came to visit he fished a half-crown coin from his pocket and proffered it to me. It was worth a good deal in those days, but I felt patronized and refused to take it. My parents were amused, pleased I suppose, that I should face up to Will who thought that money could buy anything.

Just before my ninth birthday, I went off to boarding school at Arnside in Westmorland. Earnseat was run by Mr and Mrs Barnes, Jimmy and Mum B to us. I was homesick among the strange ways and speech of the boys, most of them from the north. By a curious coincidence four of us from Earnseat were to find ourselves, ten years later, at the same college in Cambridge.

Jimmy used to read to us on Sunday evenings and I learned to enjoy Macaulay's *Lays of Ancient Rome* and the poems of Walter Scott. Several passages still echo through my mind like well-known tunes, such as the haunting coronach for a highland chief:

> He is gone on the mountain,
> He is lost to the forest,
> Like a summer dried fountain
> When our need was the sorest.
>
> Fleet foot on the correi,
> Sage counsel in cumber,
> Red hand in the foray,
> How deep is thy slumber.

I was also blessed with a good maths teacher, Mr Wright, whose guidance helped me to explore a world that has been a joy all my life.

I enjoyed games and soon found that I could run faster than the others; sports' day was like a benefit day for me.

The school overlooked the estuary of the River Kent and we used to watch the bore coming in as the tide turned. Trains would rumble noisily across the long viaduct on the line to Grange-over-Sands. Beyond the river we could see the foothills of the Lake District, where Jimmy used to take us for occasional outings to walk over the fells and round the tarns. This gave me a lasting love for the area. It was at Earnseat, while in bed with some childhood ailment, that I read a book by George Finch called *The Making of a Mountaineer*. Its tales of mountain climbs and an Everest expedition thrilled me. It may not be one of the classics, but its effect on me at the age of 11 was inspirational.

When I was given a bicycle my horizons expanded and from Reigate I explored far and wide, even riding up to London. My favourite haunt was Croydon airport, where I could watch the aeroplanes come and go. In the hangars I gazed at the different types of civil airliner, French, German and British. I was fascinated and bought flying magazines which I read from cover to cover, absorbing all the news and names. I listened spellbound to the radio reports of the Schneider Trophy races.

When my parents were in India I was taken one winter to Switzerland with Maurice Bennett, son of Gordon and Dorothy. There, at Chateau d'Oex, I put on skis for the first time. They had no metal edges nor any heel bindings. Once we had learned the basic 'stem', we went on to the Telemark turn and the 'open' Christiania. Maurice and I went out every day with *Monsieur le Guide*, as he was known. There were no ski lifts or pistes and, after a week or so, he took us on small tours that involved climbing on skins — real sealskins in those days. I loved this and became enthralled by the mountains. After that trip I took every opportunity to go to the Alps and ski.

At 13 I moved to Kingswood. Having been head boy at Earnseat and found exams easy, I was now a small fish in a sea full of bigger and brighter specimens. To live and work in such company was both stimulating and humbling. One thing I came to regret later was the streaming that required a choice to be made, even in the lower fifth form, between classical and modern courses. I chose 'modern' which included physics and chemistry, but this meant giving up Latin and missing out on Greek.

At Kingswood I found rugby a puzzling game. I was first assigned to the 'pack' with little idea what we were supposed to do. A broken collarbone put me out of the game for a season and when I returned I was given a place in the backs where I could run with the ball. Now I could see what the game was about and enjoyed it enormously.

I got to know Harold Berry, the senior maths master whose real enthusiasm was for athletics. He followed all the latest news and technical developments and he inspired me to try different events. I found I could win races over longer distances as well as sprints; and I also took up hurdling. One night we sat up late to listen to the radio commentary from New York on 'The Mile of the Century' when Jack Lovelock, a New Zealander, defeated Glenn Cunningham of the USA. Berry brought in Franz Stampfl from Austria for a coaching session: he was the man who later went on to Oxford to coach Roger Bannister.

At 14, propelled into the sixth form, I was again obliged to choose a main subject. The choice of maths was not difficult with physics to go with it, but it meant that I had to abandon, far too early, subjects like English and history which I have had to read up later in life. French was no great loss, for the teaching was indifferent, and as a bonus I was able to take up German as the language of some of the more advanced maths textbooks.

'The sons of intelligent paupers' was how Headmaster Sackett once described us pupils, not unfairly. This did not worry us: financial success was not a factor that entered into our calculations about future careers. My Uncle Will, who was a generous benefactor of the school, once gave an address in which he advised the boys to work hard in order, as he put it, 'to attract the special attention of the Chancellor of the Exchequer'. This materialist attitude was ill received: we were all idealists at that age. It was about that time that I came across Sir Arthur Eddington's book *The Nature of the Physical World*. Reading this was a galvanic experience and caused me to rethink my understanding of the world and of religious belief.

In 1936 my parents were in India so, in the summer holidays, I accompanied Berry, along with another boy, to the Olympic Games in

Berlin. Although we saw and heard Hitler at the Olympic stadium it was the athletics I found unforgettable. We saw the great British athlete Godfrey Brown lose by a foot in the 400 metres but victorious, with Roberts, Rampling and Wolff, in the 4×400 metres relay. Lovelock, an unknown in Germany, duly won the 1500 metres. And of course we saw the fabulous Jesse Owens. In the last round of the long jump, after the German Lutz Long had taken the lead, Owens had the final jump. Afterwards the announcer's voice trembled as he said:

'*Owens sprang acht Meter sechs — neue Weltrekord!*'

It was the first jump ever to exceed eight metres. Long behaved with proper sportsmanship. As far as we could see, the story of Hitler snubbing Owens after he won the 100 metres was a chimera created by the press after the war, a view Godfrey Brown later endorsed.*

The following year, a group from the sixth form spent a month at Ilfeld School in the Harz Mountains where we saw culture under the Nazis at first hand. We were taken on a trip to various parts of the area, listened to a speech by Hermann Göring in Goslar, and climbed the Brocken, home of the Valkyries in Wagner's opera. One visitor to the school was General von Lettow Vorbeck, who spoke to the boys about his adventures in East Africa during the First World War when he was commander of the German guerrilla force.

None of us really understood the appeal of Nazidom, though we could see how strongly it influenced our German contemporaries. On a school walk, I saw a notice outside a village saying '*Juden sind hier unerwünscht*' (Jews not wanted here). It was only later that I realized its significance.

When a group from Ilfeld came the next year on a return visit to Kingswood, I was assigned to look after a boy called Ribbentrop, the son of the German ambassador in London who later became Hitler's Foreign Minister. One day, the boy departed without notice and we

---

* In a letter to me he wrote, 'I think all the rubbish about the Hitler–Owens affair stems from the fact that it is viewed in the hindsight of Owens' four gold medals. There was obviously no case for his receiving special treatment after winning the first.'

wondered why. We knew little of the growing political tension in Europe.

Under Berry, Kingswood sent a team each year to the Public School Sports in London. By 1938 we had a powerful squad and became locked in an exciting contest for the trophy for top school in England. In the end we tied with King Edward's School, Birmingham. After that I entered the AAA junior championships at White City and managed second place in the high hurdles. The prizes were presented by Lord Burghley, the great Olympic hurdles champion: our paths were to cross again in later life.

With all these diversions my studies were neglected and my teacher doubted if I could manage university. He suggested that I might as well look for a job at the labour exchange, but my father found this advice unacceptably defeatist. In the event, I was accepted by St John's College at Cambridge.

Meanwhile, the shadows of war had been lengthening with the unpleasant prospect that we might soon be asked to kill fellow human beings, including our German friends from Ilfeld. One had to think the unthinkable and I was torn with pacifist feelings. When Neville Chamberlain came back from Munich with the promise of 'peace in our time', I felt enormous relief, shared, I think, by most of the population. We may have been short-sighted but, if Britain's people had not shown their primary dedication to peace then, I wonder if they would later have proved so dogged in fighting aggression. Glad anyway to put the war out of my mind, I sent in my preliminary application for the Colonial Service.

My sister had introduced me to ballet and I loved the amalgam of music, movement and colour. Wanting to emulate the great male dancers' feats of elevation I joined a ballet class, and I formed a ballet society at Cambridge. The local newspaper took me on as its ballet correspondent which gave me access to press seats at Covent Garden when the Russian ballet was performing. There I got to meet the principal dancers and interviewed the great dancer and choreographer, Leonid Massine. I spent part of my winter vacation working with a small ballet company in London but my father, not surprisingly, thought poorly of this.

At the end of the year I scrambled third-class honours in part one of the maths tripos and knew I was getting out of my depth. After talking with my father in the summer of 1939, I switched reluctantly to law and started to pore over books on Roman law and other mysteries; but the intellectual satisfaction of maths was missing.

Then war was declared. I volunteered for the RAF but was told to carry on at Cambridge until called for. Another academic year passed with a second-class result in law and a dead heat with my partner Frank Nicholson to win the hurdles in the Oxford v. Cambridge athletics match. In the summer of 1940 I set off with Philip Halliday from St John's and Earnseat for the Lake District where we joined another college friend Denys Hall and worked for a few weeks at a sawmill near Hawkshead. There, at last, I received my call-up papers: I was to report at Torquay in two weeks' time. It was June 1940. The end of childhood had arrived.

Flying

At the induction centre in Torquay I was glad to find an old friend, David Beaty from Kingswood, who later acquired fame as a novelist. Also on our course was a lawyer from Cambridge, Geoffrey Lane, who was later to become Lord Chief Justice of England. After a month learning how to march and salute, Morse code, elementary meteorology and even some simple maths, we were sent off north in a blacked-out train to Prestwick in Scotland. Protracted halts at remote stations we attributed to the engine driver, unfamiliar with this route, having to stop to ask the way.

After my boyhood enthusiasm for flying, it was a thrill to climb into the cockpit of a DH Tiger Moth. Everything seemed familiar and, after making a few turns, my instructor asked me where I had flown before. After seven hours dual, he sent me off solo. I loved the freedom of movement in three dimensions and enjoyed aerobatics and the Immelmann turn, about which I had read so often in stories of the First World War. I liked to fly upside own over the seafront at Prestwick. However, the Tiger Moth had a gravity fuel feed from a tank in the upper wing so that, when inverted, the engine would cut out and petrol would dribble out of the fuel gauge as one glided quietly down. Fortunately, it was not difficult, with a bit of a dive, to restart the engine in flight.

After six weeks at Prestwick, we were all sent back south, this time to South Cerney in Gloucestershire where we learned to fly twin-engined Oxford trainers. Those who had expressed a preference for single-seat fighters were disappointed, but at this stage in the war it was a mass-production system to train pilots. After practising cross-country navigation and blind flying, we came to night flying.

To avoid attracting enemy aircraft to the main airfield, we used a subsidiary field at night with a grass strip 'lit' by four goose-necked flares. After three circuits and landings with an instructor, I was sent off solo: climb to 1000 feet; turn 90 degrees left; check to see the flares over one's left shoulder. No flares! An enemy attack? In that case the flares would have been switched off. I searched the horizon again, looked up, and there above my head were the flares. A glance at the instruments told its own story: I was half inverted. Yanking the plane level, I broke out in a cold sweat. 'Watch the instruments,' I reminded myself. Downwind leg, flash code letter on belly light, back comes Aldis light clearance to land. I turn crosswind and then onto final approach down the line of flares. Suddenly, the aircraft begins to shudder violently — the sign of a stall. I ram the nose down and the throttles open, just in time. I had taken my eye off the airspeed indicator. A few more circuits to settle my nerves, then back into the crew room. It did not surprise me that one or two pilots were lost on these courses.

One day near the end of 1940, I was summoned to see the station adjutant. Orders had been received that I was to proceed to London for an interview at the Colonial Office. He handed me a travel warrant. I was taken aback. The next morning, instead of flying I found myself, a mere leading aircraftman, in the back seat of a Humber staff car being driven by a WAAF to Cirencester to catch the train to London. Finding my way to Whitehall, I presented myself at the Colonial Office. A guard checked my name and I was shown upstairs to a large waiting room. There I found a dozen servicemen in uniform. Others followed me in. Most of them were officers, some from the army, a few from the navy, and one other airman. They all seemed as flummoxed as I felt: a few questions revealed that all of us had applied in the past for the Colonial Administrative Service.

We were shown into a high-ceilinged room with portraits of former ministers on the walls, and offered a glass of sherry. Before the fireplace stood a greying gentleman who introduced himself as Lord Lloyd, Secretary of State for the Colonies in Mr Churchill's government. He began to speak and explained that it was important for Britain during the war to maintain control of its colonial empire for both strategic and economic reasons. This needed administrative officers. Each of us there had earlier applied and been accepted in principle for such posts. Now, the government needed us in the field in that capacity.

He realized, he said, that we might be reluctant to leave our respective units in the armed forces at a time when the country was facing a fierce enemy and even possible invasion, a feeling he entirely understood. It was for that reason that he had asked us there to meet him in person. However, in wartime, hard decisions had to be made and the government was satisfied that we, the small group in that room, could best serve the country by going to the various colonies to which we had been allocated and where we were needed. It was not intended to compel us against our will and if we declined the assignment we could return to our units and it would not be counted against us. But, speaking on behalf of His Majesty's Government, he wanted us to know that it was in the colonies that our duty was thought to lie. He hoped that, despite any personal misgivings, we would accept the appointments offered to us.

We trooped out in silence, perplexed and uncertain. In my own case, I was not only committed to the RAF but I loved flying. The thought of giving all that up and seeming to desert my RAF friends tortured me. I went home for the night and talked to my father. He observed that in wartime we all had to do what the government asked. And, knowing that the Colonial Service had long been my objective, he thought it would not make sense to refuse the government's request now.

I returned forlornly to South Cerney to pack up my kit and say goodbye. It was one of the most painful decisions I ever had to make and I am still sometimes haunted by memories of those of my friends who went on to be killed in action.

I was assigned to Uganda and told to await travel instructions.

2

Africa: First Footsteps

It was a cold January night in 1941 when the SS *Matiana*, an ageing British India liner of some 15,000 tons, sailed from Liverpool. I found myself sharing a cabin with two other men destined for the Colonial Service in Kenya. We were heading for Cape Town and had no convoy, so there was a sense of serious reality about our lifeboat drills. We slept in our clothes with life belts at hand, ready to move.

Our course took us round the north coast of Ireland and out into the Atlantic before we turned south. It was a relief to leave the bitter cold as we ran into longer warmer days, albeit an easier target for any lurking U-boats. As we approached the tropics we were surprised to learn that our first port of call would be the Cape Verde islands. A visit ashore left an impression of poverty and dirt among undernourished inhabitants in a landscape with little attraction.

As we moved into south latitudes, our concern for U-boats relaxed. We saw no other ships. Then, one morning, straight ahead, the distinctive flat top of Table Mountain lifted over the horizon. Our stay in Cape Town was short but I grabbed the opportunity to take the cable car to the top of Table Mountain.

Round the Cape of Good Hope, we skirted the coastal hills of South Africa up to Durban. From there we steamed up the Mozambique

Map of Uganda

Channel and back into the tropics until we finally berthed in Mombasa and disembarked. An Indian officer from the Government Coast Agent saw us through immigration and customs; and there, waiting for us, was our train. A reserved compartment with sleeping berths, a well-appointed restaurant car: no jungle hardships yet. On the voyage I had begun to learn contract bridge and we settled down to a game. A lady came in and expostulated: we should be looking out at our first glimpse of Africa. Quite right! She turned out to be the wife of a Kenya Provincial Commissioner.

The next morning we needed no encouragement. The train was crossing the rolling Athi plains and several blasts on the whistle alerted us to a group of browsing giraffe near the track. A little later the train slowed: there, in the shade of a thorn tree, was a pride of lions. Soon we steamed into Nairobi, an unattractive medley of galvanized iron sheds as seen from the train. We were met and taken to the New Stanley Hotel which was to be my base for a couple of days until the next train left for Uganda, and for my friends until they received their respective assignments.

Meanwhile, some kind person had arranged a game of golf at Muthaiga. Walking down the fairway, I suddenly caught sight of the unmistakable silhouette of Mount Kenya 100 miles away to the north with the glacier clearly visible between its twin peaks. When I exclaimed in wonder, our host tapped me on the shoulder and asked me to turn around. Looking in the opposite direction, I was amazed to see, floating above the clouds far to the south, the glistening snows of Kilimanjaro.

The next day I boarded the train again for Kampala. This must be the most wonderful train journey in the world and I was soon spellbound. As the train wound its way slowly up towards Limuru, African *totos* (children) raced alongside, easily able to keep pace with us. I remember thinking that these were Olympic athletes of the future, shades of Jesse Owens whom I remembered in Berlin.

Suddenly the train swung round a curve and there, below us, lay the stupendous expanse of the Rift Valley with the volcano Longonot rising up from its floor. The train came down to Kijabe before it set off across the valley floor to Naivasha, with its lake covered in pink flamingos. By evening, we drew into Nakuru where I had time to inspect the huge double-ended Bayer Garrett locomotive. Its power would be needed for the next sector in which the track climbs to Mau Summit at over 9000 feet. But, by that time, I was asleep in my bunk.

Uganda

Morning, and I awoke to a green landscape and courteous border officials as we crossed into Uganda. Past Tororo Rock jutting up into the sky, the train rolled on to Jinja and my first glimpse of Lake Victoria and the Ripon Falls, where the White Nile starts its long 3600 mile journey to the Mediterranean. By afternoon, we were in Kampala where I was met and taken to stay with A. O. Jenkins, the deputy Provincial Commissioner, and his wife.

They told me that I had been posted as an assistant District Commissioner to the West Nile district in the far northwest of the country, with headquarters at Arua. Meanwhile, I would have a couple of days to arrange my affairs, open a bank account, make some necessary household purchases and take on a cook and a servant — this last on the advice of my hostess who only knew of the West Nile by its rather daunting repute. I did not realize that the two Baganda whom I recruited would face tribal and language difficulties among the tribesmen of the West Nile which the Baganda regarded as an appallingly primitive area. Trofima Lwanga became my head boy, a combination of butler and valet. He proved charming and able, though he was never happy away from his own area near Kampala. I learned later that he was the father of twins and so entitled, among his own people, to the honorific *Salongo*. The cook was a fierce looking fellow with no front teeth, but he never settled down in the West Nile. Trofima spoke hardly any English, the cook none at all.

My father had asked me while in Kampala to call on Sir Albert Cook, the missionary doctor who had set up the first hospital at Mengo about the turn of the century. He had walked the whole way from the coast, 800 odd miles, before the railway was built — at about the same time as my father was riding in a bullock cart through India to Medak. They had corresponded over the years, but had never actually met. Sadly I have no recollection of my meeting with Sir Albert.

In due course, I set off in a government van with Trofima and the cook, and all our belongings. As the driver spoke no English, I could not ask about the various sights of interest along the dusty *murram* road. (*Murram* is a reddish laterite soil that makes an excellent hard road surface, even when wet.) We pounded along for several hours and it was not till afternoon that we arrived in Masindi, then the headquarters of the Northern Province, where I was to stay for two days. There I met Folliot Hugh Blakelock Sandford, the Provincial Commissioner — a soft-looking man of academic bent who seemed out of place as an administrative officer in Africa. His wife Jacqueline was a very different character, tall, good looking and dynamic.

From Masindi my route lay westwards to Lake Albert and I was offered a lift in his car by a High Court judge who happened to be proceeding to the same destination on circuit, along with a Crown Counsel, Audley McKisack, who was to return years later as Chief Justice and became a good friend. The drive led through lush tropical forest until after an hour or so the road emerged onto grassland. Then, topping a rise, we were suddenly confronted with one of the most stupendous views. Far below us, glistening in the sun, lay the vast expanse of Lake Albert stretching away to the mountains rising sheer from the water on its western shore. That, I was told, was the Belgian Congo which extended for several thousand miles west to the Atlantic. To the south the lake swept into the hazy distance, where I was later to find the Ruwenzori mountains hiding in the clouds. Years later I read Sir Samuel Baker's story* of how, on 14 March 1864, he was the first westerner to set eyes on this scene:

'On the west at fifty or sixty miles' distance blue mountains rose from the bosom of the lake to a height of about 7000 feet above its level.'

What must have been his feelings?

At our feet, we could see the road, winding down the escarpment and running like a narrow ribbon to a little town and port where one could just make out the funnel of a tiny looking ship. That was Butiaba and the ship was the SS *Robert Coryndon*, named after a former Governor of Uganda. This was our transport across the lake and then northwards down the first 30 miles of the Albert Nile to

---

* *The Albert Nyanza*, vol. II, p. 89.

Pakwach on its west bank. That would be my first contact with the West Nile district which was to be my home, on and off, for the next eight years.

The *Coryndon* made the trip to Pakwach once a fortnight carrying the mail. From Pakwach passengers could either take the bus 86 miles up to Arua or proceed down the river on the stern-wheeler SW *Lugard* which was commanded by a bearded old Scot who lived, when not on board, in a house overlooking the wide expanse of the river at Pakwach. His job was to take the *Lugard* every fortnight down the river as far as Nimule on the Sudan border, pushing four large barges full of freight which were fastened in front of the ship.

I was advised to go down the river as far as Rhino Camp which the *Lugard* would reach next morning. The changeover at Pakwach was a bustle of activity, noise and humming mosquitoes. On the *Lugard*'s afterdeck I met two local planters, Jock Jardine and Bill Busby, about whom many stories were told. Bill had a wooden leg and had once accompanied the then District Commissioner, one Horatio Nelson (really!), to a council meeting at a place where the people were being difficult about planting their essential famine crops. Nelson had a glass eye and, at the conclusion of his harangue, he took it out of its socket and said: 'I shall leave my eye here to see that you obey.' Whereupon Bill unstrapped his wooden leg and said: 'And I shall leave my leg here to kick anybody who disobeys.' I found it hard to keep pace with Bill and Jock in consuming endless bottles of beer and, after dinner on board, was glad to find my bunk under a much-needed mosquito net.

I awoke early the next morning to find the *Lugard* steaming down the wide river between banks of impenetrable reed. We were soon approaching the landing stage at Rhino Camp where bales of cotton were piled high ready for loading onto barges. A few buildings of corrugated iron comprised the cotton ginnery and stores. Amidst the usual noisy crowd of Africans I saw one or two white faces. As soon as we had berthed a man came up to me and introduced himself as Eric Watts, an assistant District Commissioner who had come down from Arua to meet me. We had breakfast on board and then piled into Eric's old Ford tourer, 1933 vintage, leaving Trofima and the cook to come on by bus.

Eric had with him a game ranger who reported that white rhino had been seen within a mile of the road a few miles back from the river. We stopped and went off through the bush to investigate, but after half an hour turned back without seeing anything. Rhino I learned were few and shy.

For almost 50 miles the road of well-kept *murram* led steadily upwards from the river at 2000 feet to Arua at over 4000 feet above sea level. Here the climate was noticeably cooler: bush and thorn trees gave way to open grassland savannah dotted with clumps of euca-lyptus planted round homesteads, clusters of round mud houses with thatched roofs except for the occasional mansion sporting corrugated iron. Driving into Arua township, Eric stopped at the *duka* (shop) of Sthankiya Brothers which supplied most European needs. Gujeratis from near Bombay, they were respected citizens and respectable cricketers. Next, I was taken to the *boma* — the District Commis-sioner's office — and introduced to the DC, Bill Slaughter, a big buffalo of a man with dark curly hair and a moustache. He was to be my mentor for the next two years.

Initially, I was billeted with Eric in his bungalow, one of half a dozen similar houses for the use of British officers, sited around a slight rise looking out to the west and north across the rolling plains to distant mountains. His cook would provide for both of us until I moved into a bungalow on my own. Eric suggested that I should pay him 50 cents, half a shilling, per day to meet the extra cost of food. Unused to doing my own catering, it never occurred to me at the time how ridiculously little this was, the equivalent of 2½p in modern English currency.

The pay of an administrative cadet during his first two years of probation was £350 per annum, about £29 a month. Of this, £4 went to Trofima and £3 to the cook. Later, when I moved into my own house, I took on a *shamba* boy (gardener) and a *toto* to fetch and carry and help the other servants. Even after paying for food, drink and any items of clothing made by the excellent local tailor, I was still able to live comfortably on my salary and to equip my house with bed and table linen, cushion covers and so on.

The DC gave me an initial briefing on my job. During my first two years, prior to confirmation of my appointment, I would be required to pass examinations in one local language and in law. Until then, I would rank as a cadet, but would work as an assistant District Commissioner — we were always known by the term ADC. (District officer or DO is used as a general term to cover all grades of administrative officer in the field.) Since the tribes in the district spoke several different languages, the DC told me I should first learn Swahili which was used as a kind of lingua franca and for all the court and other records of the local native administrative system. After that, a second language would have to be learned within two more years.

One other item I recollect of the DC's briefing was of his telling me that, as representative of the government, a district officer was 'in the position of Caesar's wife'. This may have had something to do with the fact that the normal dress of women of the local Lugbara tribe consisted of a bunch of leaves, fore and aft, but I found nudity in the mass soon palled.

In peacetime, officers recruited to the Colonial Administrative Service underwent a year's training at Oxford or Cambridge during which they studied law, languages, anthropology, tropical hygiene, agriculture, and other germane subjects. But during the war this was dispensed with and I simply arrived. I had to pick things up as I went along and I must have made many mistakes through ignorance or inexperience. There is a saying that the more one knows the more one finds there is still to learn. In my case I knew too little to realize how ignorant I was. However, to describe my work as a district officer I must first explain the background, the place, the people with whom I had to deal, and how the government worked. The information in the next few pages took me months, sometimes years, to assimilate. I had to start without it.

A Look Back

The first European explorers and missionaries arrived in Uganda in the middle of the nineteenth century after an 800 mile march from the coast or an even longer trek up the Nile from Khartoum. Round the northern shores of Lake Victoria they found tribes with a fairly well organized system of government under powerful 'kings'. Primacy among these tribes, for reasons of size and military prowess, was enjoyed by the Baganda: hence the name given to the whole country.

Early accounts of names were confusing because their compilers were unfamiliar with the practice in the Bantu group of languages of putting a prefix before the word stem, instead of a suffix as in Western languages, to denote the class of noun. Hence *mu* for a person, *ba* for people, *lu* for language, *bu* for land, and so on. This presented obvious difficulties to the compilers of dictionaries and to students new to the country.

A monarch, the Kabaka, descended from very early Hamitic invaders from the north-east, ruled the Baganda. It was with the Kabaka and his chiefs that, in 1900, Sir Harry Johnston signed the Uganda Agreement on behalf of Her Majesty's Government in the United Kingdom, and thus was born the Uganda Protectorate which in due course was extended to embrace other tribal areas to the north and west. In 1914, the West Nile district became the last piece of territory to be added to the Protectorate.

The main difference between a protectorate and a colony was that in a protectorate the interests of the native inhabitants were to be paramount. Most importantly, land settlement in Uganda was not open to British or other foreigners except where specially approved in the public interest, usually for some economic development. This avoided many of the problems encountered in other parts of Africa where land was alienated for settlement by non-Africans.

For administrative purposes Uganda was divided into 13 districts, each with a population between 200,000 and 500,000. In most cases the district boundaries had been drawn so as to include all or most of one tribe in the same district. Hence in most districts a single language was usually spoken and understood. But because for centuries Uganda had been overrun by tribal migrations, mainly from the north and north-east, the languages of the different tribes varied widely and often had little in common although they fell into four main linguistic groups. Lugard, the great pioneer of colonial administration, had left his mark in the system he conceived of indirect rule. The tribal administration, where it existed, was kept in place under the supervision of the central government through its District Commissioners.

The West Nile district was the only part of Uganda lying to the west of the Albert Nile; hence the name. Unlike the other districts, its boundaries were based on geographic features, the Nile on the east

Map of West Nile District

and the continental divide on the west, with international borders to the north — the Sudan — and the south — the Congo. This forms a rough rectangle, about the size of Wales, 150 miles from north to south and 60 miles east to west. The western boundary forms the watershed between the Congo basin carrying its waters westwards into the Atlantic and the Nile flowing north into the Mediterranean. Years before, European statesmen had used this feature as a convenient (for them) way of defining the boundary between British and Belgian spheres of influence in Africa without having to examine the situation on the ground. The line runs across country that rises gradually towards the south to over 5000 feet. It was unmarked on the ground except at certain crossing points, such as the road from Arua ten miles away to the little town of Aru a few miles on the Belgian side.

The altitude gradient across the District created many fast flowing rivers, all running west to east into the Nile, and the vegetation changes markedly between the different altitude zones. Fairly dense typical African bush trees, including acacia and thorn, cover the lower lying areas along the river. These areas supported a wealth of wildlife, including lion, leopard, buffalo, hippo, rhino, wild dogs, many varieties of buck and antelope, and various kinds of monkey. Most of the elephant had moved north nearer the Sudan border or across the river to the east bank, where they were protected by a game reserve free of human habitation. Crocodiles abounded in the river.

This part of Africa had been a confluence of tribal migration until the advent of foreign stable government imposed a standstill and settlement of the occupants on the land where they lived. As a result, the population of the West Nile district, some 300,000, comprised a number of different tribes speaking different tongues. In the south, the Alur in the highlands and the Jonam along the river spoke dialects of Lwoo, a language shared, though with widely varying dialects, with a large group of tribes extending east of the Nile to Acholi and Lango and as far as the Jaluo in Kenya. It is often possible to recognize members of this group by their names, the males beginning usually with 'O' (like Obote or Oginga) and the females with 'A'. Adjoining the Alur in the low lying land along the Nile were the Jonam. *Jo* means people and *nam* means river or lake, hence 'the river people'. They speak a slightly different variant of Lwoo.

On the central plateau around Arua are the Lugbara, a tribe that spreads west into the Congo and is related to the Moru in the Sudan. In the north, the Madi (no relation to the Mahdi) occupied a separate sub-district with headquarters in Moyo near the Sudan border. (Moyo was one of the few outstations in Uganda manned by a single district officer, a much-prized post I was lucky enough to obtain after a few years in Arua.) A smaller splinter group of Madi was also settled in the lowlands near the river south of Rhino Camp. To distinguish them from the Madi Moyo they were often called Madi Ajai, named after Chief Ajai, a mountain of a man always having trouble with his many wives.

Finally, there was a small group of Kakwa in the northwest corner of the district: most of that tribe lived in the Sudan. Their language which was related to that of the larger Bari group in the Sudan, was quite different from Lugbara. It was from the Kakwa that the girl came who was to become the mother of the infamous dictator General Amin. But when, many years later, I addressed him in his mother tongue, he did not understand.

Not only did the West Nile district abut on two other countries: it had actually formed part of each of those countries at different times in the recent past. It was first 'explored' (in the western sense) in about 1860 by Arab slave raiders from the Anglo-Egyptian Sudan, accompanied by the occasional European adventurer. Miani from Italy was one of the first; and Junker from Germany wrote the first description of the district during such a trip in 1877.* After the Mahdi rising in the Sudan and the death of Gordon in Khartoum, the Governor of Equatoria Province was cut off from Egypt and decided to march south with a contingent of his loyal Nubian soldiers. This was Emin Pasha, a remarkable Austrian in the service of the Khedive of Egypt. He led his force up the river into what is now Uganda and settled his

---

* W. Junker, *Travels in Africa during the Years 1871–78*, pp. 455 *et seq.*

headquarters at Wadelai on the west bank, a few miles south of where I had landed at Rhino Camp. The settlement prospered and the Nubis, as they came to be called locally, intermarried with the local women, siring descendants who became the backbone of the 4th Battalion of the King's African Rifles, a regiment that gained distinction in two world wars.

Stanley, in the journal of his transcontinental march, records his meeting with Emin at Wadelai in 1889.* Emin eventually moved to Dar es Salaam where he met his end, but he left his name to be adopted by numerous young Nubis including Idi Amin.

The next episode which seems astonishing today, was the grant in 1894 to King Leopold of the Belgians of a lease of the area for his lifetime — reputedly as a wedding present from Queen Victoria. The Belgian administrators in those early days must have had a difficult time, immensely remote from their headquarters, unfamiliar with the country, the people or the languages, lacking facilities or means of communication. Local legend tells with glee of the frequent discomfiture of the *Birigi* and how some of them were ambushed and slain by Lugbara tribesmen near Mount Liru. Several of their officers lie buried near Mount Wati where their graves, and remains of some of their old buildings, were still to be seen in 1950. When King Leopold died in 1909 the area reverted to the Anglo-Egyptian Sudan.

The first British administrator was appointed when the area then known as the Lado Enclave came again under Khartoum's control. He was C. H. Stigand, a remarkable man whose subsequent book about the district, *The Lado Enclave*, is a classic of its kind. At a later date, I was able to visit the house he built for himself in Kajo Kaji, just north of the present boundary between Uganda and the Sudan. There I found a plaque bearing the legend *Stigandus aedificavit* — a charming memorial to a time when the country was ruled not only by 'blues' but by classics scholars.

In 1914, when an exchange of territory was arranged between the Sudan and Uganda, the area was brought into the Uganda Pro-

---

* H. M. Stanley, *In Darkest Africa*.

tectorate and named the West Nile district. The first District Commissioner, the redoubtable A. E. Weatherhead, is still remembered in
Lugbara legend by his local name of 'Jerekedi'. He achieved fame
during a rebellion known as the Allah Water rising (of which there
have been more recent echoes with the belief that certain potions
could give immunity against rifle bullets). In one battle Jerekedi was
shot in the leg by an arrow which he is alleged to have removed while
he sat calmly smoking his pipe.

Weatherhead was succeeded in due course by another tough
character, C. L. Bruton. After him came an ex-naval officer, Commander O. R. Sitwell, who was still remembered in my day for his
constant and detailed supervision of local activities, a style that was
doubtless dictated by his training in a disciplined force and that
earned him the local soubriquet *dirili* — the hornet. Years later I was
privileged to find Sitwell as an old man at his home in Suffolk and to
chat with him about his memories of the West Nile.

Since those early days this remote and primitive area had been
brought into contact with the rest of Uganda by means of the fortnightly steamer service from Butiaba to Pakwach and Rhino Camp.
Roads had been built linking the main centres of population and the
many rivers had been bridged, albeit with bridges made of bamboo
which were flexible but surprisingly durable, though alarming to cross
in a bus or lorry. When swept away by a flood, which happened
frequently in the rainy season, they were not too difficult to replace. A
telegraph office in Arua provided immediate communication with the
outside world. And the arrival of Indian traders, with their ability to
adapt easily, to buy and market local crops and to sell cheap cloth,
kerosene and hardware, transformed the economy. When two large
sugar estates were established in the south of the country there arose a
need for strong manual labour which the Lugbara were well suited to
supply. A six month stint in the sugar fields would earn them enough
to build a house and support their families.

For administrative purposes the district was divided into 11 counties, seven for the Lugbara and one each for the smaller tribes. In
charge of each county was a Sultan, a title dating from the days of
Sudanese administration, with lesser chiefs under him known as
Wakils. The Sultan was appointed by the District Commissioner after

suitable consultation with the tribe. The Alur and Jonam already had a hereditary system and the DC normally accepted the *rwot*, or prince, as the Sultan unless he was clearly unsuitable.

Since there was no indigenous tribal organization for the whole district, a central native administration (NA) with headquarters in a building adjoining the DC's office serviced the chiefs with their small staffs of clerks and policemen. There, tax collections and fees were received and accounted for, salaries and payments disbursed and simple budgetary procedures controlled. Annual meetings of all the Sultans provided a forum for authoritative opinions on local policies and customary law. In their capacity as the Central Native Court, they also heard appeals from decisions of the Sultans' courts.

3

District Officer

So there we were in Arua, tucked up into the corner where east, west and north Africa meet at the very centre of the continent. And here I had to learn my trade.

Soon after my arrival in March 1941, I was sent off with Eric to tour Jonam county, my first 'safari'. We travelled down the 86 miles to Pakwach in a lorry loaded with all our kit, tents, camp beds, bed linen and mosquito nets, folding table and chairs, tin bath, crockery, cutlery, water filter, cooking utensils; and our staff sitting on top of it all.

As interpreter we had Adriano Okello, son of Ongwech. The DC's office employed three interpreters: Juma was a Nubi who spoke the local languages but no English; Aria spoke only Lugbara and Swahili; Adriano was the only one who spoke English which was fortunate, as it would enable me to follow what went on.

We were met at Pakwach by the Sultan Anderea Ali, son of Owing, who was also the hereditary *rwot*. He was to become a valued friend and mentor. Looking back now, I realize how gracious these senior chiefs were when confronted by youngsters like myself who had no experience of Africa or of government yet behaved as their equals, if not superiors. I discovered that his grandfather Ali had been an important chief when the tribe still inhabited lands on the east bank of the Nile, and that his two sons, Owing and Ongwech, had been rivals to succeed him as *rwot*. So our interpreter Adriano was the

Sultan's cousin but he never showed any sign of jealousy or ill will towards Anderea.

The headquarters of the various Wakils in Jonam were spaced out along the west bank of the river at intervals of about ten miles, connected only by footpaths through the bush or by canoe. Eric and I bicycled along the paths with Anderea and Adriano while porters carried all our kit on their heads and the servants walked. At each wakilate there was a site to pitch tents, usually overlooking the river, with a few mud huts for the staff and a kitchen. At some places there was a camp house where Eric and I could stay.

Firewood was supplied and local ladies brought hens, eggs, fruit and goats' milk for the cook to buy. A hen cost five cents (a quarter of one penny) and eggs were six for one cent. There were no cattle in this area because of the lethal tsetse fly and, since there was no refrigeration, goats' milk was preserved by adding urine — an acquired taste. Statuesque girls carrying four-gallon cans on their heads brought water up from the river. Drinking water was boiled, nominally for five minutes, before filtering to eliminate any bacteria.

At each Wakil's headquarters we spent a night or two. On the first day Eric would read through the court records and discuss with the chiefs any cases where the decision seemed to him puzzling or dubious. There might have been 50 cases since the last visit by a touring officer so this process usually occupied an hour or two. Then tax collection would be checked with the Wakil's clerk. Every able-bodied adult male was required to pay an annual poll tax of eight shillings to the protectorate government and seven shillings to the district native administration, a total of 15 shillings, the equivalent of 75 pence nowadays, but quite a substantial sum at that time. We would examine a group of old men applying for tax exemption on the grounds of age or incapacity and they would be paraded for inspection.

With the wage for an unskilled labourer at eight shillings a month, taxes would amount to about 15 per cent of his annual earnings. But two months' work would suffice to pay taxes and few families relied principally upon wages. They usually grew most of their own food, kept a few farmyard animals for eggs and milk, and caught fish if they lived near the river. Most families had plots of cash crops — cotton in the lowlands, coffee in the highlands and tobacco on the

Lugbara plateau — to provide income for their needs. Young men might go for six months to work down country on the sugar plantations and bring home a few hundred shillings. Others, during the war, would join the army: family remittances which were deducted from the soldiers' pay, were a valuable resource for the families they left behind.

Our next job while on tour was to inspect the famine reserves that each village was required to maintain. Everyone contributed to the stores of grain which were carefully preserved so that, if one year's crop should fail, there would always be enough seed for the next year's sowing. The grain was stored in thatched containers resembling small huts on stilts so that, in theory, rats could not get at the contents. The people were also required to make regular plantings of cassava, a hardy root crop that is almost immune to drought. This could be used to augment food supplies in the event of the rains failing and a bad harvest. If time allowed we would take a walk round nearby homesteads to check that this was being kept up and to chat with the people, particularly with the women who might be reluctant to voice their concerns in public.

Finally, came the *diwan* (another word imported from the Sudan), a village meeting at which the visiting district officer would give an address through the interpreter, emphasizing whatever matters needed public attention and sometimes throwing in items of world or local news. He would be followed in turn by the Sultan and Wakil and they would probably add some comment on points the DO had raised. Some Wakils would give the DO a flowery welcome. Finally the meeting was thrown open to anybody wishing to speak or to ask a question. There was often somebody, usually an older man, with a long winded complaint: the reactions and asides from other members of the assembly sometimes gave one a good idea of its merits. Occasionally a woman would appear and raise some matter of concern, perhaps about a local medical clinic or a school, that needed government attention.

When time allowed we would go out in the evening for a walk in the bush or a trip in a canoe on the river. On one occasion Eric and I accompanied a game ranger to shoot something for the pot. They each had a rifle but I had only a 20-bore shotgun suitable for guinea fowl. A mile or two from camp the ranger picked up the spoor of buffalo. We followed this for a while and suddenly came upon a small group in some thorn thickets. Eric fired at a bull but failed to bring it down and the herd crashed off into the bush. A wounded buffalo can be very dangerous when cornered but Eric and the ranger followed it up where splashes of blood marked its passage. Suddenly the beast burst from a thicket straight in front and charged directly at us. Eric and the ranger both fired and then leapt sideways as the animal came right on between them. I turned and fled for the nearest tree only to find that it was already occupied by five or six terrified Africans who had been following the hunt in the hope of a free supper. There was nowhere for me to climb and the buffalo could have got me there, but luckily he chased after another onlooker and then dropped dead. Never follow a wounded buffalo in thick bush: wait till the next morning by which time his wound will have weakened if not killed him.

After that trip I was considered ready to go out on my own and was sent by the DC to the small Lugbara county of Vurra in the highland area along the Congo border just south of Arua. For that safari I was allocated the chief interpreter, Juma Fademulla, whose father had been a Nubi chief. He spoke most local languages and Swahili, but no English. The DC held the view, rightly I think, that the quickest way to learn a language is to be forced to use it in order to survive. After ten days on tour with no English speaker, I was able to get by in Swahili. Six months later, after polishing up my grammar and vocabulary, I passed the government language exam.

Sleeping Sickness

Not long after arriving in Arua, I was put in charge of the sleeping sickness programme. SS, our term for human trypanosomiasis, had devastated several parts of the country in the early years of the century, particularly in areas near rivers and lakes. The life cycle of the trypanosome microbe involves incubation in the tsetse fly, a vector that inhabits and breeds in long grass close to water. A bite by an infected fly will infect a human (or, in a slightly different variety, cattle) and induce a potentially fatal illness. A fly that bites an infected human can start the microbe's life cycle over again. Hence, as the incidence of the disease grows among humans, the greater the chance of it being carried by a fly.

In the early days the disease spread rapidly out of control among the tribes inhabiting the islands on Lake Victoria, several of which had to be evacuated. Later it appeared in the low-lying areas along both banks of the Albert Nile, the section of the river flowing north out of Lake Albert. To control the epidemic drastic steps had to be taken in order to break up the life cycle of the trypanosome by separating the host vector from its human prey. The most likely points of infection were the watering places where humans fetched water from the river, so the whole population on the east bank of the Nile was moved out of an area within about 40 miles of the river. Some of them moved east into Acholi district but most moved across to the west bank to join their fellow tribesmen, the Jonam.

The rivers flowing down to the Nile from the highlands to the west were well defined and human visits to draw water could be confined to selected points on each river. The grass and undergrowth 100 yards up and down stream of each watering place were regularly slashed so as to keep the fly out of contact with humans. But these measures could never be 100 per cent effective and an additional check was introduced. Every month, itinerant medical assistants, specially trained in a process called palpation to identify the early signs of the disease in the glands of the neck, would examine the whole population living in affected areas. Anyone suspected of infection would be sent to the nearest hospital for a blood test and, if necessary, for treatment. By treating infected people promptly they could be removed from the cycle of infection.

All this required a high degree of organization, much of which was initiated by Jim Dakin, a New Zealander whom I never met but whose legacy I inherited. A separate corps of SS inspectors had been established to supervise the work on the ground and to ensure that everybody attended the monthly inspections for palpation. Gangs of labourers were maintained to keep the grass cut short around approved watering places. The chiefs imposed penalties on anybody found drawing water from places other than the approved points or for failing to attend for inspection. These rigorous provisions had, by the time I arrived, greatly reduced the incidence of the disease but we had to keep up the precautions if another outbreak was to be avoided.

Supervising this work involved me in monthly trips to visit places hundreds of miles apart, in order to pay the labour gangs and to make spot checks on river clearings. If there was a new case I needed to find out where he or she got infected. It was obvious that I needed transport, so I made enquiries.

A Goan customs officer stationed on the border at Vurra was being transferred to headquarters and wanted to dispose of his car. This turned out to be a 1934 six cylinder Chevrolet tourer that had seen better days but was basically a beautifully simple machine. He asked 450 shillings (£22.50) which was almost a month's salary for me, but I scraped it together and became the proud owner.

It was evident that the car, which I called Fanny, needed attention. On a trip to inspect SS staff in Aringa, 60 miles north, I found one tyre worn through to the canvas. The spare had an ominous swelling where a piece of rubber had been inserted between tube and tyre to cover a hole in the tyre. This made for a bone-shaking ride as I bumped my way back to Arua and I immediately ordered four new tyres which would take a month to arrive on the next fortnightly boat but one. In the meantime I had got to know Brother Fanti, the bearded Italian head of the technical school at the RC mission, and he suggested that, if I would let him have the car for a month, he would dismantle and overhaul it as a project for his trainee mechanics. I would pay for any new parts plus a modest subvention to the school. Done!

A month later I had a splendid car which, during the next five years, would carry me all over Uganda and into the Congo and would never let me down. Brother Fanti had replaced the radiator with one discarded from another car and it worked well; but the filler cap protruded several inches above the bonnet like a steam engine funnel. A year later, during a drive to Kampala, she started to misfire badly, but I drove the remaining 80 miles on five cylinders; and in Kampala they replaced the cylinder head which turned out to be cracked. But she never let me down and in five years Fanny chalked up 80,000 miles with minimal attention. I was sad to part with her eventually — for £85.

4

Outstation

The mail arrived in Arua once a fortnight by the boat across Lake Albert. It reached us on a Friday and the outgoing mail closed on Saturday so it was a rush if one needed to get off a prompt reply. As letters from England took up to two months to get there, I did not normally feel any urgency to dash off a reply but preferred to digest letters at leisure. I soon fell into this slow rhythm of the mail and became absorbed in my new life. I found the official mail full of interest with its circulars from the Secretariat in Entebbe about new government policies or staff postings, questions from provincial head-quarters about cotton production, school curricula or touring returns replies to our own earlier letters, or queries about the accounts which were passed swiftly to our Indian accountant. Entebbe, which I had not yet visited, seemed a distant nether world whose denizens were known only by name and constituted a kind of demonology, remote from the pure air of the outstation.

Family, England and the war seemed very far away. Isolation from my family was not a new experience for me. As a boy at school in England with parents in India whom I might not see for months or years at a time, I had become used to letters that took months to arrive and replies that were out of date when they did. My elder brother and sister had their own problems: we saw each other only occasionally and corresponded infrequently. I had perforce become self-sufficient and doubtless self-centred. Now that I have a family of

36

my own I realize how my mother in particular must have suffered from our long separations.

In due course, I moved into a house on my own and had to get used to living by myself. Solitude held no fears for me: I had plenty of books to read, gramophone records to play, letters to write. Nevertheless I lacked company, especially in the evenings. Apart from the DC and ADCs, the British officers comprised a district medical officer, sometimes a second medical officer, and an agricultural officer. From time to time this core of staff would be augmented temporarily by a forest officer, a geologist, or some other specialist. Most members of staff were married and at any time some of them would usually be out of the station on safari. There was no club in Arua where one could drop in for a drink or a chat with colleagues or their wives.

The junior ADC was always responsible for seeing to the proper upkeep of Arua township. For this, we employed about a hundred work-men, collectively known as the station labour. They were organized in gangs of ten, each with its own leader, under the overall command of a headman called Silimani, a Nubi and former NCO of the KAR (King's African Rifles). Grass had to be cut to prevent mosquito breeding, roads maintained, trees planted, refuse collected and 'night soil' disposed of. This last unsavoury task was always carried out by men from the small Okebo tribe for reasons I never discovered.

I used to walk round the station with Silimani most mornings to keep an eye on things. This might have been a tedious chore but for two things. When the station was first laid out the DC of the day saw that regular grass cutting lent itself naturally to the creation of fair-ways and greens for a golf course. So a nine hole course was developed, providing us with relaxation in the evenings while keeping the mosquito population at bay. It also gave added interest to my early morning tours of inspection: woe betide the ADC if a fairway was found not properly mown when the DC went out to play his evening round of golf.

The second interest I developed was in planting trees. We were restricted mainly to eucalyptus, cupressus, or silk oak (grevillia), but I managed also to get some flowering trees — jacaranda, flamboyant, and cassia — to help beautify the place. This work started an interest which has never left me.

Besides golf we had a tennis court. Sometimes on a Saturday we would organize a game of cricket for which we could just about assemble 22 players by roping in missionaries and a number of Indians from the bazaar. Some of these were pretty skilful bowlers. On one occasion Peter Williams, younger of two doctor brothers at the Africa Inland Mission, scored 100, an unheard of achievement and considered slightly bad form. When I was umpiring I gave him out — BTL (batted too long).

I was interested in developing sport among local youngsters. Cricket was a mystery for most Africans, except for a few in Kampala who had learned it at school or college. My own field was athletics and I encouraged schools to hold sports. We developed sufficient interest to inaugurate a district sports' meeting every year in Arua, with teams from each county. We had at first no hurdles, my speciality, but I enjoyed challenging and sometimes beating fancied local lads over 100 yards. It was a few years before we were ready to compete with the rest of Uganda but eventually I was able to take a team from the district down to Kampala to take part in the Uganda AAA championships.

The Lugbara used to give nicknames, often scurrilous, to British officers stationed in the West Nile. Just as Sitwell was the hornet, Bill Slaughter was Abdullah, for reasons I could never discover. I was ostrich on account of my long neck.

It was the Lugbara custom to celebrate a funeral by a dance. The drumming was loud, incessant and monotonous, with an obbligato of horns that played only one note. The whole village would turn up and would consume quantities of millet beer, a bitter tasting soupy brew. The close relations would whiten their faces with ash. Meanwhile the women would emit penetrating ululations: from time to time one of them would break away from the circle of dancers and run around the periphery producing a piercing wail as if overcome by emotion. All this would go on for hours and could be heard from miles away. Since funerals were an everyday occurrence, the sound of drums could almost always be heard from one direction or another.

One afternoon I heard drumming of a very different character and went to investigate. I found a group of young Acholi visitors playing four drums tuned to different pitches on which they could play a kind of melody with exciting rhythms. I was sorry not to have a tape recorder: I stayed and listened to them for an hour.

The Missionaries

When white men started to arrive in East Africa the local inhabitants found difficulty in understanding the distinction between church and state, between the missions, with their services and holy writ, and the government with its councils and courts of law. The Muslims anyway saw no need for such distinction: the Koran was both scripture and law. When I asked Muhammad Ali, the township chief in Arua, about his religious convictions he answered succinctly, 'Dini yangu serkali tu.' My religion is government.

The Christian missions played a vital part in the people's social development, notably through education, which they provided with financial support from the government. The first missionaries arrived in Uganda towards the end of the nineteenth century; but the West Nile district was the last area to be assimilated into the protectorate and Christian missionaries did not arrive there until the end of the First World War. Hence the Lugbara and the Alur had a lot of ground to make up in terms of education and literacy.

The Roman Catholics were represented in the area by the Verona Fathers — an Italian mission whose special talents for practical and technical education were apparent in their buildings with fine roofs of red Roman tiles, a pleasing contrast with the commonplace thatch or corrugated iron. In addition to their main establishment in Arua, they had schools in every county. At Nyapea in the Alur highlands, an excellent secondary school was staffed by American Brothers. Here it was possible to hold an intelligent discussion with senior pupils and I was interested to hear how their families handled the potential conflict between the tribal customs of their illiterate parents and the aspirations of their educated children.

When Italy declared war in 1940 the Italian missionaries became enemy aliens which presented a problem for the government. Eventually a sensible *modus vivendi* was worked out whereby the Italians were nominally interned within their own mission compounds and allowed to get on with their normal jobs. Only if they wanted to move elsewhere were they required to seek permission from the DC. I think the Italians were as embarrassed about this as we were, but they were a convivial lot and we sometimes had a laugh together about the vagaries of international politics.

The Protestants were represented by the Africa Inland Mission which had only a small establishment in Arua. The solitary British missionary eventually joined by Dr Ted Williams and his wife to start a medical facility. Ted was a man of conviction and vision. After setting up a clinic at Arua, he aimed to found a leper colony. In due course I went with him to look at a site in the bush and to plan an access road for vehicles. Now, 40 years on, Kuluva is a thriving hospital with more than 100 beds. Ted's interests were wide: he did valuable research into the incidence of certain diseases, and he was later made an honorary game warden. He was awarded the CBE when he retired. He was joined in Arua by his father and younger brother Peter, an ophthalmologist, and by his father, an immensely practical man who helped me, years later, to align a new road to Erusi, a hilltop village in the far south which could, till then, only be reached by a ten-mile walk from the road.

Rabies

A friend in Masindi had a pair of bull terriers and I obtained one of their pups which I brought home with me in the car after a visit down country. He was an attractive brindle whom I called Paddy. We became fond of each other and he accompanied me everywhere — to the office, in the car, on safari. I knew that there was rabies in the district but reckoned that Paddy would be safe if I kept him always by me.

One day when he was fully-grown I noticed that he was unsteady on his back legs. I knew that this might be an early symptom of the disease and decided to lock him up overnight in the spare room. Wire mosquito gauze on the window would allow him air. But, when I went into the room next morning, he was gone. A gaping hole torn in the mosquito wire told its own story.

This was alarming and I set off at once to find the headman in charge of the station labour. I told him the position, explained the danger and offered a reward for the dog's recapture. He went off to spread the word. To my relief Paddy was found fairly soon and brought back to the house on a string. He seemed quite quiet. I had consulted the local assistant veterinary officer, a helpful African, and he advised me that the only safe course was for the dog to be destroyed. He would then take the brain tissue for microscopic examination. I locked Paddy up in the garage and went to get my shotgun. When I was ready, we opened the garage door and Paddy wandered slowly out, blinking in the sunlight, and advanced trustingly towards me. I waited until he was about three yards from me and shot him. As the brain would be needed for examination, I had to aim at his shoulder, but thankfully it killed him instantly.

The vet later reported that the microscope had revealed the presence of 'negri bodies' in the brain, a condition that always accompanies rabies. Specimens were then sent to Kampala for further tests and a few weeks later we were informed that the results were positive for rabies.

I was thankful, at least, that I had not killed the dog needlessly. I then had to consider my own position and whether any other human contacts might be at risk. The long incubation period of the disease which may be up to a year, allowed us a little time. I did not think he had bitten anybody and the servants assured me that he had not licked any open cut or wound on their hands. I did have a small scratch on one hand, now healed, but I could not be sure that Paddy had not licked this earlier. The medical officer thought it would be prudent to give me a course of anti-rabies vaccine, but this had to be obtained from South Africa which took two or three weeks. When it arrived I had to have large doses injected every day for two weeks — two shots under the skin, one each side of the abdomen. It soon made me very sore and it was uncomfortable to fasten my belt.

Not long after that we had a report of a man dying in Koboko, 40 miles to the north, with symptoms that sounded suspicious. Ronald Ladkin, a young English doctor who had recently arrived on first appointment as a government medical officer, went out, and had the gruesome task of sawing open the man's skull to obtain a specimen of his brain, a process he carried out on the clerk's table to the dismay of the assembled relatives. The ensuing tests proved positive for rabies.

Since then I have been a staunch supporter of the strict quarantine laws that have kept the UK free from rabies.

In later days of sophisticated drugs and elaborate prophylactic precautions before any venture to the tropics, it is interesting to recall the advice on personal health which I received from the Colonial Office before leaving London. It was precisely nil. It was not till I arrived in Arua that I was taught that water must be boiled for five minutes and then filtered before drinking. One should also see that the cook washed his hands before handling food, a precaution which I rarely bothered to enforce. Mosquito boots made by an Indian cobbler in the bazaar provided comfortable protection against the irritation of bites round the ankles in the evening. And mosquito nets on beds avoided both the annoying buzzing of insects in one's ears and their bites. It was little comfort to be told by the medical officer that only the female mosquito carried the malaria parasite, whereas only the male emitted the telltale buzz. Mepacrine and paludrine were not yet known. I survived for 18 months without malaria but finally succumbed to my first, and worst, bout when exposed to the cold up high on Ruwenzori. The treatment was heavy doses of quinine till the fever abated.

More troublesome for me was dysentery. The bacillary variety left me prostrate and the MO treated me with Epsom salts. This seemed to make things even worse while eliminating the bacilli, so one had to drink copious quantities of water. It was several years later that, after another attack, a doctor told me of 'M & B 693' and the new sulphur drugs, one of which would clear up the problem as if by magic. Amoebic dysentery became a continuing nuisance and the treatment with injections of emetine for two weeks left one pretty weak. Antibiotics had not yet been discovered.

When Dr James Hunter arrived to take over as DMO, he and his wife came to live next door to me. He was a splendid doctor and later became Director of Medical Services. We formed a friendship that lasted until he died in Edinburgh 50 years later. Occasionally we would go out together to investigate some health problem: once we had to swim a river in flood after heavy rain to reach our camp.

One day James came to ask my advice about a patient in the hospital who had developed gangrene following a wound in his leg while hunting. He was a man I knew called Bilal, well educated, tall and handsome, a Nubi and a devout Muslim. The only hope of saving his life was to amputate the leg but Bilal steadfastly refused. He believed that amputation would leave him with only one leg in the hereafter and through all eternity. I went to talk to him but his mind was clear and unchangeable. Since the days of Sudanese administration there had always been a substantial number of Muslims in the district, most of them settled in Arua or in a township in the north called Aringa. I consulted a *mwalim*, a religious teacher whom I knew, and he confirmed that Bilal's belief was genuine and well founded in Islamic doctrine. I had to advise James that he must accept the man's decision. It would be unthinkable to operate against his wishes. Bilal died two days later and was widely mourned by his community.

5

Ruwenzori:
The Portal Peaks

In wartime home leave was out of the question and we were encouraged to take a fortnight's local leave every year. Eric went off to Kenya where his brother lived and, after a year in Arua, I began to wonder about doing the same. But fate fortunately intervened in the shape of a letter from Rennie Bere asking if I would like to join him for a climb in the Ruwenzori mountains. He was the DC in Acholi, over to the east of the Nile, had become run down with overwork and was being sent on sick leave to recuperate: he had persuaded the doctor that mountaineering would be the best tonic. I had never met him but knew of his formidable reputation as a mountaineer.

I was thrilled at the invitation and accepted with alacrity. I had read about the Ruwenzori. The first report of them in modern times was by Stanley in 1876 in the course of his first journey across Africa. But way back in AD 150 Ptolemy had written about the snow clad 'Mountains of the Moon' where the Nile was said to have its source in a lake between two high peaks; and Ruwenzori is the only range whose snows feed the Nile. The mountains were first climbed in 1906 when an expedition led by the Duke of the Abruzzi reached the top of most of the major peaks including Margherita which at 16,763 feet is the highest point.

I had some misgivings about my own lack of experience beyond ski touring in the Alps, but Rennie reassured me. Instead of going for one of the higher peaks involving snow and ice climbing, his aim was to explore the Portal Peaks, a hitherto unclimbed group on the eastern flank of the main range. At only 14,000 feet they barely reach the snow line. I had no proper mountain clothing or boots but equipped myself as best I could and, in due course, set out across Lake Albert and south to Fort Portal. After begging a bed from Dr Barnetson, whom I had known in Arua, I went round to the DC's house where the Beres were staying. Rennie's beautiful wife Maree met me with a warm welcome. Rennie was a big man with a kindly face, slightly deaf. We were to become lifelong friends.

The next morning we packed our kit and food on the back seat of Fanny and set off to drive 40 miles down the eastern flank of the mountains to the bridge over the Mobuku River. There we turned off onto a track and drove three miles up the valley to the chief's head-quarters at Bugoye where 20 men were assembled. These were our porters, men of the Bakonjo tribe who, like so many mountain folk, were stocky, strong and cheerful. In addition to our own kit and food Rennie had ordered blankets and *posho* (corn meal) which we bought for the porters. All this was eventually divided up into loads of about 50 lbs. Rennie and the chief then selected a headman who produced chits from leaders of previous expeditions testifying to his competence. With his help we then selected the necessary number of porters, wrote down their names and agreed rates of pay. Finally each man picked up the load he preferred and fixed round it a grass rope tied to a headband so that the weight fell on his forehead and back. And off they set up the path.

We said goodbye to the chief and asked him to keep an eye on the car. In those days cars had no keys and could, in theory, be driven off by anyone knowing how. Then Rennie and I followed the porters. For an hour or more we marched uphill along paths through fields and homesteads. A porter would often stop, put down his load and add to it some delicacies brought to him by a wife or mother whose home they were passing.

After a while we entered a region of rainforest with huge trees con-cealing any view. The path got steeper and, in the late afternoon, we reached the top of a ridge and arrived at our first camp site. There, in the shelter of an overhanging rock, the porters lit a fire. They used cigar-shaped packages. These were about 18 inches long and consisted of bark cloth that was kept smouldering indefinitely by being tightly wrapped in dry grass and a banana leaf. A few puffs into one carefully opened end would transform the spark into a flame. With this fire lighter slung round their necks, it would always be possible to light a fire, even in the wettest conditions and on trips lasting several weeks.

We pitched our small tent nearby and got to know the cook whom Rennie had already earmarked among the porters. He would get a higher rate of pay for his trouble. We also carried a small primus stove. Our diet was simple and eaten in or near our tent. We soon stretched out into sleeping bags and dozed off.

The march next day was rigorous. We had to descend 500 feet to cross the Mobuku, then climb up over a shoulder, then down again to a place where we had to cross the Bujuku River on a fallen tree trunk. The porters crossed with their heavy loads, using the sticks they carried to keep their balance. Rennie and I followed cautiously: a fall into the torrent of glacier water would not have been nice. We were now moving up out of rainforest into a region where everything seemed permanently wet and the trees were festooned with 'old man's beard' which gave the place a fairy-tale appearance. After a long day we camped at Nyinabitaba. The altitude was about 8500 feet. It started to rain and it became difficult to keep dry and warm. The porters were better off in a large rock shelter.

The third day saw us up to the base of a long ridge leading towards the southern end of the Portals, but our progress was painfully slow. Mist shrouded the mountains, there was no path, and dense bamboo forest up to 40 feet high covered the slope and made it difficult to find a route. At one place, elephant had trampled a track up the hill which we were glad to use. Next, we came into a wilderness of giant heather growing to a height of 20 or 30 feet. The headman had to hack his way through the undergrowth and over fallen trees which gave us a miserable time slipping and sliding, trying to avoid falling.

It's hard to describe the difficulties of climbing through a forest of giant heather. Imagine Lilliputians three inches tall scrambling through thickets of normal heather. Add to that a lattice of boughs from fallen trees lying a few feet above the ground, covered with a carpet of lichen and moss concealing the branches beneath, all this wet and slimy. First one had to prod with a stick to find where *not* to step. Having decided where next to place your foot you had to reckon that the bough may be rotten and will certainly be slippery. We had great difficulty finding anywhere to pitch a tent on this unstable surface and spent a cold and uncomfortable night.

We set off again next morning. The heather gradually thinned and, by afternoon, we emerged onto better ground where we could make a camp near the foot of the cliffs guarding the Portal Peaks. I tried to cook a rice pudding on our little primus stove, but the rice was still hard after having been boiled for more than an hour. At 12,000 feet, the boiling point of water is too low to cook rice, but we managed a few mouthfuls mixed with soup and chocolate!

The next day we set out to look for a way up the cliffs, taking with us just the headman and one porter. Our first choice was the south peak, known locally as Rutara which had been clearly visible from the road but was now shrouded in mist and cloud. Eventually we reached the foot of a rock cliff which Rennie thought would be possible to climb and we made some slow progress until we reached a very steep face which was wet and slippery, clearly beyond us. I had noticed from below a wide cleft that seemed to slice diagonally upward from the left so we made our way laboriously along the base of the cliffs until we reached the place where the cleft started. To our relief this turned out to be relatively easy to climb and we called it the boulevard. Gradually we made our way up until, after a couple of hours, the slope began to ease. By now we were in thick cloud and could only surmise that the south peak lay on our left. This involved quite a short climb up to a flat rock area. Rennie went off to explore the other side causing me some anxiety because visibility was so poor. Whichever way he went, the slope went down. We were on the summit at 14,050 feet, but photographs were out of the question. It had taken us about five hours since leaving camp. We shook hands, grinned and turned to go down, taking great care to find our route back into the boulevard. From there we made good time down out of the cloud to the foot of the cliffs and back to our camp.

Back in camp I began to feel unwell and started to shiver uncontrollably. Rennie felt my brow and diagnosed fever. We had brought no drugs, a mistake I never made again. I crept into my sleeping bag and spent the night alternately shivering and sweating. In the morning we realized that we could not go on to explore the range further and would have to head back down. Rennie may have been disappointed but I was beyond caring. We had at least made the first ascent of Rutara.

Of the next days I remember very little, but I managed to stay upright and keep going. Two days later we reached the car and, by evening, had arrived at Fort Portal. My host was away but an African doctor came to see me, took my temperature which was 104 degrees, took a blood sample, and started me on heavy doses of quinine. My head was bursting but within four days my temperature had subsided, though by then I felt like a wet rag. Barnetson returned and insisted I stay for another week before he would allow me to travel. He telegraphed Arua to explain my delayed return. So, ingloriously, ended my first expedition to Ruwenzori. Rennie reported our first ascent to the Alpine Club in London and later described it in his book *The Way to the Mountains of the Moon.*

6

Safari

In due course Eric was transferred to Kampala and I became the sole ADC in Arua. This meant extra work, but I relished it. When the DC was on tour I was in charge of the office; on his return we might have only a few days' overlap before I went out to tour another county. Our aim was to tour each of the 13 counties at least twice a year and it was not long before I became familiar with most parts of the district.

On tour, surrounded by people talking and ready to talk, one could get closer to tribal hearts and minds. As I became more familiar with the languages, I began to understand better how the people really thought and to learn some of their folk tales. These often gave human personalities to wild animals — Mr Leopard and Brother Jackal — and reminded me of stories about Brer Rabbit and Brer Fox on which we had been brought up and which, I supposed, had come from Africa originally.

There were also local legends like that of Dribidu, known as the father of the Ayivu or southern Lugbara, who had come across the Nile from the east and made his first settlement on the slopes of Mount Wati. Thereafter he sired the people of Terego and Vurra and acquired the terrible name of Banya, the cannibal. The story goes that a hawk, passing near his home one day, dropped a heart which Dribidu picked up, cooked and ate. Finding it delicious he killed many different animals and ate their hearts in an attempt to discover which

49

one it was that had tasted so sweet; but he could never recapture the same savour. One day when he was old, his adult sons and daughters went off to work in the fields, leaving their many infant children to the care of their grandfather. As soon as they had gone Dribidu killed one of the children, took out his heart, and ate it. At last he had discovered the origin of that sweet taste. He buried the child's body underneath the house. When his sons and daughters came home they were horrified to find that several of their children were missing. They finally unearthed the dreadful secret and Dribidu Banya was driven out into the bush.

Books were an important part of safari kit and I had a good supply: some of them I had brought out from home, others my father sent to me from time to time. Elspeth Huxley's *Red Strangers* became for me the touchstone of writing about Africa with its luminous evocation of tribal life whose equal I have never seen. Another I remember in particular was J. W. Dunne's *An Experiment with Time* because it challenged my scientific scepticism about paranormal phenomena. He sets out evidence for his contention that future events can be experienced in dreams and proposes a personal experiment in which, every morning on waking, one notes down all that one can recall of one's last dream before it fades from memory.

Safari gave me an ideal opportunity to put this into practice and before long I began to notice a surprising correlation between the notes I had written and subsequent events. One day, for example, I climbed a hill in Madi and was confronted at the top by a huge boulder of a distinctive shape. Alongside it stood a thorn tree that provided the only means of getting to the top. On looking through my notes that evening I was amazed to see an outline of the boulder with the nearby tree that, on waking, I had drawn. Another time I visited Rhino Camp and sat on the deck of SW *Lugard* looking over the ship's rail across the long vista of reed and elephant grass on the far bank. That evening, I found a note describing a scene on a balcony looking over a similar type of rail to distant fields. I am always sceptical about the evidence of other people's experiences of the paranormal but it is difficult to be sceptical about one's own.

When it became time to tour Jonam again, I made sure to take a government rifle, a .404, heavy enough to deal with large animals if necessary. At every village I heard complaints about the depredations of hippo which came ashore at night and caused much damage to the villagers' crops. I was shown their heavy footprints in confirmation. Food supplies were scarce and something had to be done. One evening Sultan Anderea and I went out on the river in a big dugout canoe. We sat on small stools while four men paddled and we soon came across a family of hippo in a wide bay. They would come to the surface to look at us, showing only their snouts, eyes and ears above water. After a few seconds they would twitch their ears and go down again with a snort and a puff of spray. They offered a very small target, perhaps 12 inches wide and four or five inches above the water. If the shot was a fraction too low it would ricochet off the water and fly over the hippo's head, if too high it would deflect harmlessly off the heavy skull bone. The margin of error was very small and one had only a few seconds in which to take aim. After watching them for several minutes Anderea identified the bull which should be my target and we waited quietly while he gave us several looks of inspection from about 100 yards away. Finally, while everyone in the canoe kept very still to avoid rocking, I drew a bead, squeezed off and was knocked backwards by the recoil. The head simply disappeared. Anderea clapped me on the shoulder with approval.

'*Umepiga*,' he shouted. 'You got him.'

I was not so sure; but there was no splash of the bullet striking the water. I supposed I must have hit him between the eyes and killed him instantly. I could hardly believe it.

We paddled on downstream for a few minutes before we sighted more telltale puffs of spray from a large group of hippo, this time farther out in the stream. We drifted quietly towards them while they watched us with interest. There seemed to be two bulls, but they kept their distance. The water was less calm here and the canoe was rocking gently which made it difficult to hold the rifle steady. At last I had what seemed a fair opportunity for a shot, but rushed it and missed. We decided to try once more and paddled on until we found a group of hippo in relatively shallow water. At last I made a good shot: the hippo reared, splashed, kicked and eventually disappeared. The paddlers cheered: this time there could be no doubt that he was fatally shot. Anderea explained that the body would first sink to the bottom.

After a few hours, as the gas in its stomach expanded, it would float to the surface and the villagers would come and drag the carcass ashore. They would be delighted, he said, and feel some recompense for the damage to their crops.

It happened as he said. Next morning news came to the camp that both hippos had been recovered. They were being cut up and my cook was dispatched to collect a share of the meat. That evening I dined on hippo steak: it was slightly tough and had a fishy taste.

A few days later we camped at Mutir, near Emin Pasha's Wadelai. There the villagers complained about elephants marauding through the crops they had planted on the far bank. The east bank was a game reserve and closed to habitation on account of sleeping sickness, but the people were permitted, as an emergency measure against famine, to plant crops there. This led to conflict with the herds of elephant that enjoyed uprooting and devouring the growing maize. Anderea and I went over to have a look and soon came across a herd of 30 elephant that took little notice of us. I had never been so near such a large herd.

Elephant hunting was controlled. A licence costing £10 permitted the holder to shoot three elephant and a single good tusk weighing about 50 pounds would more than cover the cost of the licence. (The biggest tusks I have ever seen were from an elephant shot by another DO, Sandy Field: they weighed more than 180 pounds each and are now in a museum in England.)

I had no licence, but these beasts were damaging important food supplies at a time of shortage and Anderea asked me to shoot one as a control measure to frighten the herd away. We got near one of the bulls and, with such a huge target, I found it difficult to know where to aim. My first shot seemed to have no effect apart from alerting the rest of the herd to danger. They immediately gathered round the wounded beast and started to trundle off at a steady trot. I tried another shot which I should not have done because by then the range was too long, almost 200 yards. Luckily I dropped one of the herd, though probably not the same one I had shot first. Anderea congratulated me on such a shot but I was ashamed. I had taken an unjustifiable risk with the second shot and the wounded elephant had got away. I never shot elephant again.

A final episode during that memorable tour happened the next day when we were again out in a canoe close to high reeds on the east bank. We heard a sudden snorting and crashing sound in the reeds. Hippo! When disturbed, hippo make straight for the water, and I knew that this one would smash through our canoe if he emerged at that point. Anderea was sitting behind me with his rifle at the ready, but we could see nothing. Suddenly a huge shape burst from the reeds about ten yards in front of the canoe and plunged into the water. There was a deafening report and I felt a blast of hot air by my left ear. Anderea had loosed off a shot and missed me by a hairsbreadth.

Wild animals were not the only hazard we faced. All along the river mosquitoes filled the air and in some places they would go on biting by day as well as by night. At Mutir, instead of the usual shorts, I had to wear long trousers and mosquito boots in the morning while working at the Wakil's headquarters.

By now I felt reasonably at home in Swahili, but an incident during that safari satisfied me that I could now *think* in the language. Walking with Anderea one day we passed two old men sitting rather mournfully by the side of the path. With no particular forethought I exclaimed:

'*Wanajisikitikia sana.*' (They are feeling very sorry for themselves).

In Swahili it is possible to put much of a sentence into one word by adding all the appropriate prefixes to the verb stem. I had done this automatically without having first to translate in my mind. It was a luminous moment in my process of learning about Africa.

On another safari, with Sultan Ajai in Madi, I had my first serious encounter with tsetse fly. We had to visit Rogem, a village near the Nile, and this involved cycling for ten miles along forest paths from our camp at Ofaka. On the way back I felt a sharp prick on my hand grasping the handlebar, then another, then one on my neck, then more. They were all over us and we could only wave them off with one hand while trying to steer with the other. I kept pedalling, but several times came near to falling off. It was a nasty hour before we reached camp.

The next day a man came in to report white rhino in the vicinity. I set off at once with my camera. Progress was slow through the thick bush but after an hour our guide motioned us to silence and we crept slowly forward for another 50 yards. Then he stopped. I saw nothing. Suddenly a huge brownish rock started to move and I realized that this was a rhino. There were two of them but the light in the forest was too poor to get a photograph. After a minute or two they lumbered slowly off and we returned to camp. I never saw white rhino again and I expect they are now extinct in the area.

Another hazard on safari was the pit latrine or *choo* which was provided at each camp site. It consisted of a hole in the ground about 12 feet deep, covered by a floor of wooden beams coated with hardened mud leaving a hole in the middle over which one had to crouch. A small mud and wattle hut with a thatched roof and, with luck, some kind of outer fence to provide privacy, surmounted the whole structure. On tour once in the Alur highlands, with a Dr Bruce to examine recruits applying to join the army, I was in occupation of the *choo* when the floor gave way. Down I went, scrabbling furiously with my hands and knees on the sides of the pit before finally coming to rest in the netherworld. Fortunately for me, that pit had not been dug quite as deep as the health regulations required — or it had been filled up over the years — but it still took me some time to climb out, shocked and sore. White ants, invisible under the coating of mud, had eaten away the beams supporting the floor. When he saw my condition, Dr Bruce was convulsed with laughter: it took me a while to appreciate the joke.

Another time, in Offude, I had just finished my business in the *choo* and stood up to button my shorts. I had not noticed that the hut was already occupied: hornets had built their nest hanging from the roof and my head disturbed them. I was stung 12 times on the head before I could escape. The pain and the swellings subsided in a few days with no ill effects, but I was more careful after that to examine the roof of a *choo* on entering.

There were plenty of hills in the district and, when on tour, I liked to leave no mountain in that area unclimbed. This often puzzled or amused the local chiefs, who were not always keen to accompany me. Some of the hills, I believe, had never before felt the print of a human foot. On one hill, Luku in Madi county, I was warned that evil spirits resided and dangerous animals abounded. Nobody had ever climbed it and returned to tell the tale! When I persisted, the sick list among those expected to accompany me quickly lengthened. Happily we returned from the summit unscathed.

I would look out from my house in Arua every morning and see the elegant shape of Mount Wati 20 miles away to the north. It was not long before I found an opportunity to go and climb it. This proved a good day's excursion, a climb of 2000 feet from its foot to the top, from where I could enjoy splendid views all round the district.

Further to the north one could make out another mountain of about the same height, but with a distinctive flat top and steep sides of bare rock. This was Liru. A geologist friend told me that the technical name for this type of formation was 'inselberg'. (As so often happens, the foreign name sounds more poetic than its translation 'island mountain'.) Ronald Ladkin shared my interest in climbing, so when we had to make a joint safari to examine a health problem in that area we naturally grabbed the chance and one afternoon cycled over to the foot of Liru. We found that its flat top was riven by a deep cleft with steep sides of bare rock, out of which it would have been difficult to climb. We decided to go for the eastern summit but once on the bare rock the slope steepened alarmingly. There were no handholds and we could adhere only by careful placing of our rubber-soled shoes. Then I slipped on a steep pitch and slid down 20 or 30 feet before I could stop, thoroughly skinning my knees and elbows. Trying again, we worked our way round to an easier line and finally reached the top, a rather barren place. The other summit looked about the same height, but there was no way to reach it without first climbing down quite a long way. We had no appetite for that. I was sore from my fall and did not enjoy the eight mile ride back to our camp.

7

Law and Order

The Pax Britannica was a novelty in Africa. Even those tribes which had developed their own system of rule by the chiefs were accustomed to indulge in warfare and raiding against their neighbours. But the British administration rested firmly on order, and the rule of law is its first requirement. Hence judicial matters figured large among the duties of a district officer.

There was a dual system of law. Native Courts dispensed justice within their own tribal areas and applied 'native customary law' — a phrase that allowed for a good deal of flexibility in its interpretation. These courts had very wide powers in both civil and criminal matters where Africans were concerned. Only capital cases, effectively homicides, and cases involving non-natives, were reserved for the protectorate courts. Most cases were dealt with in the court of the Wakil sitting with his elders. More serious cases went to the county court presided over by the Sultan, who could also hear appeals from the Wakil's court. At the top was the District Native Court comprising all the Sultans sitting together to hear appeals from the counties. Considering the differences of language and customs it was surprising that this court, with its preponderance of Lugbara members, worked as well as it did.

One of the duties of a DO on tour was to inspect the records of each Wakil's court. He had to satisfy himself that there had been no illegality or miscarriage of justice, and check that fines had been collected and debts paid. The DO had power to vary or overrule the decision of a native court if he thought it ran contrary to natural justice or exceeded the court's powers; but a wise DO would be reluctant to intervene in matters involving customary law, a subject on which we were not experts. There was another difficulty: the case records were written in Swahili by a clerk to whom that language was usually as strange as it was to us. Nor was he trained as a court reporter. It was not difficult to be misled about the issues and the evidence. For these reasons I learned to approach cases cautiously and, where necessary, to discuss them with the Wakil in the presence of the Sultan. If it seemed to me essential to intervene, I always preferred to refer the matter back for review by the Sultan's (higher) court than to substitute my own decision; and I would try to explain my reasons to the chiefs concerned.

In parallel with this system, there was Protectorate statute law as enacted by the Legislative Council, a body originally advisory to the Governor but later developing into a proper parliament. The Penal Code was based on English Common Law in a codified form that was fairly standard throughout the British dependent territories. There were also codes of procedure for civil and criminal cases and a statutory law of evidence. A separate system of courts administered these laws under a High Court manned by a Chief Justice and Puisne Judges. Every few months the High Court would progress on circuit to each district to hear capital cases or occasional appeals from the magistrates' courts.

All DOs were ex-officio magistrates, starting as 3rd class magistrates with limited powers. As a 1st class magistrate the DC had much wider powers, except in the larger towns where there were full time professional resident magistrates. Few of us DOs had any legal training and newly appointed officers had to rely heavily on the wisdom and local knowledge of their DC. Although I had read law for a year at Cambridge I was entirely inexperienced and was fortunate to have Bill Slaughter to guide and advise me. Though not professionally qualified he had a natural understanding of jurisprudence and a keen interest in this aspect of our work. I was glad to repay his help by gaining high marks in the government law exam, after which I was promoted to 2nd class magistrate.

Being exposed to both systems of law I became interested in some of the curious anomalies and possible conflicts of law to which this dual system gave rise. For example, whereas adultery in English law was at most a matter of civil suit for damages, the native courts treated it as an offence against tribal custom, punishable by imprisonment, as well as a civil cause for compensation. Because of the practice of 'bride price' which the future husband paid to the father of the bride, the woman's father would have no sympathy with his daughter if she later ran off with another man or merely left her husband. Either way, her father would be required to repay the bride price — usually three head of cattle plus a few goats — to the injured husband.

The legal technicalities of bigamy were also interesting in a society which recognized monogamy under Protectorate law and polygamy under native customary law. Although Protectorate law established bigamy as a crime, it only applied where the first marriage had been registered under a monogamous system. By a curious twist, a monogamous marriage contracted by a man who already had a wife under native law would not constitute the offence of bigamy under Protectorate law.

An added complication was a provision whereby magistrates were empowered to deal with certain civil disputes under Islamic law — a provision I only once had to apply several years later and, fortunately, only after I had studied Islamic law in London for the Bar exams.

Owing to wartime shortages of manpower the High Court sometimes had to extend to a DC the power to try a homicide case; and by the same token, the Attorney General was sometimes unable to supply a professional Crown counsel to prosecute cases. So when Bill Slaughter was assigned to try a murder case I was asked to prosecute before him. This gave me valuable experience and led to my being asked later to prosecute another case before the Chief Justice, Sir Norman Whitley, sitting in Arua. I was warned that he was not always an easy judge to please but I determined to stand my ground. We had one or two minor clashes in court during the trial, but this did me no harm and we grew to respect and even to like each other.

It was during this trial that I first encountered the problem of double interpretation. The accused and the witnesses were Lugbara, and Aria, our Lugbara interpreter, spoke no English. Questions to witnesses were put first in English to Adriano who translated them into Swahili. Aria then repeated them in Lugbara; and the answers came back through the same laborious channel. Knowing how easy it is for error to creep into a single process of oral translation it is not hard to see how difficult it was to be sure that the answer emerging after four successive translations accurately represented what the witness meant. Finer nuances of meaning in which some lawyers delight could never survive such a process of attenuation. One could only try, by repeating questions in a different form if necessary, to eliminate misconceptions as far as possible. This inevitably dragged out the length of the trial, much of the time being spent waiting for questions and answers to travel down and up the pipeline. The effect of this upon an irascible judge can be imagined.

In due course Bill Slaughter left the district on transfer and the new DC who succeeded him had no taste for, or interest in, legal matters. Finding that I was available and willing, he had me promoted to 1st class magistrate so as to relieve him of judicial duties. Not long afterwards, a murder case occurred in Jonam for which the High Court was unable to provide a judge. I was appointed, probably on Whitley's authority, to try it under extended jurisdiction.

I was all of 25 years old and to try a murder case was a heavy responsibility; but I relished it and worked hard to ensure that the case was well and carefully tried. In my judgement I made sure that I covered all the relevant points of fact and law. In this case the culprit had killed a man who claimed to be a witch doctor and was threatening to put a spell on him and his wife that would lead to their deaths. This the culprit implicitly believed; and I believed him; so did the two Assessors — elders of the same tribe who used to sit with the judge in such cases to advise about tribal customs and give their assessment of the facts. They believed the story of the accused but observed that his correct course was not to take the law into his own hands but to report to his chief, who could have dealt with the witch doctor under customary law.

Under the Protectorate law which followed English law, there could be no defence of provocation for what was a premeditated killing; nor could self-defence be argued. At the end, I had to pass sentence of death which was mandatory.

The case went on appeal to the court of appeal for eastern Africa, sitting in Nairobi, and I awaited its judgement with some trepidation. When a copy of the judgement arrived in Arua, I was surprised and pleased to read the words of the Court's President, none other than Sir Norman Whitley at that time. 'This case has been so well tried by Mr Posnett that there is no need for the Court of Appeal to go into the matter further.' This was an accolade that later stood me in good stead when I applied to the Bar Council in London for exemption from some of the normal requirements for call to the Bar.

The trial judge had the further duty of advising the Governor whether or not he should exercise the royal prerogative of mercy. In this case I had no difficulty in recommending that the sentence be commuted to imprisonment because of the state of mind of the murderer. In due course the Governor did consider the case and accepted my recommendation for mercy. I felt much relieved.

A year later I was having supper one evening with Ronald Ladkin when there was a call at the door and a uniformed policeman informed us that there had been a fight in the town and a man was lying dead. Ronald and I jumped into a car and drove a mile to the place where a crowd had gathered. Another policeman showed us the body of a man lying in the road. Blood was seeping from the wound in his chest. Ronald examined him, confirmed that he was dead and told the police to take the body to the mortuary, where a postmortem examination could be done next morning. The assailant had not run away and he was taken to the cells by the police.

In due course I was again asked to preside at the trial and I had to consider whether I ought to disqualify myself because I had been so close to the event. I decided there was no reason to do this merely because I had seen the body. When the case came to trial the crux of the defence was that both parties had been inflamed by drink at a beer party. The accused came from the Congo and tribal insults were exchanged. The accused had lost his temper, pulled his knife and that was that. The facts were not in dispute and, however one looked at them, they could not meet the legal definition of provocation such as would reduce the offence from murder to manslaughter.

Yet again I had to pass sentence of death. Again the appeal was dismissed. I advised the Governor that it was not a premeditated killing but a drunken affray that did not call for the death penalty. I recommended commutation but this time, wrongly I thought, my advice was not followed and the accused was later hanged.

8

Congo

With a long frontier intersecting tribes indiscriminately, it was important to maintain a good working liaison with our Belgian counterparts across the border. The nearest Belgian post was Aru, only 14 miles from Arua, where a single Belgian administrative officer was in charge. Aru was a smaller town than Arua, and the *Administrateur*, Benoit, had few, if any, other officials with whom to consort. Since his wife Marjorie was English they were glad to exchange visits and to cooperate with us where necessary. We worked on a basis of common sense rather than strict legality. Wanted criminals who ran across the border were caught and handed back with minimal formality.

When Benoit was later transferred to Stanleyville, he and his wife invited me to visit them there. So when I became due for a further spell of leave I resolved to explore the Congo. I decided to drive south as far as Irumu, whence I could fly to Stanleyville. I would leave the car in Irumu and, on my return, drive on south towards the fabled Lake Kivu before coming back into Uganda at Kabale in the far southwest, where James Hunter was by now stationed.

In due course I set out in the redoubtable Fanny along exciting roads through mountainous country to the west of Lake Albert. We had only sketchy maps of the Congo and it was a relief to arrive for an overnight stop in Bunia where I found a small hotel. The next day, after passing the Kilo Moto gold mines (which later became famous when Amin allegedly raided them), I reached Irumu. The town was set on an upland plateau at an altitude of over 5000 feet. I found a hotel where they agreed to let me leave my car for a week while I flew to Stanleyville.

Next morning the plane arrived on schedule. It was an old three-engined Junkers 52, an aircraft that had been in service in Europe for many years and was remarkable for having a corrugated metal skin. This one was operated by the local subsidiary of the Belgian airline SABENA. We flew west at modest altitude across the endless green carpet of the Ituri forest. It was like an ocean and no place for a forced landing. Only once did I see any clearing and that was a small airstrip which we passed over an hour after leaving Irumu. I was glad I had not attempted the 600-mile drive by road.

Our approach to Stanleyville was signalled by more frequent clearings in the forest and eventually a glimpse of the silver waters of the great Congo River. We landed and stepped out into a warm and humid atmosphere: Stanleyville is about 1000 feet above sea level. Marjorie was there to meet me and drove me to their house. I spent my days there seeing what I could of the town and taking photographs. It seemed a large metropolis after Arua. At that time BOAC was running a flying boat service across Africa from west to east and this involved a night stop at Stanleyville *en route* to Lake Victoria and Mombasa. I got to see one of the boats moored at its buoy in the river: the current here was faster than the Nile and the boat was tugging at its moorings.

Stanleyville was at the upper limit for navigation from Leopoldville and the sea. A mile upstream there was a series of rapids which provided a happy hunting ground for local fishermen. One day Benoit took us out in a fisherman's canoe. The river seemed wider than the Nile at Pakwach and surprisingly fast flowing.

From talking with Benoit I was able to get some idea of how the government worked. As pure administrators they seemed first class, but where they differed from us was in their view of the country's future. Secondary education for Congolese was rare and no attempt was made to bring Africans into the higher echelons of government. Politics was not encouraged. During my stay a mutiny broke out among African troops at a military establishment in the south and I was able to report what I learned about this when I got back to Uganda.

The time came for me to return to Irumu and I bade farewell to Benoit and Marjorie. Half an hour after takeoff I noticed the pilot was making a turn through 180 degrees and saw that the port engine was windmilling. (No feathering for those propellers.) Soon we were losing height over the outskirts of Stanleyville. A couple of nuns were sitting behind me and I heard one of them say to her companion (in French):

'It's surprising how similar this looks to Stanleyville.'

Indeed it did!

We touched down and I felt the plane begin to swing left. Without a tricycle undercarriage in those days a large aeroplane on the ground could only steer with its engines: with the port engine dead there was little the pilot could do to correct the swing. Finally there was a jolt and we stopped. There were some excited exclamations by the crew and we were invited to climb down the usual ladder at the back. We were at the far end of the field. The plane had collided with an anthill.

It was two hours before a replacement aircraft was ready and during our wait I made the acquaintance of a fellow passenger. John Birch, a British officer from West Africa, was on his way to Goma on Lake Kivu to examine and report to the British government on the famine in Rwanda. When, several hours later, we arrived at Irumu, he was dismayed to be told that the plane could not take him on to Goma. It was scheduled to fly to Costermansville via Goma, but because of the altitude it could not take off from Irumu at full load. Passengers for Goma would be off-loaded. Furthermore, as it was now late, there would be a night stop at Irumu. I suggested that John should join me for the long drive down to Goma. He accepted and we had a convivial evening at the Irumu hotel.

There followed three fascinating days on the trip and I cannot do better than quote an account John himself wrote. An abbreviated version is included in his autobiography.*

'Posnett's car is an old 1934 Chevrolet tourer, capable of a top speed, I should say, of about 35 mph. (Rubbish!) We went first

---

* John P. Birch, *The Merchant Venturers' Servant*.

to see the plane off. It took practically the whole length of the runway. With my extra weight I doubt whether it would have made it. We then set off south for Butembo and soon got into the Ituri rainforest, the home of the pygmies. We saw only a few, ugly little dwarfs. It must be depressing for them living in such a vast damp and gloomy forest. There was a slow drizzle that seemed to have been going on since the beginning of time.

We came out of the forest into open rolling country and a mass of cloud to our left showed where the Ruwenzori mountains lay. At midday we arrived at Beni and lunched at a pleasant little hotel. After lunch the car refused to start and Posnett decided to dismantle the pump. He produced his tool kit which consisted of a screwdriver and an adjustable spanner the size of a sledgehammer. However, a Frenchman staying at the hotel rescued us with a complete set of tools, did most of the dismantling, and finally told us, incorrectly, that the diaphragm was faulty. So we decided to stay the night.

That was a happy decision, for towards evening the clouds cleared from the Ruwenzori and we had a magnificent view of the whole range, covered with snow. We walked up to St Gustave Mission to get a better view and Posnett climbed on the roof of the church to get a photograph. Four fathers from the mission came out and greeted us, glad to meet someone new, and took us back for coffee, bread and cheese. They were pleasant people, two Dutch, one Belgian and one French. Back at the hotel we had a drink with the helpful Frenchman. He had owned a transport business in Burma and took part in the retreat into India with the British forces.

Next morning Posnett took the fuel pump round to the SHUN garage where a little African mechanic in a Tyrolese hat soon found out that the trouble was only a faulty filter gasket. He soon cut a new one, but in fitting the pump back he broke the pump gasket. I made a new one out of the cover of the *Political Quarterly*!

We finally left Beni at midday, making for Lubero. The road, winding and steep, passed through magnificent hilly country. Past Butembo we took the 'mines' road, so winding and danger-

ous that only one-way traffic is allowed, southbound and
northbound on alternate days. (On Sundays you trust to the
good Lord.) Most of the day's drive was at an altitude between
5000 and 7000 feet.

Lubero itself, at 7000 feet, is right on the equator. They said
that the dining room of the hotel was in the northern hemisphere and the sitting room in the southern. We took a short
walk and noticed that the altitude made us puff. It was a simple
little hotel with excellent food. We had strawberries and cream
for tea by a roaring fire of eucalyptus wood. It's the strawberry
season all the year round here, they told us. In the evening a
convoy of 20 lorries of the Force Publique arrived, returning
from Rwanda where they had been taking famine supplies.

Next morning there was a nip in the air. We climbed again
with a dizzy number of hairpin bends to over 8000 feet. We
passed plantations of pyrethrum with picturesque houses
perched on hills, then through bamboo forest and out into open
savannah where we could see the road ahead winding away up
into more hills. Finally, we came to the top of the Kabasha
escarpment from where we had a magnificent view down over
the Lac Edouard plain with the ring of (Virunga) volcanoes
going up to 14,000 feet in the background. The road cut out of
solid rock, zigzags down the escarpment in a terrifying series of
hairpin bends.

Across the Parc Albert Game Reserve we saw little game
before reaching Rutshuru. There we found no petrol to be had
so pressed on through a rather eerie region of volcanic mountains and lava beds. There had been an eruption last year and
the lava streams were only now cooling down. We arrived at
Goma and stayed at the Hotel des Volcans. Lake Kivu is really
beautiful. The volcano behind Goma (Nyamulagira) was glowing red, and throwing a spectacular light on the cloud above.

As Posnett was leaving for Kabale next day we had a pleasant
farewell dinner. His offering me a lift from Irumu had been a
fortunate chance for he took me through some of the most
spectacular country in the Congo and I would not have missed
it for anything.'

It was fortunate indeed: it gave me agreeable company on such a memorable trip. John kindly refrains from mentioning that the car's old canvas hood disintegrated during the drive leaving us exposed to the elements, but we did not mind and the weather was fine. Now I could add the Kabasha escarpment to my collection of Africa's greatest viewpoints. John's mention of Rutshuru reminds me that 15 years later my wife and I were back there on the first day of independence for the Congo which the Belgians had so precipitately left to its tragic fate.

I went on by myself through Ruhengeri to re-enter Uganda at Kisoro. The road from there climbs 3000 feet up the escarpment to Kanaba Gap and then winds through bamboo forest and the Kigezi hills. I arrived in Kabale as if in a fantasy world to be welcomed by James and Netta Hunter.

During the week I spent with them I suggested to James that we should climb Muhavura, the nearest of the volcanoes. We camped in Kisoro and set off early with a guide. Ascending gently at first over grass covered foothills and then through denser undergrowth where the guide cut a way, after two and a half hours we reached the foot of the final cone at about 8,500 feet. From there on it was like going upstairs without a pause for almost five hours — and the stairs got progressively steeper near the top. We also felt the lack of oxygen and had to make frequent stops for breath. James weighed over 15 stone and I was anxious about his condition but we finally struggled on to the summit at 13,547 feet. There we found a lovely little tarn of fresh water. Sadly, we were in thick cloud so we got no view. A two pound can of peaches in syrup which, with some misgiving, I had brought in my pack, was consumed with relish before setting off down. We had climbed 7,500 feet from the roadhead and the descent was extremely jarring on our knees: we both suffered for a day or two afterwards.

I had a lot of new experiences to digest during the long drive back to Arua.

9

Flying Boats
and a Transfer

When Owen Griffith arrived in Arua as a newly appointed administrative cadet, he brought a breath of realism into our sugar coated
lives. He had been wounded in action with the Welsh Guards in
North Africa, mentioned in dispatches, and invalided out of the army.
His presence was a constant reminder of how cocooned we were, far
from the battlefields where the world's future was being decided and
where lives were being risked and lost, including those of some of my
friends. In the office, it was helpful to have another pair of hands.
Owen also augmented, and raised the standard of, our meagre
resources for evening games of golf and bridge.

Moyo

Another staff change occurred when Chris Marshall, the DO Madi
based in Moyo, was posted elsewhere and I was asked to take his
place. This was pleasing news. It meant I would have my own
command 100 miles distant from any other government authority.
However, the assignment was to be on a part-time basis so that
every month I would spend a week or two in Arua. Looking back I
suspect that this proviso was due to the DC's wish not to be involved
in court work which would still be left to me. I thought that the

arrangement would be manageable and looked forward to exploring my new territory.

By then there had been changes in my own domestic staff. Trofima and the cook had returned to their homeland in Buganda and had been replaced respectively by Ongei, an Alur, and Samueli, a Lugbara cook. Both were old hands for whom safari held no fears and each month we moved to and fro between Arua and Moyo with little difficulty.

The larger part of the population in Madi sub-district lived on the east side of the Nile, a flat and fairly arid area at an elevation of only 2000 feet above sea level. One reached it by a road that wound down a steep escarpment from Moyo to Laropi on the river where a ferry was based. This was a simple pontoon construction which four men propelled with long poles and paddles, and the crossing took about 20 minutes. Laropi is the lowest and I suspect the hottest place in Uganda. It is the only place where I was ever overcome by real heat exhaustion.

The DO's house in Moyo was a delightful change from the standard public works' design of houses. Red brick walls and pillars supported a high thatched roof over a floor plan with two side wings set at an angle of about 30 degrees to the central section which comprised a single large living area with open verandah at the front looking north towards the Sudan. One wing housed a bedroom and bathroom, the other a dining room and kitchen. With its high ceilings and shady verandahs, the house was remarkably cool to live in despite Moyo being lower than Arua in altitude.

Soon after I took over we were informed that BOAC wanted to introduce a flying boat service from Cairo up the Nile to Lake Victoria, with a night stop at Khartoum. Between Khartoum and Port Bell, near Kampala on Lake Victoria, there would need to be refuelling stops at Wadi Halfa and, if practicable, Laropi. It was amazing to think of flying boats alighting at such a remote spot but a senior executive from the airline duly arrived in a light aeroplane which landed on the small grass airstrip at Arua. From there I drove him the 100 miles to Moyo and then down to Laropi. After a good look round he seemed satisfied and said that engineers would follow to prepare the necessary installations for fuel storage, boat and lighter berthing, and buoys for the flying boats. All this gave me an interesting break from the routine of district administration.

Soon the cargo on the *Lugard*'s fortnightly trip began to include unusual items such as fuel bowsers, boats, buoys and building materials. Being used to slow moving government procedures it was fun to see how quickly things could be done in the commercial world. There were soon petrol storage tanks, buoys moored in the river, a new jetty and motorboats alongside. It would be only a matter of time before our old car ferry with its four paddlers was motorized. Two years later, homeward bound at last after the war, I found myself boarding a flying boat at Port Bell on Lake Victoria for the two-day journey to Cairo and had the sweet experience of alighting on the river at Laropi and seeing some of my old African friends there. It is rare to see a project come to fruition and be able to enjoy its fruits.

The frontier between Madi and the Sudan was a fairly arbitrary line unmarked on the ground. There were inevitable problems over trying to control crime and trade across the border. I made it my business to get in touch with the DC of the neighbouring district in the Sudan and to arrange a meeting at Nimule, about ten miles downstream from Laropi but a much longer circuit by car. The DC turned out to be a Wordsworth, a distant relative of the poet, and we enjoyed a satisfactory dialogue, reaching agreement on how to handle a number of matters. I stayed the night with him at the Nimule rest camp and what started as an official meeting soon became a friendly celebration over far too many glasses of whisky. When, after my return to Moyo, I sent a report to the Provincial Commissioner I received a quizzical reply that mingled approval with a degree of reserve. Sandford was a master of the *double entendre* and obviously knew his man.

While at Moyo, I was determined to climb Otze, the great mountain towering over the Nile above Laropi which is visible in clear weather from Arua 100 miles away. It proved a good day's work on foot. Ascending first through a fertile valley with fields of sweet potato and cassava amid upland woods, we then left the inhabited areas and plodded up the long west ridge in light scrub. This allowed fine views north into the Sudan with the Nile, like a silver streak, disappearing into the haze. Once on the summit, we could gaze down on the river 3000 feet below and on the little jetty at Laropi, a moment I still like to remember.

I had to return to Arua while the DC took local leave and at that time a tragedy occurred in Jonam. Owen Griffith was down there on his first solo safari. One day I received an urgent message to say that Sultan Anderea had been murdered. This could lead to serious unrest and my first reaction was to jump in the car and head for Pakwach. But I could not leave the station unmanned, and after a little thought, I sent for Juma, the head interpreter. Being a man of great experience and sense, whom I trusted, I asked him to go down to Jonam to give Owen any assistance he needed. I scribbled a note to Owen saying that he could rely on Juma for advice about local politics and added a warning about one particular fellow whom I knew from a previous encounter was jealous of Anderea and, I feared, unscrupulous.

Juma returned a few days later along with a policeman and the man accused of the murder. It turned out to be the very man I had mentioned in my note. He had apparently come up behind them when the Sultan and Owen were standing looking across the river. Raising a *jembe*, a local hoe with a sharp edge, he crashed it down on Anderea's head, smashing his skull. The shock for Owen, who had been standing within a yard of him, must have been intense. Fortunately, the culprit made no attempt to assault anyone else and was arrested at once. That was a case I did not try.

In due course the DC returned from his leave which he had spent with friends down country. He was a bachelor and I had tried not to notice one or two signs about his private life. One day, the agricultural officer came into my office with a worried look, closed the door behind him, and leant over my desk.

'Dick, I have learned that the DC is keeping boys! Did you know?'

As it accorded with things I had observed, I knew at once that this must be true. I suppose I nodded, but I replied weakly,

'What do you expect me to do about it?'

The AO was obviously appalled and, knowing the tribal view on this sort of thing, I was well aware of the danger, but could think of no course of action that was not fraught with difficulty. I made discreet enquiries and ascertained that the DC had indeed brought back two young boys from Toro district and they were living in his servants' quarters. One of my problems was that, having spent all my service in this remote outstation, I had no personal contacts at headquarters to confide in and consult. It seemed much too dangerous anyway to commit anything to a letter.

It happened that very soon after this I was told of my impending transfer to Jinja in Busoga. I was to exchange places with Peter Gibson and ten days later he arrived in Arua. At a suitable opportunity I took Peter aside and told him about the DC. I confessed that I had done nothing about it because I did not see what I could do. As a newcomer to the station he felt much the same way. I felt very uncomfortable about having to leave him to cope with such a nasty situation.

Some months later I heard that the DC had been replaced and shortly afterwards he left the country. I never enquired how it had all come to light. Thankfully, Peter remained a good friend and, ten years later, I was happy to preside, as registrar of marriages, at his wedding in Entebbe.

❋ ❋ ❋

Jinja

Jinja is located at the point where the Nile flows out of Lake Victoria to begin its long journey to Cairo. The river was bridged for railway and road: the dam and hydroelectric plant were not built until many years later. The town was a metropolis compared with Arua — it had a railway station, a cinema, and an army barracks with several British officers. There was a large Indian population and a wide variety of shops. The British must have numbered well over a hundred, with a lively club and some unattached women which was a nice change for me. The DC's office occupied the end of one wing in a large office complex which also housed provincial headquarters and all the technical departments servicing both the Eastern Province and Busoga district. We were small fry in that large pond and I think this affected the regard with which the DC was held by the Basoga.

Busoga district had none of the attractions for me of the West Nile. Mainly flat and wooded, it had no views, no mountains, and no rushing rivers aside from the Nile. I could not speak the language which is similar to Luganda, and they did not use Swahili. Many of them spoke English, but I felt I lacked the insight into their minds which only knowing the language can give. I was due to take the government exam in a second language, but for that it was too late to start on Luganda. Instead, I sat the lower standard Lwoo paper, for which my practice in Alur and Jonam stood me in good stead. Fortunately, the senior ADC, Tom Cox, was a qualified examiner in Lwoo and for the oral exam he sat me down with an Acholi police-man. Acholi is not too different from the Jonam dialect and I managed to converse fairly freely. Tom made due allowance when my Alur accent intruded and he passed me without further ado. I should then really have got down to learning Luganda, but I felt uninspired by the work in the district and let things slip.

I was allocated the house Peter Gibson had previously occupied overlooking the golf course and lake. Because of rabies in the West Nile, Peter had asked me to take over his dog, a lovely golden retriever bitch called Juno which soon became attached to me and was a good companion. If I did not take her to the office in the morning she would turn up there 20 minutes later and flop down under my desk. One day she did not appear. When I went home for lunch she was not there. The servants told me that she sometimes went down to the lakeside, presumably to scavenge on the leavings of fishermen. They feared that a crocodile had taken her. I drove all over the town looking for her but to no avail. I sought help from the local chief and offered a reward, but Juno was never seen again. I was very distressed and wrote abjectly to Peter.

Ruwenzori: Mount Gessi

When the war in Europe ended there was a rush for home leave to Britain. We could not all go at once and I was in no hurry. I wanted to accumulate enough leave to allow me to return to Cambridge for a year to complete part two of the law tripos. The college could take me for the academic year 1946/7 by which time I would have been in Uganda for more than five years and be due for almost a year's leave.

This left me another 12 months to serve and, meanwhile, gave me time to take three weeks' local leave. I wanted to have another go at Ruwenzori and, after a lot of letter writing, we made up a party of three with Peter Hicks as the leader. A railway engineer and surveyor, he was also a considerable mountaineer with a number of difficult ascents to his name on Mount Kenya and elsewhere. Peter Allen, a DO from New Zealand, would make up the party.

Allen and I planned to meet at Bugoye on 1st December 1945. Hicks could only get away three days later but he planned to catch us up at the foot of Mount Gessi by travelling fast and light. By that time we hoped to have reconnoitred a route up Gessi. This is one of the northernmost peaks of the Ruwenzori range and is named after the Italian explorer who in 1876 circumnavigated Lake Albert and saw the distant snows of Ruwenzori without quite realizing what they were. Gessi consists of a long ridge with two summits, Iolande the higher at 15,470 feet, and Bottego at the northern end of the ridge. The mountain was first climbed in 1906 by the Duke of the Abruzzi's expedition which reached both summits. Since then it had only been tackled once, many years later when Dr Noel Humphreys reached the top of Iolande after breaking his arm and setting it himself.

Before implementing our plan, I went for a few days to see James Hunter in Kabale where I suffered another bout of malaria. By now paludrine had become available to help deal with it, but I sent telegrams to the two Peters to warn them that I might be unable to join them. Fortunately the message never reached Allen and I managed to get to our rendezvous on time. Meanwhile Hicks had sent telegrams to inform us that he was down with a severe bout of tonsillitis and could not come. His telegrams also failed to arrive, but Hicks did and by 6 December he had caught us up.

Allen and I had failed to find a route up to the Gessi ridge and we now intensified the search. Hindered by bad weather we got turned back twice by rock faces on the west of the mountain. We moved our camp round to the Bukurungu valley on the eastern side and from there found a way up to the ridge. We came to a rock face split by a crack which we nicknamed 'Mummery's Crack' (after the classic climb on the Grépon), but by then it was late, the weather was bad, and we had to turn back. It was only on 11th December that we finally established a bivouac high on the eastern flank of the mountain and sent the porters back to camp. I recorded the next day in a letter at the time:

I got up at 4.50 to light the primus. It was a fine starry night, but clouds were moving up the valleys from the east. It was very cold and took half an hour to boil water for cocoa. We were off by 5.30, Hicks leading with a hurricane lantern. Now and again I relieved him of the lantern so that he could get a second handhold on a difficult move. But we wriggled our way up to the ridge and turned north towards 'Mummery's Crack'. By now it was light enough to see and we left the lantern there. We also placed slips of paper at intervals under stones to mark the route for the return journey, in case the clouds closed in.

At about 8.15 we reached the foot of the glacier and stopped to brew tea and eat a chapati and jam. A wind had sprung up and we were soon enveloped in cloud. After roping up, Hicks led off. It was steep, about 45 degrees: it would have been very steep to ski on, that's how I judged it. There was enough snow to kick steps and no danger of avalanche so early in the morning. Hicks was using a compass because we could see nothing. We reached a level place, then had to go down a snow gully, up another and finally up some very loose and rotten rock which I kept dislodging onto the unfortunate Allen who was following. After a shout from Hicks, who was out of our sight ahead, we were there, with a nice little cairn to our left. To cap it all, the clouds suddenly cleared and we had half an hour of magnificent sunshine. We gazed around at all the other peaks as the clouds lifted. Margherita, the highest of all, was pure white to the southwest. The Portal Peaks were now below us. And Bottego, the second peak of Gessi, lay about a mile away across a broken rocky ridge. Hicks used the opportunity to take survey bearings for a map he was preparing.

After leaving a note in a tin in the cairn to record our names, we set off to climb Bottego which had not been done since the first climb 40 years before. It was slow going, down and up and further than we thought. Finally, we came up to a huge boulder which required some juggling with the rope to climb onto. On top were five stones, presumably put there by the Duke's party. We could only go up one at a time and Allen decided not to bother with those last 15 feet.

It was after midday when we started down and we were all beginning to feel the strain. Hicks was pale and had a bad headache. Once past the Iolande summit we took a glissade down a snow slope which made us all feel better. We plodded on across the glacier until we got to the steep snow slope leading down to the rock ridge. My hat blew off and, in our efforts to rescue it, we found the snow very soft. After Hicks had moved across to grab the hat, I shouted to the others that we should glissade again and started off, leaving them little option as we were still roped. We arrived at the foot of the slope in exhilarating style. We undid the rope and carried on down the ridge, picked up the lantern at 'Mummery's Crack' and plodded on down until at last we saw our bivouac. The porters were there and we gave them a shout which they answered with joy. Packing up the tent we went on down to our earlier campsite in the valley. When we reached this at about 6 p.m. Gessi was clear and we were able to point out to the porters our route up the glacier which had left a faint line on the snow. It was only three or four miles away in a direct line but far above us now.

We were all exhausted. Allen was elected cook by a majority of two to one. My contribution was to open the inevitable can of peaches we had saved for the day of victory. Two days later we were back in Fort Portal. It was only 54 hours since we had left the summit of Gessi.

When I got back to Jinja I was not sorry to learn that I was to be transferred again, this time to Soroti in Teso district. There it was flat, hot and mosquito ridden but at least there were wide open spaces — and some interesting mountains up near the border with Karamoja. The people were black and tall and I liked them. They spoke an Hamitic language that few Europeans have mastered, but the district also contained isolated pockets of people speaking a Lwoo dialect which made me feel more at home.

I was in Teso for less than a year before it was time for me to go home on leave. Fanny was sold, farewells were said, and I was soon boarding the flying boat at Port Bell for the two-day trip to Cairo. It was a strange feeling to land at Laropi; it left me wondering which world was the real one and which a dream. Two days in Cairo waiting for onward transport gave me the chance to see the superb museums before I picked up a Dakota flight to Malta. There, after getting stung by a jellyfish, I finally caught a flight home to England and to a reunion with my family.

It was 1946. I had been away for five years, during which time we had not seen each other. My parents had moved to Dorset. My sister had married. My brother had been badly burnt when the Hudson he was ferrying to North Africa caught fire on takeoff in Bathurst in West Africa; but he had recovered and had distinguished himself in coastal command before leaving the RAF with a DFC. It took time to pick up all the threads before going back to being a student again.

10

Lawyer

Back at Cambridge I was glad to find a few friends from earlier days and to share rooms at St John's with Denys Hall. Others had not survived the war. We were now rubbing shoulders with fresh-faced 19-year-olds straight from school. Although with our experience we might be more motivated, our habits were less ascetic: we drank more and our memories were less retentive.

Wanting to make the best use of the time available while I was on leave from Uganda, I decided to take the Bar exams at the same time as doing my degree course. A firm of crammers in London advised me that to complete both parts of the Bar exams would normally take two to three years. Despite this negative advice, I started on their correspondence course for Part I which I planned to sit in December, only three months away. One of the subjects on the curriculum was English land law which would be followed in Part II by conveyancing, neither of which interested me. I discovered that alternative subjects could be offered, mainly for the benefit of overseas students, one of which was Islamic law. I thought this might be useful in Uganda where the Sudanese and Arab influence has left a Muslim minority in certain areas.

The crammer did not cover the subject so I cast around in Cambridge and found a charming young Indian postgraduate student named Sharma who agreed to tutor me for a modest fee. Neither of us imagined that 30 years later we would meet again in India when he was Governor of Andhra Pradesh, or that one day he would become President of India.

December came and I hurried down to London to sit the exams. Then, wanting to return to the Alps after six years away, I went to Arosa with the University Ski Club. One day at the top of a ski lift I saw the familiar face of an old prewar friend from St John's, Hans Wilmersdoerffer. He was one of several fellow students who, at the outbreak of war, had been arrested and interned as enemy aliens.

'Hans!' I shouted with delight.

He came over and clasped my hand.

'My name is now John Wilmers,' he said quietly.

He had changed his name to avoid the wartime prejudice attaching to anybody with a German name. After initial internment in Canada, he had been cleared as a genuine anti-Nazi from a Jewish family and had then joined the SAS and fought in the Mediterranean theatre.

When the ski team left for the university races in St Moritz, John invited me to come with him to Sils Maria, a small village ten miles up the Engadine valley, where he planned to stay for a few days with Swiss relations of his. I knew of Sils Maria as the birthplace of Christian Klucker, whose book *The Adventures of an Alpine Guide* I treasured. I recalled the couplet:

Sils Maria ohne Klucker
Ist wie Kaffee ohne Zucker.

In Sils I met John's relatives, including the Stiebel sisters. Elisabeth and I became fond of each other and this led to our marriage six months later.

John and I found companions with whom to ski and had a memorable day climbing Piz Corvatsch on skis (with skins) long before any cable car had been thought of. Professor Bezzola led the way up for six hours without ever ceasing his flow of talk on all manner of interesting subjects. From the summit glacier I had my first view of lovely Piz Bernina and of the mountain immortalized for me as a boy in Ernst Udet's film *The White Hell of Piz Palü*.

Back in Cambridge for a few months' intensive study, I managed to scramble second class honours in the tripos but, with little time for training, I failed to make the university athletics team. I had to be content with a place in the relay team for the low hurdles.

Elisabeth and I then settled down in London. The Bar finals were due in December which left me a bare six months to prepare, comforted by the crammer's advice that I could not hope to cover the syllabus in that time. In the event, to their surprise and mine, I got a second class, confirming Posnett's first law: 'Don't be deterred from your purpose by negative advice.'

The finals had included a paper on the Islamic law of inheritance, a complex set of rules which vary depending on which of the several Sunni or Shia sects is involved. After the exams I paid a courtesy call on Professor Vesey Fitzgerald, the leading Islamic scholar at the Bar. He had been our examiner and surprised me by saying that I had written a first class paper, but took the gilt off the gingerbread by pointing out that I was the only candidate who could write decent English.

A Road and a Revolt

It was early 1948 when we returned to Uganda. I was again assigned to the West Nile district, home for me but an adventure for Elisabeth. When our first child was due, I took her down to stay with Rennie and Maree Bere in Kampala and returned to Arua to await events. In due course, a telegram arrived from Rennie announcing: 'Summit reached with boy as third on rope.'

It had been a difficult delivery and Elisabeth must have felt alone, but in those days it was unusual for the father to be present at a birth. A week later I drove down country from Arua to pick up my wife and newborn son whom we named David, but who was always called Daudi, the Luganda version of the name he shared with the former Kabaka of Buganda.

Although I was happy in Arua among old friends and familiar places, I began to feel frustrated working under an uninspiring DC. Frank Steele arrived as a new cadet and soon proved to be a kindred spirit. We made some interesting trips together, including one into the Congo. But I was not putting my legal training to good use and could see little prospect of promotion. I wrote to apply for a transfer to the Legal Department.

Meanwhile, I took Elisabeth and the infant Daudi to tour the Alur highlands. The sub-county of Erusi, 5000 feet up in the far south of the district, was an area of prolific coffee growing but it could not be reached by road. Heavy bags of coffee had to be manhandled on bicycles ten miles down to Parombo. I asked for funds to build a road and was allotted 1000 shillings — £50! I spent several days working out the best route for a road that would have to climb 2500 feet from Parombo to Erusi. With some careful traversing and circling a hill, I marked out a line for the ten-mile route which, apart from one short stretch up a ridge, was nowhere steeper than a one in ten gradient.

Six months later the road had been completed within budget and entirely by manual labour. We were able to drive up it in a lorry, to the immense delight of the populace, especially the children few of whom had ever seen a motor vehicle before. That night the hills throbbed with drumming as everybody assembled for an all-night dance. The future prosperity of Erusi was now assured.

Soon after that we received reports of a disturbance among the Lugbara of Offude county who were refusing to pay their taxes. The Sultan, who bore the inappropriate name of Risasi (Swahili for 'bullet') was ineffective and frightened. The DC consulted me. I said that one of us should obviously go there to find out what the trouble was and I offered to go. He asked me if I would like to take a police escort but, knowing the friendly Lugbara, I thought that would be ridiculous and might even be provocative. Instead, to avoid any appearance of alarm, I took my family and my trusted friend Juma, the head interpreter and an influential figure.

Camped in Offude I noticed a rather tense atmosphere. I summoned a public meeting at which I announced that I had come to hear all their complaints and would listen to them carefully, but subject to one condition: before I would hear them they must pay their overdue taxes. I added that if anyone refused to pay I would have to impound his cattle. This was not received with pleasure, but I had found out beforehand the names of two ringleaders and called them up. When they refused to pay, I sent Risasi out with Juma and two local *askaris* (constables) to take one bullock from each of their herds.

By the time the public meeting reconvened the next morning, more than a hundred had paid up and I listened to them for some hours. Their complaints were not serious and I was able to resolve them without difficulty; a better chief would have done so by himself. So ended the Offude revolt. Risasi was discreetly retired and his county amalgamated with neighbouring Maracha under the efficient Chief Maskini (whom I was to meet again 30 years later.)

A Legal Career?

In due course my application for transfer to the legal department was approved and I was posted to Mbale in the Eastern Province to act as Resident Magistrate. During the six months while the incumbent RM was on leave I came to see what one could expect from a career in law. It would be a comfortable life mainly in civilized places and with good prospects of promotion, but I would be dealing with the affairs of those in trouble of one sort or another — rather like a doctor whose patients by definition have problems of a bodily sort. I missed being involved in the lives of the people and in their future which I had found so enjoyable in the administrative service; and I felt excluded from the important activities, policies and decisions about the district and the tribes which were the province of the DC.

After six months I was moved to the Crown Law Office in Entebbe, where my duties as a Crown Counsel covered criminal prosecutions and occasional civil actions involving the government. If I hoped to pursue a permanent career in the legal service I would first have to work for two years in a barrister's chambers in England and the Attorney General in Uganda kindly arranged such an attachment for me. Meanwhile I was sent off on circuit with the High Court to conduct the prosecution in homicide cases. During that trip I enjoyed meeting friends and colleagues in various up-country stations but this only served to bring home to me more clearly how, in the legal department, I was getting sidetracked from the beating heart of the country which lay in the care of the political administration.

I realized that a moment of personal crisis was at hand: I had reached a crossroads and must decide now, once and for all, which way to go. After a few days of agonizing, I wrote to the Attorney General to say that I had changed my mind and did not feel able to accept his offer of an attachment to chambers in England. I sent the letter off and felt that I had crossed the Rubicon. There would be no turning back and any thought of a career in the law was at an end.

It was difficult to explain this very personal decision to others; and the government, not without reason, saw little to admire in my changes of mind. I could expect no more favours from superiors whom I had disappointed.

11

Buganda
and the Kabaka

The kingdom of Buganda which covered a large area around the northern and western shores of Lake Victoria, was a province of the Protectorate. The Baganda, numbering almost two million, were by far the largest tribe in the country. They also claimed a degree of primacy because of the treaty status accorded them by the Uganda Agreement of 1900 which recognized their hereditary ruler, the Kabaka, and his chiefs as the official authority in domestic affairs, subject to certain conditions and under the supervision of the protectorate. And from 1950 it was in Buganda that I was to spend much of the next nine years.

Under the Kabaka, the Katikkoro, equated to a prime minister, and are supported by a minister of finance and a chief justice who presided over an extensive system of courts. The Lukiiko, an assembly of tribal leaders, was slowly developing into a parliament with some of the members being directly elected. Ministers who had been responsible only to the Kabaka now became answerable also to the Lukiiko whose members were becoming increasingly politically aware and motivated.

Whereas in other territories the rising tide of African politics was directed mainly towards achieving national independence, the

Baganda, or their leaders at least, pursued a rather different course. They liked to regard the Uganda Agreement as a treaty between sovereign states and demanded that relations between them should be conducted only with the Governor, not with his subordinate officials. Originally, the British Protectorate had been represented in Buganda by a Provincial Commissioner and District Commissioners, who dealt with the Kabaka's ministers and chiefs in a way similar to the pattern in other provinces. However, because of the Agreement, their supervisory functions had to be exercised with discretion and more in the form of liaison and advice. This sometimes led to resentment when the sensitivities of the Kabaka or his ministers were aroused.

Sir Philip Mitchell, who was Governor from 1935 to 1940, sought to alleviate this friction and introduced changes that were designed better to reflect the proper relation between Protectorate and Buganda government officials. The Provincial Commissioner became the Resident. In 1944, under his successor Sir Charles Dundas, District Commissioners became assistant Residents, while the duties imposed by central government statute were shifted to a new post of Protectorate Agent. These well-meant changes were, however, not well received.

'The Lukiiko feared that this change would require that their officials deal entirely with the Resident, and they saw in this an attempt to lower the status of Buganda. The incident illustrates how suspicion and hostility affect even the most trivial aspect of Protectorate–Buganda relations.'*

In practice, the changes proved to be largely cosmetic and, except in Kampala, the functions of the assistant Resident later came to be combined with those of Protectorate Agent in the same officer.

Supervision of the Buganda courts on behalf of the Protectorate was vested in a Judicial Adviser, and it was in this post that I spent some of my time. It involved examining court records and, although the judicial adviser had the legal power to review the decisions of the Buganda courts, his position *vis-à-vis* the Omulamuzi (chief justice) of

---

* D. A. Low and R. Cranford Pratt, *Buganda and British Overrule.*

the Buganda government was obviously sensitive. Fortunately, I was able to establish close and cordial relations with the Omulamuzi of my day, Joseph Musoke, and we consulted each other freely. On one occasion, we made a trip together to Bukoba in Tanganyika to discuss with the authorities there some matters of mutual concern.

The Buganda courts were generally well run and effective. Working under customary law as well as local enactments of the Lukiiko, they handled crime and civil disputes of a fairly substantial nature. Among these, they had to deal with complex disputes about land tenure, often flowing from the extraordinary *mailo* system — a legacy from the Uganda Agreement of 1900 which introduced the English concept of landlord and tenant. This was superposed on, and gravely distorted, the existing traditional arrangements for use of the land by tribal clans. A register of *mailo* land was maintained after a fashion, but many transactions went unrecorded and the absence of proper survey made the description of boundaries too vague to be definitive and open to endless dispute. This led to frequent litigation and cases from the magistrate's court were often taken on appeal to the county court and the central court, over which the Omulamuzi presided.

There was also provision for a further appeal in certain cases to the judicial adviser, sitting as a court. Civil cases concerning land matters were often difficult to unravel from the written records; and I was at a further disadvantage being unfamiliar with the Luganda language in which all court records were kept. I rarely found it necessary or prudent to interfere with the decision of the lower court.

Local lawyers would sometimes appear on behalf of litigants and it was in the course of such proceedings that I came to know Ben Kiwanuka, who later, in 1961, became Uganda's first chief minister. Later still he was appointed Chief Justice of Uganda only to fall foul of Amin who had him atrociously murdered.

Self-Rule: Tribe or State?

The clan system was a strong factor in Buganda society. Each clan had a totem animal which members of that clan were forbidden to eat. No man might marry a woman of his own clan. The children took the father's clan except in the case of the Kabaka, whose children always took their mother's clan thus neatly avoiding the creation of a royal clan. When Kabaka Daudi Chwa died in 1939 there were two main candidates to succeed him. His own favoured heir was thought to be his eldest son Prince George Mawanda, a commanding figure whom many thought to be a fine potential leader. He was also a good all-rounder at cricket which he had learned at school in England (and he later played for Uganda). This may have won some British hearts, but George's mother was one of Daudi's tribal wives, not married in church, and this swung the Lukiiko (where the church was influential) towards Mutesa, the son of Daudi's church marriage and named after his great-grandfather. He was still a schoolboy when he became the second Kabaka of that name. He later spent two years at Cambridge, but I never found him an easy companion. He had a mind of his own but kept it wrapped up.

During periods as an assistant Resident in the 1950s, I was able to tour Buganda and get to know the people in their homes and on their farms. After the wide-open spaces and hills of the West Nile I found less attraction in the low-lying wooded countryside around Lake Victoria. Struggling to pick up the Luganda language I felt a stranger. Chiefs and staff were impeccably polite, but I could not help feeling that I was an outsider whom they regarded with quiet tolerance. I began to understand the deep tribal feelings below the surface and to realize that I was now sailing on a much more dangerous political sea.

In the West Nile, with little indigenous political activity beyond parochial affairs in the various tribes, it was difficult to envisage the concept of self-government. In Buganda I met a different situation. Here, in a kingdom that had managed its own affairs since long before the advent of white men, I had no difficulty in conceiving of self-government as a practical possibility. Indeed, the Kabaka's government already governed effectively in matters within its wide powers. Their problem was analogous to that of the princely states in India — how to fit the kingdom into the larger state as it moved towards independence.

An organization calling itself the Bataka — literally clan landholders — had become politically active. It was not a national movement like those in some other African territories, but a purely Buganda tribal organization, concerned mainly with local affairs but critical both of the British and of conservative elements in the Kabaka's government. It evoked strong popular support and on two separate occasions, in 1945 and 1949, plunged Buganda into serious disturbances involving riot and arson. This placed the Kabaka's government in a quandary over whether to support the protecting power and face public opprobrium or risk conflict with the Governor and Resident.

By 1950 the Kabaka and his ministers were becoming increasingly anxious about the safety of Buganda's constitutional position under the Uganda Agreement. The Colonial Office in London was known to be in favour of closer union between the three East African territories, at least in economic matters such as railways and customs' management. A suspicion grew up that Buganda would be thrown into the melting pot along with Kenya and Tanganyika. The Baganda feared that the power of their own government would be eroded and that the government of Kenya, which they perceived to be dominated by white settlers, would hold sway. For several years this fear was the main bone of contention between Buganda and the Protectorate. But when the concept of an East African federation was abandoned and self-government for Uganda alone began to emerge as the policy in London, the politicians in Buganda foresaw another and this time more serious danger. This was that Buganda would be absorbed in a unitary state in which its powers would be submerged by those of the other tribes in the surrounding districts and in which Buganda would become a minority influence. The Lukiiko refused to agree to Buganda taking part in a nationwide legislature embracing not only all the tribes but also representatives of the Asians and Europeans.

The British aim was to build a stable country where the rule of law prevailed and which was governed on lines something like the Westminster pattern of parliamentary democracy. Lugard's system of indirect rule had served the British government well in the past and it was of course agreeable to the tribal chiefs who retained their positions and, generally, to the people they ruled. But it did not create the machinery or the political education needed to build a strong democratic central government. It had been taken too easily for granted that local governments in Buganda and other districts would develop and produce leaders who could aspire to government on a national scale. In practice it left a legacy of enhanced authority and power in the hands of tribal and district leaders which often proved to be a stumbling block in the way of later administrators who sought to engineer a new single self-governing state. Only in some realms like sport, for example, was there an active process of nation building.

When in 1952 Sir Andrew Cohen arrived from the Colonial Office in London as the new Governor, he faced a dilemma whose vital importance had not, I think, been fully foreseen. He was anxious to give African leaders more say in the country's affairs, but at the same time his ambition to lead Uganda towards independence as a unitary state made him impatient of their conservative or tribalist attitudes. He wanted them to make their own decisions, but he wanted them to do it his way. Cohen found that loyalty to the tribe and suspicion of, even hostility towards, other tribes were to put major obstacles in the way of his policy. Pondering this at the time, I scribbled a clerihew:

Sir Andrew Cohen
Wanted to get Uganda going;
But he reckoned
Without Mutesa II.

A collision with the Kabaka and his government was, with hind-sight, almost inevitable and the clash came to a head in 1953. Reports of a speech given in London by the Colonial Secretary, Oliver Lyttleton, which did not exclude the possibility of future plans for federation in East Africa, aroused suspicions. In order to safeguard Buganda's position the Kabaka asked for Buganda affairs to be transferred from the Colonial Office in London to the Foreign Office so as to reflect its proper treaty status; and for a timetable to be prepared for the independence of Buganda, separate from the rest of Uganda. It was even canvassed that Buganda should issue its own passports. These proposals for the separation of Buganda commanded wide popular support: even the Uganda National Congress, ostensibly a nationwide political party, came out in support of the Kabaka's demands.

This cut directly across Cohen's aim of an independent unitary state. The Kabaka was asked to sign an undertaking that he would neither oppose, nor encourage the Lukiiko to oppose, Buganda's progress as an integral part of the Protectorate and that he would submit names of Buganda representatives to sit in the Protectorate legislature. Mutesa knew that these undertakings would be unacceptable to his ministers or to the Lukiiko and he refused to sign. For some years British policy had aimed to transform the Kabaka into more of a constitutional monarch who would act on the advice of his ministers and of the Lukiiko. When the Kabaka informed Cohen that he could neither act nor speak against the Lukiiko's will, the Governor was hoist with his own petard.

Cohen was advised by his officials that the Kabaka's refusal constituted a breach of the terms of the Uganda Agreement of 1900 which required the Kabaka to accept and follow the formal advice of the Governor on important matters. When Mutesa still refused to comply, the Governor withdrew recognition from him as Kabaka and he was deported to England. This brought about a major crisis of administration.

At the time I was serving as senior assistant Resident in Kampala, but I had been neither consulted nor informed of what was afoot. Before leaving for Entebbe that morning the Resident, John Birch,* warned me to await a telephone call and be prepared to put the security plan into operation. The call came at about midday, giving me the bare facts with which I quickly briefed the other assistant Residents. It was a surprise to us all, for we had not been taken into confidence about the issues that had led up to the deportation. We fanned out round the country to explain the situation to the chiefs as best we could with the instructions we had been given, setting out only the bare bones of the Governor's side of the story.

The implications for the practical administration of the country appalled me. I did not see how the position could be held in the face of what seemed to me inevitable — the hostility of the whole tribe and of its leaders. Efforts to sell the British case and to get support for the appointment of another Kabaka were doomed to failure. Mutesa had not been universally popular, but now he had become a martyr. Getting him back became the sole objective of his tribe.

---

*   Not the same person as the John Birch quoted in Chapter 8.

After months of discussion a constitutional committee of Baganda was formed under the chairmanship of Sir Keith Hancock, an outside expert, and it eventually came up with proposals for constitutional change which, if the Lukiiko accepted them, would satisfy British requirements. But the Lukiiko would accept them only if Mutesa himself agreed and if he were returned to office.

By that time Alan Lennox-Boyd had become Secretary of State for the Colonies and he came to Uganda to assess the situation for himself. He called a meeting that was attended not just by the senior officers who had advised the Governor but by the district officers most concerned with Buganda affairs in the field. We sat in a semicircle in the Governor's office facing the Secretary of State who had the Governor on one side of him and Gorell Barnes from the Colonial Office on the other. Each of us in turn was asked his view on the situation. John Birch said that we must hold to the line and refuse to allow Mutesa to return. Philip Coutts agreed: any climb down now would make our position impossible. Bill Bell concurred. It came to my turn and I realized that if I said what I really thought my position under Cohen and with my colleagues was bound to be affected. But if the Secretary of State asked for our individual views he was entitled to the truth. I said that we could not continue to rule Buganda or make any political progress without the cooperation of the ministers and Lukiiko; and that could only come if we allowed the Kabaka to return. It must have been obvious that I regarded the deportation as having been a grave mistake but Cohen listened carefully: I think he had probably reached the same conclusion himself. But I was glad when Jake Jacobs, the assistant Resident in Masaka district, spoke out to the same effect. It was many years later when I read his biography* that I realized how reinstatement of the Kabaka must have appealed to Lennox-Boyd's predilection for traditional rulers and monarchy.

Meanwhile, a case was launched in the High Court of Uganda seeking in effect to challenge the legality of the Governor's actions. The case attracted wide popular interest, especially the arguments eloquently deployed by Kenneth Diplock QC, who appeared for the

---

* Philip Murphy, *Alan Lennox-Boyd: A Biography.*

Lukiiko, to the effect that the Kabaka had only wanted to tell the truth to his people. The Resident, John Birch, was called to give evidence and was roughly handled under cross-examination.

In the event the court held that, as an 'act of state', the matter was not justiciable by the courts. The Chief Justice went on to add that the claim of the Secretary of State to be acting under Article 6 of the Uganda Agreement was unjustified, for somewhat technical legal reasons. This undermined the position of the British government which had claimed all along to be acting under the terms of the Uganda Agreement. It was in effect a victory for the Kabaka and his government; and it led inexorably to the ultimate return of the Kabaka to Uganda, albeit as part of a deal involving various constitutional changes. Eventually the Kabaka returned to a hero's welcome from the populace. A new constitution sought to explain the reversal and perhaps cover up British embarrassment. But it was a severe blow to Cohen's standing. The enhanced prestige of the Kabaka and the pride of his tribe turned out unfortunately to be a contributory factor years later in the collapse of the independence constitution when Obote sent troops under Amin to capture or kill the Kabaka, who was lucky to escape to London with his life.

12

New Horizons

In between assignments in Buganda and spells of leave I served two tours of duty during the 1950s in the Secretariat at Entebbe which was the headquarters of the Protectorate government. This was a fate viewed with horror by many field officers. All my service hitherto had been in the field working with Africans and their leaders in the context of their own tribal administration. Now I had to learn how the government of Uganda worked and how it linked with the Colonial Office in London. I did not enjoy the formality, the consciousness of seniority, and the prim rules of procedure, but I learned how to get on with colleagues and, more important, superiors. Inferiors there were none: I was at the bottom of the heap.

When Sir Andrew Cohen arrived in 1952 it happened that my colleague John Champion was selected to be the new Governor's private secretary. This left a vacancy in the post of clerk of the executive and legislative councils to which I succeeded. These councils were the equivalent of the cabinet and parliament and I soon discovered what unexpected power the clerk wielded. The conclusions of ExCo, as it was known, were enshrined in the minutes framed by the clerk; and these conclusions constituted the written record of vital policy decisions. When discussion in council had wandered ambiguously, I was not above putting into the minutes a clear decision that I thought the Council ought to have reached. The Governor usually accepted this.

Papers submitted to ExCo by the departments were sometimes long on technical argument but short on precision about the political decision required. I soon began to see the importance of clear drafting beforehand if the proceedings of the council were to be properly focused. Occasionally, if I could not put this right on the telephone, I would be reduced to sending a paper back for clarification. By persisting in this I found that the Governor could wind up discussion in ExCo with yes or no answers to many of the questions put before it. This made my work easier and, hopefully, that of the departments more effective.

By now our family had grown, with Roland born in Kampala and Monica three years later in Zürich. But Elisabeth was increasingly unhappy with our life together in Africa and she decided to go back to live in Switzerland, taking the children with her. It became difficult to maintain contact except when I was on leave in Europe and, after three years apart, a divorce was granted in a Swiss court. Meanwhile, I had to get used to a bachelor existence.

Olympics

I had become involved in the administration of the Uganda Amateur Athletic Association. African villagers could enjoy athletics without costly equipment or complex rules and without the need to collect 22 people to make up a team game. Several years earlier, in Soroti, I had come across a tall young man of the Teso tribe who had suffered a childhood deformity of one leg, possibly due to polio. As a result, his other leg had become unusually well developed. His name was Patrick Etolu and I taught him the basic elements of high jumping and the 'western roll' technique. It soon became apparent that his good leg endowed him with a prodigious spring.

When I was working in Kampala, Etolu came down to the Uganda championships and easily won the national high jump title with a jump of over six feet. A month later, in the triangular match against Kenya and Tanganyika, he won again with an improved height. Uganda also won the sprints and the long jump, but was outclassed in the distance events. We realized that we now had athletes who could compete on equal terms with other countries and could match the British qualifying times and heights for the Commonwealth Games.

We set up an Olympic Committee in Uganda, of which I became the chairman, and we entered our first small team for the Commonwealth Games to be held in Vancouver in 1954. We included Etolu, two sprinters and a long jumper. For family reasons, I decided not to go with the team — a painful decision. It was at those games that Roger Bannister beat John Landy of Australia in their epic mile race. I listened avidly to the radio reports that came through to us in the early morning. One day I was astounded to hear that Etolu had won the silver medal in the high jump, beaten for the gold only by the number of failures. He had jumped 6 feet 7½ inches, much higher than his previous best. I was overjoyed.

We now turned our thoughts to the Olympic Games which were due to be held in Melbourne in two years' time. I applied to the International Olympic Committee (IOC) for Uganda to be admitted. We had to satisfy certain conditions, notably that the government did not control the national Olympic Committee. In due course we were invited to send a representative to attend a meeting of the IOC at which our application would be considered. The next meeting, it turned out, was to be held in early 1956 during the winter Olympics at Cortina d'Ampezzo in the Dolomites; fortuitously, I was to be on leave at the time in Switzerland.

The journey from Sils Maria to Cortina by bus and train required a number of changes and took most of the day. At Cortina, a group of young ladies in smart uniforms was waiting on the station platform to welcome arriving teams and dignitaries. I approached one and introduced myself. She took some moments to grasp that I was really the representative of an African country, and then asked for my luggage. I indicated my rucksack and skis. This led to another look of surprise, but at last I was shown to a waiting minibus and driven to my hotel where I was delighted to find that the Norwegian team was also staying. I became friendly with its members over the next few days and was allowed to come and watch their skiers practising for the downhill race. I was provided with free passes to all the Olympic events and for all ski lifts, and given a badge that enabled me to go more or less anywhere I pleased.

The British member of the IOC, Lord Burghley, was sponsoring the Uganda application and he asked to meet me. Having answered all his questions, I reminded him that we had met before when he was presenting the prizes at the AAA junior championships in London in 1938. By now crippled with arthritis, he had been a fabulous athlete in his youth and, as a hurdler, a particular hero of mine. During the 1920s and early 1930s he had won countless championships in both the high (120 yards) and low (440 yards) hurdles, including a number of Commonwealth Games titles. A superb victory in the 400-metre hurdles at the 1928 Olympic Games in Amsterdam crowned his career. To me (and possibly to him) this was more important than the fact that he was a scion of the great aristocratic house of Cecil, the sixth Marquis of Exeter, and a direct descendant of William Burghley, one of England's greatest statesmen under Henry VIII and Elizabeth I.

There was a sequel to this story when I went as Governor to Bermuda in 1981 and found Lord Burghley's name on the list of my predecessors. But by then his health was failing and he died before we could meet again.

Two weeks in Cortina were full of excitement. I was able to ski all the major racecourses and other classic runs, and could watch the races from privileged vantage points. This was the year when Toni Sailer from Kitzbühel (der Blitz aus Kitz) won four gold medals for Austria; I remember the calm and seemingly effortless way he handled the demanding downhill course. I also watched bobsleigh races and figure skating, but what sticks in my memory is the historic ice-hockey match between Canada, the reigning champions, and the USSR. It was held one evening under lights in the open-air stadium when the temperature was minus 20° Celsius. I put on every piece of clothing I possessed, starting with pyjamas, and still found my face and feet freezing. Who won? I forget!

After the games I had to make my way back to Zürich and the easiest route was by train via Innsbruck, where I had to change. Leaving Innsbruck in the afternoon I fell into conversation with a lady sitting opposite me. We found a common interest in skiing and she wanted to hear about the Olympics. She asked if I knew St Anton. For me that was a name full of romance, the home if not the birthplace of downhill racing, the Arlberg Kandahar, and the 'Arlberg crouch' introduced by the great Hannes Schneider. I had to admit that I had never been there. She stared at me.

'You can't call yourself a skier until you have skied at St Anton.'

After a pause she brought out a railway timetable.

'This train will halt at St Anton in about 20 minutes' time. You could get out and spend the night there, ski in the morning and still be in Zürich tomorrow afternoon.'

I spelt out the objections to such a sudden change of plan, but she brushed them aside. I realized that this might indeed be the chance of a lifetime; anyway I would be hard put to look the lady in the eye if I stayed on the train with her.

It was dark when the train pulled in to St Anton. I bade farewell to the lady and climbed down onto the platform with my skis and rucksack. I set off to look for a night's lodging and, on about the fourth try, found a room in a pension. When I telephoned Zürich, my explanation of the change in my plan seemed to carry little conviction.

The next morning there was a thick mist hanging over the slopes. I took an early cable car up to Valluga which was still under a blanket of mist with a visibility of about 20 yards. I had only a small tourist plan of the ski runs and it was not prudent to ski off into the murk with no idea of where I was going or where any run would finish. But I felt obliged to catch the midday train to Zürich and, having come this far, I could not bear to turn back.

I could only move slowly, stopping at each marker post to look for the next and with no sense of direction or slope in the whiteout. It seemed steep and endless, but I was able to navigate by the markers, though I did not know which piste I was following. I had only one mishap when I plunged over the side of a ten-foot drop that was invisible. It took me almost two hours of intense concentration to make a run that would normally take 20 minutes. Fortunately the markers I was following led me back at last to the railway station and I was in time to catch the train, drained but fulfilled. I knew that someday I must come back to St Anton.

Skis on the Equator

The mountains on Uganda's eastern side include a series of long-extinct volcanoes. The largest, Mount Elgon, shaped like an inverted pudding bowl, presents no serious climbing difficulties despite its altitude of 14,178 feet. I first climbed Elgon in 1950 with Owen

Griffith, Barry Cartland and Pip Coutts by an unusual route from the south. We camped in the crater where it snowed overnight and then descended down the western side after climbing the volcanic plug, named Jackson's Summit after the eponymous former Governor. On later expeditions I was able to climb Elgon from both the north and the west.

Napak, otherwise known as Kamalinga depending on which tribe's language one adopts, is further north on the borders of Teso. The fractured remnants of its crater rim provide an imposing gateway through which the road runs into Karamoja. Although of modest height at 8424 feet, the climb involved a long march south to a point where one could climb up to the ridge and from there back north-wards to the summit. Getting back to camp during a hot afternoon with the temperature around 100 degrees, I had to go slower and slower, halting frequently, until at length I struggled into camp and doused my head in cool water before collapsing in my tent, totally exhausted.

To the east, near the Kenya border, Moroto mountain stands behind the township of that name in Karamoja. I climbed to the 10,000 foot summit guided by a naked Tapeth — a tribe of hill people who probably predate the arrival centuries ago of Hamitic cattle-owning nomads from the north. I still use the home-made walking stick I purchased from him for one shilling.

Finally, there was Debasien, 10,050 feet, otherwise known as Kadam which I climbed in a convivial party including Sir Andrew Cohen and Rennie Bere. Cohen wanted to take a radio 'to keep in touch' which gave rise to a limerick:

> When the Governor went up Kadam
> He insisted on taking a pram
> He said 'As you see
> It isn't for me:
> It's to carry my radiogram.'

The top of Debasien is uninteresting, a large flat expanse of rock, but the expedition gave us three splendid days of stimulating talk.

Cohen was succeeded as Governor in 1956 by Sir Frederick

Crawford, with whom I used to play golf. He once confided in me that he would rather have been a professional golfer than a colonial Governor; I sometimes uncharitably wondered if he might have been better at it. His kindly advice certainly helped me to bring my handicap down into single figures.

In Entebbe I got to know David Hadow, an entomologist at the Vitus Research Institute, and we agreed to join forces along with his brother for another expedition to the Ruwenzori mountains. We aimed to climb the highest peak Margherita (16,815 feet) which I had not done before. And, ever hopeful, I borrowed an old pair of wooden skis, thinking of the snowfields on the glacier and plateau below the summit.

After four days of slogging up through rain soaked forest, swamp, and alpine flora, we reached Cooking Pot camp where the porters sheltered under a huge rock overhang. The next day we moved up to the small bivouac camp at the foot of the Elena Glacier and sent the porters back to Cooking Pot camp. From the bivouac we hoped to ascend to the wide summit plateau of Mount Stanley, from which Margherita and the slightly lower Alexandra rise. We awoke the next morning to find ourselves in thick cloud. We set out up the glacier but after two hours we were still enshrouded in cloud with no visibility. I decided that the danger of losing our way on the open slopes of the plateau was becoming too great and we turned back sadly to retrace our steps to the hut. After a rest I grabbed the skis which a mystified porter had carried up there and climbed up a few hundred feet. The skis had only the most primitive leather bindings but somehow I fixed them to my climbing boots and set out to ski for the first time at over 16,000 feet within a few miles of the equator.

There was no improvement in the weather the next day. When the porters arrived we returned to the lower camp, leaving the skis at the bivouac hut for the benefit of any future skier. They are probably still there. My third and last Ruwenzori expedition had ended without much success but had been a splendid adventure.

Whitehall

The Colonial Service, of which I was a member, differed from the Foreign Service. We were not based in London or paid by the British government. We were a loose knit service employed and paid by the respective colonial governments for which we worked. The Colonial Office in London, on the other hand, was a department of the British government staffed by the home civil service, and its members did not normally serve abroad. One of its roles was to select and appoint members of the Colonial Service and assign them to the various territories that would employ them. Although the Colonial Office was often the butt of jibes by officers in the field, it was an efficient and enlightened organization whose guidance and overall control were generally beneficent. Andrew Cohen was typical of the best of the Colonial Office where, as he told me, people were expected to say what they thought — a practice I had sometimes indulged too freely for my own good in Uganda. In order to improve mutual understanding between the Colonial Office in London and the service in the field, there was a regular exchange of officers between the two. Those coming from the field to London were known as beachcombers. I decided to apply for such a secondment, partly for professional reasons and partly in the hope that it would enable me to see more of my children in Europe.

Then one day a young lady walked into my office in Entebbe and handed me a letter of introduction from an old school friend, Ken Mole. Ken had a dazzling record as a classics scholar, organist and spy behind the Japanese lines in China before deciding in his thirties to become a doctor. Shirley, who brought his letter, had been a nurse at St Mary's in London while Ken was a medical student and she was now an air stewardess with BOAC. Being on my own in Uganda, I was only too glad of company and drove her to Kampala for dinner. We kept in contact when she passed through Entebbe on duty.

Approval came through at last for my secondment to the Colonial Office for a period of two years.

Before starting work in London, I went with the Uganda team to Cardiff where the Commonwealth Games were about to start. We met athletes from all over the world and the event that is marked most vividly in my memory was the mile (the Commonwealth Games had not then converted to metric distances) in which the great Herb Elliot of Australia outran even the star Kenyans in world record time.

After the games, a special athletics meeting in London gave me an opportunity to introduce Shirley to my favourite sport and to meet the Uganda team. The assistant manager was Basil Bataringaya, who had been a good quarter miler as a student. (He was later to enter politics and serve as a minister, but eventually fell foul of Amin and was assassinated during the terror years.) After chatting with Shirley, he smiled and said to her:

'You must come back to Uganda.'

I had told Shirley that I would never marry again, but walking down the Upper Richmond Road one morning I was struck by the powerful conviction that if I were to put my life back together again I must marry her. When she returned from an overseas flight a few days later, I proposed marriage and she accepted. She was one of six sisters in a close knit family, all musicians. She had been the youngest girl to play the double bass in the National Youth Orchestra of Great Britain, was a qualified nurse, and had attended Winston Churchill on his transatlantic flight to meet President Eisenhower. I doubt if her parents considered me a suitable match for their daughter. I did not even play an instrument to augment her mother's orchestra. But we both felt sure; and I could now look ahead with confidence.

✳ ✳ ✳

Work in the Colonial Office followed a steep learning curve. I was assigned to the department dealing with intelligence and security, subjects about which I was largely ignorant. We were a small team: the boss Duncan Watson, who was to become a lifelong friend, and two desk officers of whom I was one and Bill Formoy the other. I discovered and tried to rectify my many blind spots.

I began to learn about the various intelligence agencies. Bill and I were inducted into the mysteries of signal intelligence during a visit to Cheltenham. Every week one or other of us would attend a meeting of a subcommittee of the Joint Intelligence Committee to say our piece about colonial matters. There we would meet other departmental representatives in the same trade. In this way I gradually learned my way around Whitehall.

For relaxation I joined Roehampton Golf Club. One Saturday morning, while I was standing on the first tee looking for a partner, a

tall dark man approached and I recognized an American I had met at
the US embassy. We agreed to play together and from this simple
happy coincidence flowed a series of events that led to a lifelong
friendship with Osborn Webb. From a distinguished New England
family and a better golfer than I, he introduced me to Wentworth
Golf Club. There one day we played the notorious west course — the
'Burma Road' — in the morning and the east course in the afternoon,
along with two of his colleagues from Washington, one of whom was
later to visit us in Kampala. Osborn's mother and uncle Earl were to
come and stay with us in Kampala and, years later, did much to help
us when we went to live in New York.

When a security crisis arose in Nyasaland (now Malawi), I was
required to pay an urgent visit to investigate serious allegations that
had been made about a plot by some militant Africans to murder
senior British officials. It was an eye opener for me to see how such
matters were handled in central Africa by contrast, I thought, with the
more sensitive policies in Uganda. The outbreaks of violence had been
attributed to the activities of the African National Congress, led by Dr
Hastings Banda. The source of disaffection there, as in Buganda, was
a fear of being absorbed into a Central African Federation which the
whites in Southern Rhodesia were perceived to dominate. When the
Governor declared a state of emergency more than 1000 African
leaders were arrested and the use of undue force led to a number of
innocent Africans being killed.

On my return to London, I had to report to the Secretary of State,
Alan Lennox-Boyd. I wondered afterwards whether my impressions
had influenced some of the staff changes that came to be made.

In due course Lord Devlin headed a judicial enquiry and his critical
report led Lennox-Boyd to tender his resignation. This the Prime
Minister Harold Macmillan promptly and rightly refused. Because a
debate in the House of Commons was expected to arouse criticism,
ministers needed to prepare themselves. A weekend meeting with
officials was set up at Chequers and, in the absence of Duncan
Watson, I was summoned to attend. Among the others called in was
Charles Wilks, a beachcomber from Kenya with whom I had become
friendly. We drove down to Chequers together on a fine Friday
afternoon and were fascinated to see the place where so many former

prime ministers had received famous visitors and dealt with momentous affairs of state. At dinner we found ourselves in the company not only of the Secretary of State but also of the Lord Chancellor Lord Kilmuir, the Attorney General Sir Reginald Manningham-Buller, and Julian Amery, who was Minister of State in the Colonial Office. (He came from a famous family: his father had been a cabinet minister and his brother was hanged for treason.) It was over the brandy after dinner that the real pronouncements of policy came through and this, I thought, was how Britain had been governed — and generally quite well governed — for generations.

On the Saturday morning we got down to drafting a paper for parliament. Somebody asked the date and the reply came:

'It's the nineteenth of July.'

'Good Lord!' I exclaimed, 'It's my birthday.'

Laughter and good wishes came from all round the table.

'And I am getting married a week today,' I added to more cheers.

Then we got back to work. Later Shirley was surprised to get my phone call from Chequers.

The government weathered the storm in the House of Commons, but the writing was on the wall: the Central African Federation did not long survive.

13

Independence for Uganda

Returning to Uganda in 1960 I found myself assigned once more as Judicial Adviser in Buganda, a post that disappointed me because it made no use of the experience I had acquired in London. However, the cheery presence of Dick Stone as Resident and of his wife Mavis made our lives agreeable. They became valued friends and we had a delightful tour together to the Sesse islands on Lake Victoria. We were also pleased by the news that Charles Wilks and his wife Barbara were back in Kenya after his stint as a beachcomber in London, and were posted almost next door as DC in Kisumu. It was to them that we would go to spend our first Christmas back in Africa.

Shirley resumed her nursing career and was appointed sister of the gynaecological theatre at Mulago Hospital. There she worked under Dr Richard Trussell who was doing groundbreaking investigations into uterine cancer. Mulago enjoyed a high reputation for research done there. We later came across an unassuming physician called Denis Burkitt who had identified the eponymous Burkitt's tumour, thereby earning himself international recognition and a cover story in New York's *TIME Magazine*.

Off-duty, Shirley pursued her musical life, playing the double bass in the Kampala orchestra, teaching piano, and even tackling the solo part in a performance of Mozart's A major piano concerto, for which her mother led the orchestra while on a visit from England. The following year, when a conductor was suddenly needed for a production of *The Merry Widow* at the Kampala National Theatre, she stepped confidently onto the podium where her orchestral experience stood her in good stead.

In July 1960 the Belgian Congo was plunged, ill prepared, into independence. I was keen to observe this event and arranged to drive to Rutshuru with Shirley on 1 July. Apart from new flags, little seemed to have changed. The border guards paraded smartly and asked me to take their photograph. The Belgians in the hotel were relaxed and unworried. But 14 days later Belgian refugees from the violent events further west started to pour across the border to Uganda with only what they could carry in their cars.

Meanwhile, next door in Rwanda, the loosening of Belgian control over the UN Trust Territory allowed the Hutu majority to rise against the ruling Tutsi and unleash a wave of violence that sowed the seed for the country's fearful subsequent bloodbaths. Tutsi refugees in their hundreds came walking over the hills to Uganda carrying on their heads baskets containing all their possessions. I was appointed to take charge of the refugees' problems and had my first experience of these tall, slender, handsome and dignified people, whose ancestors long ago had come all the way from the Ethiopian highlands with their longhorn cattle. Now they were destitute. Shirley was assigned to provide necessary immunization for the refugees and the UN High Commission for Refugees lent us a hand in the persons of Warren Pinegar and Temnomorov, a Russian who himself had been a refugee from the Bolsheviks. Warren and Tem were both based at the headquarters of the Commission in Geneva where, some years later, we were to renew our friendship.

In 1961, our daughter Janina was born in Kampala and six weeks later we took her with us on the two-day train journey to Mombasa for a holiday by the ocean. Travel became a way of life for her.

✽ ✽ ✽

The constitution of Uganda was being rapidly adapted to a more advanced electoral and ministerial system. In 1961 countrywide elections were called on a common roll with a wide suffrage. They resulted in victory for the Democratic Party which followed a moderate line and had some association with the Roman Catholic Church. Its leader was Ben Kiwanuka, my old lawyer friend, and he became Uganda's first Prime Minister. I was happy to be appointed as permanent secretary to the newly created Ministry of Labour and Social Development even though these were areas in which I had no special experience. Stanley Bemba, an upright ex-soldier who had no strong political feelings, was the minister.

Events were moving fast in Africa: almost before we knew it Tanganyika and Zanzibar had become independent and later fused into the United Republic of Tanzania. We had always expected Uganda, with its more advanced educational system and thriving economy, to lead the way; and it came as no surprise when our timetable in Uganda was speeded up. There were to be fresh elections in 1962, followed by independence in October of that year.

We returned from leave in Europe in March 1962 to be greeted at the airport with the surprising news that I had been given the job of organizing the independence celebrations. Once I got used to the idea, I recognized how many opportunities it offered. I was allocated £250,000 for the exercise and, with a bare six months in which to prepare, there was no time to be lost. Jake Jacobs joined me and we set to work.

Since the celebrations had to be countrywide we needed to involve each district through its DC and his team. Jake concentrated on the design and production of all the decorations. I had always had a yen for fireworks and engaged Brock's of London to send out two technicians to take care of that side which included a huge 'set piece' structure and distribution of fireworks to the districts with appropriate instruction on safety.

There was no stadium adequate for the central functions and we engaged Dexion to build us a temporary structure which we could resell afterwards, to accommodate 50,000 spectators on the disused Kololo airstrip where there would be room to park the large number of vehicles. Invitation lists, domestic and foreign, involved wide consultation: finding accommodation and providing transport for all the visitors from abroad was a major operation. On top of this, the Duke and Duchess of Kent were to pay a ten-day visit which required the most detailed minute-by-minute planning in liaison with their staff. A local doctor had to be in attendance on the royal party during their tour and the officer nominated was the same Denis Burkitt.

The programme of events was ambitious. Besides the formal cere-monies in public and in the parliament, there were to be a church service, a grand ball, a banquet, lunches, football matches, canoe races, a military tattoo, a state drive, and many other events. All these were to take place within the space of a day or two either side of Independence Day, and each had to be organized and dovetailed with invitations, seating plans and traffic arrangements. The whole pro-gramme had to be agreed with the Governor, who by then was Sir Walter Coutts, with the elected ministers, and with the royal party. In the midst of the preparations, there was an election. This brought the Uganda National Congress to power with a new set of ministers who were not always ready to accept plans to which the former govern-ment had agreed. It was an interesting and testing exercise in admin-istration, with the inevitable frustrations and setbacks.

I enjoyed having to draft the speeches to be made on the main occasions by the Duke, the Duchess (at the opening of the new Mulago Hospital), the Governor and the newly elected Prime Min-ister, Milton Obote. For the royal visitors I used a formal style, but for Obote I drew on Jefferson and Lincoln. I was surprised when my drafts were accepted with few alterations.

In the main stadium we had to arrange a seating plan on the dais for heads of state, heads of government, ministers, governors, arch-bishops and heads of other religions, ambassadors, representatives of the UN and the Commonwealth, captains of industry, generals, air marshals — the list seemed endless. The danger of hurt feelings opened my eyes to the importance of precedence and what diplomats call 'placement' with the French pronunciation. I asked Shirley whom she would like to sit next to: she chose the Aga Khan whom she had met while she was flying.

The high point was to be the Duke handing over on behalf of Her Majesty the documents of statehood that would terminate Britain's sovereignty over Uganda. This was planned to occur at midday in the main stadium and to be saluted by an RAF fly-past involving various planes of differing speeds. We had to calculate the timing so that the whole formation would pass overhead just after the Prime Minister finished his speech. The RAF needed a signal ten minutes in advance to organize the formation, whose component flights would already be airborne.

I had practised reading Obote's speech at the speed I thought he might adopt, with pauses for applause, and I marked on my copy of the text the time intervals from paragraph to paragraph. An RAF radio operator was positioned close behind me on the dais and, when I judged there were nine minutes to go, I gave him the ten-minute signal. The PM's delivery, however, was unhurried, with measured pauses for applause, and I soon realized that he was going to overrun my estimate. I ceased listening, crossed my fingers and scanned the sky anxiously. At last I saw the formation approaching low from the north. Obote had reached his penultimate sentence: then the last sentence. The planes were almost upon us. His final words and the applause were drowned by the roar of the formation passing overhead. It was a close run thing! To friendly congratulations on the perfect timing, I thought 'They little knew!'

✳ ✳ ✳

The tumult and the shouting dies; the captains and the kings depart. An independent state had been born. It was October 1962.

Foreign Affairs

I was appointed to head the newly created Office of External Affairs and the embryo Uganda Foreign Service. We were starting from scratch without experience in the field; we had no prepared foreign policy, no trained diplomatic staff and no premises abroad except in London. I collected staff and set myself to read the classic texts on diplomatic practice so as to be able to handle with a semblance of professionalism the formalities of accreditation when these were sought. I drew freely on the expertise and advice of the diplomatic representatives now arriving to set up embassies.

Prime Minister Obote chose to be his own Foreign Minister which was an advantage to me. It gave me access to the top man and meant that his approval was the final word; and he was usually able to make decisions quickly. That he had less time to spend reading papers or looking into details, made it easier to convince him than it otherwise might have been. It also meant that he was quick to accept, or on occasion reject, advice. On some matters he had gut feelings with which it was difficult to argue. When both the People's Republic of China and the Republic of China, Taiwan, sought to establish missions, he declined to choose between them and insisted that we accept both. It was not, he argued, for Uganda to take sides. If they did not like it, that was their affair.

With me he was generally straight and friendly, though he was secretive on certain matters which he did not want known to civil servants. Gradually I came to recognize the areas in which he was moved by preconception or prejudice. I discovered that he suffered from an obsession about security. When it was proposed to increase the strength of the army I asked him what external enemies Uganda could possibly have to fear that would justify this heavy cost. He claimed to fear attack from the Sudan or from Zaire. I said I thought this unreal. I warned him that a large underemployed army could present a danger to political stability and a potential threat to his own position, as the experiences of other countries had proved, but he was not to be persuaded. I did not know at the time whether his fear was genuine or whether he had other more sinister motives. But the writing was on the wall: later events were to show that he was developing paranoid suspicions about tribal and political opponents within Uganda, a condition not untypical of autocrats, the archetype being Stalin. In the end, it was the army that was to prove Obote's nemesis.

The Foreign Minister of Zaire was the first foreign dignitary to pay an official visit and this gave rise to a problem of interpretation. The visitor had no English and Obote spoke no French. So when the two statesmen met I was called in to act as interpreter. I found it a severely testing exercise. Since then, I have always admired the skill and accuracy of trained interpreters, notably those who provide simultaneous interpreting at the UN.

At that time the British government was struggling with the intractable problems of Southern Rhodesia and the break-up of the Central

African Federation. This was to be exacerbated by Ian Smith's uni-
lateral declaration of independence. In an effort to develop a
concerted Commonwealth approach, Harold Macmillan was corres-
ponding directly with other Commonwealth prime ministers, a group
that now included Obote. Obote's views were naturally in line with
those of other African leaders and I had no difficulty with that. But I
could see the need to draft Obote's letters in terms that conveyed a
cool, thoughtful and realistic approach and that would show him as a
statesman to whom Whitehall should pay attention. I explained to
Obote why, in drafting letters for him to send to Macmillan, I used
language he himself might not have chosen, but which I calculated
would have the effect he desired upon minds in London. He took the
point, signed the first letter as drafted and thereafter was generally
content to accept my advice in this correspondence.

To have a Briton as head of his Foreign Service had to be an embarrassment to Obote and this was exemplified when he had to attend a
regional conference of Foreign Ministers in Khartoum. Since he could
hardly be seen to take me as his adviser, I sent my Ugandan assistant
to accompany him. Once the machinery of the new department was
set up and running fairly smoothly my prime concern had to be to
train a successor to take over from me; and I had a reasonable
candidate for that role.

Soon after independence, Shirley had produced a son Dickon who
enjoyed the option of becoming a citizen of Uganda. Archbishop
Leslie Brown baptized him at Namirembe Cathedral, using the liturgy
of the Church of South India where he had served before coming to
Uganda, and in recognition of my father's role in the formation of
that Church.

I now had to think about the future of my family and of my own
career. I saw no long-term future for myself in the Uganda civil
service, but I had no particular job in mind in Britain. When a friend
was successful in his application to join the Commonwealth Relations
Office I decided to throw my hat into the ring. The selection procedures for the CRO and the Foreign Office were unified and, for

various reasons, it was to the latter that I was attracted. The British Foreign Service covered strange and exotic countries outside the Commonwealth, most of them using interesting foreign languages. It also covered the United Nations. By comparison, the countries of the Commonwealth seemed pale, cosy and unexciting. Moreover what I had seen of the CRO operation in Kampala had not impressed me.

I went to Obote to explain that I had in mind retiring from Uganda and asked if he would have any objection to my applying for the British Foreign Service after I had worked in that capacity for his government in Uganda. His reaction was sympathetic but he asked me to stay on for a year as permanent secretary for trade and industry, a department that was going to have to negotiate trade agreements with various foreign governments. I agreed to this and went on to ask if he would act as one of the two referees I was required to name in my application to the British Foreign Office. He smiled with surprise and, I think, enjoyment.

'Yes,' he said, 'It would be good to have a friend in the enemy camp.'

In due course he received a letter asking his opinion on my suitability. He was tickled and showed it to me.

'What do you think I should say?' he asked.

I resisted the temptation to draft a reply for him and merely mentioned the points on which he ought to express a view. I did not see his final reply but I felt that a recommendation from a Commonwealth prime minister should carry some weight in London.

In due course I was advised that, in view of my age (44) and experience, I would be excused the written exam and the psychological tests for suitability. I was bidden to go to London to report for three days of selection tests and interviews. I had to indicate my competence in foreign languages and to name one in which I would be given an oral test. Anxious not to be type cast as an African specialist and fearing that my Swiss accent would count against my German, I offered French which I brushed up with the help of the French ambassador.

In London I met my 21 fellow applicants who came from many walks of life: one was Peter Derrick, a district officer from Kenya, but few of them enjoyed my own experience of work in a government ministry, let alone running a Foreign Service. This proved to be my great advantage because of the way the tests were designed. To start with we were each handed a folder that had been compiled like a mock-up of a government file. It included minutes, correspondence, news clippings, Hansard reports, and other papers of more or less relevance to the subject. It asked whether a Ministry of Foreign Trade should be relocated in the north rather than in overcrowded White-hall. We were allowed two hours to prepare recommendations to 'the Minister'. It took half an hour to read through and to decide which papers were relevant. I noticed a glaring omission from the minutes on the file which failed to mention that the ministry would be dealing with foreign governments whose embassies were all in London. I made this obvious point in a memorandum which took about 30 minutes to write: writing papers like that was all too familiar to me. I handed it in and, having nothing else to do to fill the time allowed, went out for a drink at a nearby pub where Peter Derrick shortly joined me.

After further interviews and mock committee meetings came the final selection board.

'Why do you want to join the Foreign Service?' I was asked.

'To be frank, I am not sure that I do, but I need a job and I have some experience in this field. Also, as we are building selection pro-cedures for the Foreign Service in Uganda, I am interested to see your methods.'

'What do you think of them?'

'I think they are flawed because they tend to assume an under-standing of government procedures and so to discriminate against anybody without that kind of experience.'

'Oh! We make allowance for that,' they said, but I was uncon-vinced.

Finally, they asked if I would accept appointment to the CRO. I explained my reasons for preferring the FO.

I returned to Uganda to await events and, a month later, received the results. Four of our group had been selected, including Peter Derrick. I was placed first and was offered an appointment to the FO.

Kilimanjaro

Uganda had been my home for 23 years — almost all my adult life.

Going away, perhaps never to return, left me with a hollow, homeless feeling.

I had been invited to accompany the GOC (East Africa) on a visit by air to the Northern Frontier district of Kenya, a romantic area I had never seen. I left my family with the Wilkses in Kisumu and drove on to Nakuru where I was picked up by the GOC's Canadian Beaver plane. We flew high above the Aberdares, thickly forested mountains that had once been the haunt of Mau Mau, and landed at Nanyuki to pick up General Goodwin. After taking off, we flew north-east across dry plains stretching to the northern horizon with Mount Kenya looming up to our right. Two hours later we landed at Wajir, the most distant administrative outpost before the Somalia frontier.

The cluster of low whitewashed buildings resembled a film setting for *Beau Geste and the Foreign Legion* with an entry gate surmounted by a low crenellated tower. The surrounding land was flat and arid, red laterite dotted with thorn bushes through which the occasional train of camels plodded slowly along with its austere-looking Somali herdsmen. Inside the town were a very few Somali shops, the district headquarters, a rest house where we were to spend the night and the Wajir Yacht Club, to which we repaired after General Goodwin had inspected his troops. Though hundreds of miles from the nearest water, it still sported a naval type stepped flagpole and, in the visitors' book, we found interesting signatures, including that of Jack Profumo with a picture of a young woman whom we happily supposed to be Christine Keeler.

The next morning we took off and headed northwest for Moyale on the Ethiopian border. There we met the DC and I went for a short walk across the border to take photographs. After a simple lunch we took off again and flew south towards Marsabit, passing over a huge meteorite crater half a mile across and hundreds of feet deep with near vertical sides. I could find no trace of it on the map. The mountain massif of Marsabit rises to 7000 feet and the Rendille tribe, which has little contact with the outside world, inhabits its dense forest.

Back at Nanyuki we dropped General Goodwin off, having discovered that we were both destined to be sailing back to England on the same ship. I flew on to Nakuru, where I picked up my car for the long weary drive back to Kisumu.

Before moving to Mombasa for our voyage home there were two more things I had to do. One was to climb Kilimanjaro, for which I had arranged to join forces with three RAF officers from Nairobi. The other was to visit our friend Sandy Field in the Serengeti where he was now the warden of the national park. After a night in Nairobi we headed south for the Tanganyika border at Namanga and from there round the base of Mount Meru to Marangu where we assembled in the hotel with the RAF men.

It is a long steady plod up this enormous extinct volcano, at first through woodland, then tree heather and finally through open heath land with tussock grass and the inevitable giant lobelia. It was a nice change from the oppressive rainforest of Ruwenzori. We camped on successive nights at 9000 feet and 12,000 feet. On the third day, we came to the immense expanse of the saddle between the mighty main crater of Kibo and the subsidiary rock peak of Mawenzi. This plateau stretches for more than a mile, rising gradually to the Kibo hut at 15,500 feet where we spent the third night. I was sick all night, poorly acclimatized. Our plan was to climb Kibo (19,340 feet) the next day and we started before dawn. The scree of the final pyramid gets progressively steeper and I soon found myself having to go slower and slower. Eventually I could only take each step with difficulty and at about 18,000 feet I could go no further. I told the others to go on without me and assured them that I could find my own way back to the hut. They reluctantly agreed and I sat down to consider the prospect. After a while I tried again, but any attempt to move up was halted as if by an invisible wall. Sadly I realized that I had to turn back 1000 feet below the summit. As soon as I started down I felt as right as rain: such was the perplexing effect of altitude.

Having reached the summit, the others came down late in the afternoon fairly exhausted. They had intended to try and climb Mawenzi the next day but, after some discussion, they decided to go down with me. I suspect that they were unduly and generously concerned about my condition. The climb up had taken us four days: going down we made it in one and a half, albeit with blisters and sore knees from the pounding our legs took on the descent.

After a day to relax in the hotel at Marangu I set off with my family for Ngorongoro where we spent a fascinating afternoon in the crater among the hundreds of animals. I was advised that the track from there to the Serengeti park headquarters at Seronera required a four-wheel drive vehicle, but obstinately decided that we could manage it in our trusty Ford Galaxie. The shifting sands certainly caused wheel spin but we managed to keep moving and to get across the dry river-beds along our route. Unfortunately the wind was on our tail which deprived the radiator of air and the engine boiled continually. To remedy this I would turn the car round and head into the wind for a few minutes while the engine cooled off before swinging round on course again for another few miles. Repeating this manoeuvre several times we made steady but slow progress.

Once we saw what looked like an oil derrick in the distance. Then we thought it was a crane, then it was a giraffe, but when we got close it turned out to be a thorn tree — our first and convincing experience of a mirage.

At Seronera we were well looked after by Sandy Field, taken for a drive and had splendid close-up views from his Land Rover of lion, cheetah and leopard.

The time had now arrived to make for Mombasa. We reached there in two days' drive and checked in at a seaside hotel to wait for our ship. Next afternoon, there was a gentle call of '*hodi*' at the door of our chalet and there was Anna, our beloved *ayah* who had come unprompted all the way from Kampala, two days' journey by train, to see us off. Such loving devotion to the children was deeply moving. When we finally embarked, Anna was there at the quayside to wave goodbye. We felt wretched.

On the ship we renewed our acquaintance with Dick Goodwin who was given a salute from the air by his air wing as the ship steamed out of harbour. On the next day we heard of the assassination of President Kennedy and, shocked, wondered what kind of world we were heading for. Sailing up the coast, round Cape Gardafui, through the Red Sea, the Suez Canal and the Straits of Sicily, past Stromboli to Barcelona and Gibraltar gave us time to prepare our minds for the new life that lay ahead.

14

United Nations

Myself when young did eagerly frequent
Doctor and Saint and heard great Argument
About it and about; but evermore
Came out by the same Door as in I went.

(Omar Khayyam)

The Foreign Office in London had a daunting reputation for intellectual brilliance and sophistication, of which I was very conscious when I entered its portals early in 1964. To start with, I was interviewed by Johnny Graham of the personnel department; he put me at my ease and helped my morale by rehearsing my record in a way that made it sound impressive. He asked me if I had any preferences for future postings. I said that I did not want to go back to Africa yet, nor did I want an Arabian or Middle East post, but I would like the United Nations as a quick way to learn about parts of the world of which I knew nothing.

At a time when third world countries were plunging headlong into the ocean of independence, the FO and CRO were recruiting older men with experience in those fields. 'Over-age' applicants like me were treated differently, judged more on our record, and excused the written examinations and psychological tests. It cannot have been easy for the personnel department to fit former Colonial Service officers into the diplomatic pattern but they did their best to make use of such talents and experience as we brought with us.

We the colonials (for I have never been able fully to cast off that character even when wearing a diplomat's clothing) had lived among, and become imbued with responsibility for the welfare and development of, those in our charge. In a protectorate like Uganda their interests were paramount: it behoved us to understand their language and their customs, to safeguard them from the evils of famine, disease and disorder, and to open their minds to new possibilities in the way of higher education and eventual participation in government. Furthermore, although the Colonial Office in London selected Colonial Service officers, they were appointed to serve, and to be paid by, the government of the particular territory to which they were assigned. The result was that most officers developed a loyalty to the government of their own territory and indeed to the territory itself, rather than to London. Since most district officers could expect to spend their whole working lives in a single territory, joining the Diplomatic Service could be quite a culture shock. It was not easy for us to change our spots although my previous experience in Whitehall and among the diplomatic corps in Kampala was an advantage.

Mainline diplomats, on the other hand, sometimes found it difficult to understand the mindsets of third world leaders, for example in Africa, which were strange to them. The wide disparity between different African strains, tribes and countries were not always fully appreciated in Whitehall once the Colonial Office, with its accumulated expertise, was disbanded.

Soon after I joined the Foreign Office it was amalgamated with the Commonwealth Relations Office to form the joint Foreign and Commonwealth Office. At the same time the two services were unified and renamed the Diplomatic Service, a reversion to an earlier title that had been abandoned when it was joined with the old Consular Service. While the Diplomatic Service differed from the Colonial Service in many respects, there were areas of commonalty between them which helped to ease the transition when I moved from one to the other. In both cases, directly or indirectly, one was working for a democratically elected government and I had acquired some familiarity with the vagaries of ministerial politics and with the accepted procedures of a civil service. At a more basic level, one was working for a government which could be relied upon to pay one's salary and pension.

Indeed the British government underwrote the pensions of officers retiring from the Colonial Service and provided protection for them against the inroads of inflation.

The differences in outlook between the two services stemmed from the different jobs they had to do. Since the Diplomatic Service operates both the FCO in Whitehall and our embassies abroad, its members can expect to spend part of their careers in London, where they are involved to some degree in framing British foreign policy. In the field, a diplomat is accredited to, and provides the channel of communication with, the host government. He is in regular contact with London by the very efficient system of telegrams and is rarely obliged, except in an emergency, to act solely on his own initiative. Along with the interchangeability of staff between London and overseas, this gives the service a degree of homogeneity in its functioning which makes the Diplomatic Service a well-oiled machine and a highly effective tool for the government to use in implementing its policies. It also tends to engender a certain professional ruthlessness in diplomatic dealings with 'the other side', however friendly.

In foreign posts members of the diplomatic corps tend to club together, often seeing more of each other than of the people of their host country. This is not wholly sterile: intelligence gathered by other embassies can often help to enrich a diplomat's own picture of a situation and there is a good deal of useful sharing of information. But diplomats' lives in capital cities are generally sheltered and comfortable, with the protection of diplomatic immunity from both local taxation and prosecution, notably for motoring offences. This tends to isolate a diplomat from the man in the foreign street. Indeed, members of the Diplomatic Service were discouraged from becoming too closely involved in public or social matters in foreign countries. It was called 'going native' and was frowned on because it might taint the impartial accuracy of an officer's reporting and his assessment of where Britain's interests lay. Britain's interests were always paramount for the Diplomatic Service officer; and this was a lesson I often found hard to remember, notably when returning to Uganda as High Commissioner in 1979.

※ ※ ※

In London, I was first assigned as as a desk officer in Arabian department dealing with Aden and the Yemen. Alongside me sat Charles Powell, also newly joined but 20 years younger than I and later to achieve notice as Margaret Thatcher's private secretary. Mig Goulding, an accomplished Arabist, became a friend whose expertise on the turf led me to make my first and only bet on a horse that duly won the Derby. Mig went on to achieve distinction at the UN before returning to Oxford as the head of a college. I found it difficult to keep up with the quick minds of these and other bright young men while I was trying to master the intricacies of Foreign Office procedure. Under this kind of pressure it was easy sometimes to overlook the strict security regulations requiring papers always to be locked up; and after another frightful lapse I was spoken to by Tom Brenchley, the head of department:

'I wonder whether you are really suited to this profession.'

'I wonder too,' I replied; and I did, though for rather different reasons.

But after two and a half years in London, my telephone rang one September afternoon. The personnel department reminded me that I had expressed an interest in the UN.

'One of our delegation in New York has fallen ill during the General Assembly and we need a replacement. Are you ready to go?'

'Yes. When?'

'Within the next two days. You can come back home for Christmas and then go out on a permanent basis with your family in January.'

So began a four year stint in New York and a much longer friendship with the place for my family.

The General Assembly of the United Nations convenes the representatives of all the member states (who then numbered about 130) in New York each year from September until Christmas. Most of the work is done in six main committees, in each of which every member state has a seat. Hence, the committees are large, unwieldy, and slow moving. Plunged into this maelstrom, I depended heavily on the tolerant tutelage of Brian Barder, with whom I shared duty in the fourth committee, the committee on colonialism. I grew accustomed to long anti-colonial polemics which seemed a far cry from my own experience in Uganda. Indeed, the Uganda representative on the committee was a young man I had myself appointed to their Foreign Service three years previously; he had no compunction about seeking my advice when he had to answer queries or submit reports for Entebbe.

As 'United Kingdom' we were seated next to 'United Republic of Tanzania' and I was amused to hear their delegates speaking together in Swahili, hoping no doubt not to be understood. At last I had to put them wise and we became good friends. I soon learned that many of the Africans on the committee were highly educated and extremely professional, having much more diplomatic experience than I had. Jimmy Aggrey Orleans from Ghana was a delightful colleague who recounted an incident in which a journalist, unaware that Jimmy had been educated at the Sorbonne, had sought to explain a French phrase to him. (Jimmy later became High Commissioner in London.)

Lord Caradon, formerly Sir Hugh Foot, was the head of our mission. He had a distinguished record as a colonial administrator in Palestine and West Africa, and eventually became Governor first of Jamaica and then of Cyprus. He was the embodiment of the best in the Colonial Service and, for me, an understanding mentor. (His father Isaac Foot was a Methodist lay preacher who had been friendly with mine.) Once when I sought to argue that Spanish colonial rule in Latin America had not been wholly devoid of benefit, he teased me for being an unreconstructed colonialist. When an ambassador was due to arrive from newly independent Botswana I thought that going to meet him at the airport would help us to establish a good liaison that could be helpful later. As this involved a morning's absence from the mission, I went to ask Caradon's permission. He smiled.

'Very good of you my boy, but I think I'll go myself.'

Our daily routine required an early arrival at the offices of the UK mission on 3rd Avenue. We had to read the telegrams that had come in overnight from London and other posts, draft papers and statements, make telephone calls to other delegations, arrange meetings and generally prepare for the day ahead. At 9.00 a.m. the whole delegation, which sometimes included visiting specialists or ministers from London, would gather in the conference room to discuss any particular problems facing us in committee. Lord Caradon liked to lead from the front and for all of us to make up our own minds. He once criticized a telegram I had sent to London asking for instructions. I should have stated our intended course of action and left it to the FCO if they wished to express any reservations.

After that meeting we would jump into cars and drive the seven blocks to the UN building in time to be in our seats in committee by 10.00 a.m. Diplomats of all countries share many common problems and follow similar professional practices. In their duties and conduct at the UN diplomats are analogous with barristers for they speak to their briefs in committee but are friendly fellow professionals once outside in the lobbies. In the bar one day I felt free to express sympathy with my Russian colleague over the implausible case he had been obliged to argue.

At the end of the day's proceedings we would return to the mission to deal with any paperwork and draft telegrams to report to the FCO. Any telegram that concerned a British dependency would also be repeated to the territory in question. After that the social round would start.

Hurry home to change or pick up one's wife and then out to a cocktail party with one delegation or a dinner party with another — sometimes two or three engagements in a single evening. At these gatherings much of the 'behind the scenes' work was done to pave the way for useful progress in the next day's committee meeting. It was a hectic schedule which I found stimulating and demanding. In the years that followed I was sometimes reduced to taking tranquillisers when the stress began to affect my ability to make sound decisions quickly and to hold everything together. I soon realized the good sense behind the policy of having all UK mission staff living in Manhattan instead of in the suburbs, as some other missions did.

At Christmas I went home to collect my family. We returned on a Cunarder in January with Florence, a qualified Ugandan nurse whom we had brought to help look after our children along with her own baby. Innocent of the residue of colour bar which we were to discover in New York, we had our application for an apartment in a cooperative turned down because our nanny and her baby were 'coloured'. Later, when we were settled in another apartment block, Florence was not allowed to use the main elevator. She had no friends in New York. Soon the pressures and loneliness became too much for her and we sent her home to Uganda with her baby. But diplomats were generally a privileged class with tax exemptions on liquor and petrol and a near immunity from speeding or parking tickets. Resentful New Yorkers knew of our DPL numberplates as 'double parking licences'.

For my family New York offered a novel, often exhilarating, experience. Janina and Dickon attended day schools and brought home tales of wonder: their English background and prior education seemed to give them a favoured position. Shirley discovered a rich and welcoming world of chamber and orchestral music but, when invited to audition as a double bass player for Stokowski's American Symphony Orchestra, she declined the invitation, putting first her obligations to her family and as the wife of a British diplomat.

Pacific Islands

After the First World War responsibility for administering Germany's former overseas possessions was assumed by members of the victorious allies under League of Nations Mandate — Tanganyika by Britain, Ruanda–Urundi by Belgium, Nauru by Australia and, among others, a group of islands in the western Pacific known collectively as Micronesia (or 'small islands') by Japan which was on the winning side that time. After the Second World War these mandated territories became Trust Territories under the United Nations, and the USA assumed responsibility for Micronesia* which became known as the US Trust Territory of the Pacific Islands.

Apart from the General Assembly the UN maintained three standing bodies — the Security Council, the Economic and Social Council and the Trusteeship Council. The membership of these Councils comprised the five permanent members — USA, USSR, UK, France and China — plus a number of other member countries elected for three-year terms. It was the function of the Trusteeship Council to oversee the administration of the territories by the respective administrative powers and this was done by sending missions periodically to visit and inspect each territory.

It was to such a mission that I found myself appointed soon after

---

* Not to be confused with Polynesia ('many islands') or Melanesia ('black islands').

my return to New York with my family in January 1967. We were to go for a month to the US Trust Territory of the Pacific Islands. Our leader was Angie Brookes, a large and charming Liberian lady who sensibly liked to be called 'Madam Chairman', not 'Chairwoman'. The other members of the mission came from France, Australia and Sri Lanka.

For me, it was a wonderful chance to see the Pacific for the first time, taking in first Honolulu, then flying on to Midway and Guam, the administrative capital of a territory whose islands sprawl for 1000 miles across the sea. It was from here that first the Spaniards and more recently the Japanese had ruled their possessions in the western Pacific. Now the large airfield was populated by huge B-52 bombers which were used in the Korean War and then in Vietnam.

Exploring the island I was enjoying the marvellous scenery when, on rounding a curve in the road, we came across a simple monument to one of the world's most remarkable epics of seafaring. It was there in that quiet bay in the year 1521 that Magellan, his crew starving and without water, made his first landfall 99 days after leaving the coast of South America. I could only stand in wonder and contemplate the scene.

From Guam we flew to Saipan in a Grumman amphibian that had been put at our disposal, a friendly little machine that landed as happily on water as on land and could clamber up from one to the other to park. In Saipan the Japanese had established sugar plantations: one could still see some of the rusting machinery and the statue of a forgotten Tokyo tycoon. We saw the high cliffs from which Japanese people had thrown themselves to their deaths to avoid capture by the Americans. We also visited Tinian, the island from which the plane took off to drop the first atomic bomb on Hiroshima, and which was now almost deserted.

Then we set out in our trusty Grumman to visit a string of far-flung islands, each with its separate history and people, held together loosely and artificially by the territory's US administration which we were there to inspect. In Palau the district administrator looked like any other Micronesian but he was called Macdonald and was proud of his distant Scottish ancestry — a sign that the ripples from the Highland clearances have spread half way round the world.

In Yap red-mouthed betel chewing youngsters hurtled about on mopeds with flower decked topless girls on the pillion. I met an old man who was the sole survivor on a driftaway canoe that had been lost for five weeks before landing in the Philippines 1000 miles away. The only language we had in common was German which he had learned when the island was a German colony before the First World War, after the original Spaniards had left and before the Japanese took over. No wonder the people found it difficult to develop a character of their own. And no wonder the Americans found it hard to develop any sense of nationhood among such different and widely separated islands. Yet that was what the UN Trusteeship Council, with its anti-colonial lobby, would look for.

We then went to Truk where one could still see on the bottom of the lagoon the hulks of Japanese ships sunk by the American forces which had caught them at anchor. In a cave on the hillside above, I came across a naval gun from a British ship captured in Singapore by the Japanese and transported improbably to Truk.

Our next two hour hop took us to Ponape. There we saw the amazing ruins of Nan Madol, an earlier and unwritten civilization that had used huge basalt blocks for building but left no clue to their identity. This remains, I believe, one of the great, unsolved mysteries of archaeology.

The Marshall Islands, named after a British naval officer John Marshall, were more recently notorious as the site of atomic bomb tests at Bikini and Eniwetok. Kwajalein had a considerable US naval presence and we were taken on a launch to visit a neighbouring island. On our return the coxswain at the helm approached the dock at some speed, aiming to halt impressively at our landing. Unfortunately he found himself unable to engage reverse gear. As we were standing on the deck I saw that we were going to collide with the dock wall: I grabbed Angie's considerable bulk and pulled her down onto a bench just before we struck. Her astonished protest was stilled when she saw the others in the party tumbling about at the impact.

Our last visit was to Majuro, a larger island at the southern end of the chain and destined to become a tourist attraction. There we paused for breath and to write up notes. One day we took a boat trip across the large lagoon, part of which was exposed to huge Pacific rollers that required the boat to climb at full throttle 40 feet up one side before hurtling down the other. I understood then how 2000 miles of open sea could affect the ocean's behaviour. Nevertheless, when somebody produced a pair of water skis, I accepted the challenge: sadly the boat's power was barely sufficient to get me surface borne.

On the long journey back to New York I pondered the problems of small islands in the post-colonial era. I had clear views about the administration of the territory and happily took over the drafting of our report. In due course the UN Trusteeship Council, as was its way, 'took note'.

* * *

That exercise over, Teddy Youde, our head of chancery, asked me to move to a section of the mission that dealt with economic affairs. When I denied any expertise in that area, he reminded me of my stint in the Ministry of Trade and Industry in Kampala.

'Anyway,' he said, 'you are not expected to be an expert on economics. You just have to know who to listen to.'

I was to take over from John Taylor, whose skill and experience, wrapped in charm, guided me through the mysteries of the Economic and Social Council (known as ECOSOC). The great advantage for us was that it met every summer in Geneva.

When the UN was set up after the war the choice of venue for its headquarters posed a complex political equation. Geneva, situated in a neutral country with all the old League of Nations facilities left behind, was in many ways the obvious choice. But, having played no part in the Allies' hard won victory, the Swiss could exert little influence. The new organization was largely the brainchild of Roosevelt and Churchill in the Atlantic Charter; hence it was viewed with suspicion by China and the USSR, and to some extent by France. London was to host the 1948 Olympic Games but was still recovering from the ravages of war and would have been hard put to provide the permanent facilities required for the United Nations Organization. It was anyway desirable to keep the UNO separate from the government and capital of the host state. New York, with its excellent facilities and communications, and a site presented by Rockefeller, was the best possible candidate. As a sop to the Swiss it was agreed to hold ECOSOC's annual meetings each summer in Geneva, where the old Palais des Nations' conference facilities could be used. Also, the WHO and ILO were based there. (To London went the IMCO, to Montreal the ICAO, to Rome the FAO and to Vienna the IAEA.*)

In Geneva, sitting in the fading grandeur of the Palais des Nations with its 1920s' architecture, one could imagine statesmen of that era like Eden, Benes and Ciano feeling at home in the high-ceilinged pillared halls. It seemed an improbable setting for discussion of the world's current economic and social problems, like seabed minerals or the brain drain.

Being able to move with my family to Geneva during June and July gave us an idyllic retreat. We were able to escape the summer heat of New York and, at weekends, could explore the Jura and Haute Savoie. There, following de Gaulle's like effusion in Quebec, the walls were splashed with the slogan '*Vive la Savoie libre*'.

In Geneva, we were welcomed by our old friends Warren Pinegar and Temnomorov, who had helped us with refugees in Uganda. Tem lived across the border in France and enjoyed showing the children his collection of antique armour. Unexpected visitors from Africa one year were the Wilks family: we took them for a picnic at which Shirley slyly fed them frogs' legs, for which she has never been forgiven.

My son Daudi was by then reading medicine at Geneva University and was a frequent caller. One weekend he came with us up to the glacier above Les Diablerets. When young Dickon became obstreperous, Daudi picked him up and gently dropped him in a snowdrift. The same afternoon, Daudi and I chose unwisely to ski down the glacier when, at 2 o'clock of a June afternoon, the snow had become like treacle. I had an awkward fall and something cracked in my ankle.

---

*   WHO – World Health Organization; ILO – International Labour Organization; IMCO – Inter-Governmental Maritime Consultative Organization; ICAO – International Civil Aviation Organization; FAO – Food and Agriculture Organization; IAEA – International Atomic Energy Agency.

We had no alternative but to ski on down and I kept the boot tightly laced during the long drive back to Geneva. An X-ray revealed a fractured metatarsal: a cheerful Spanish doctor said he would treat me on condition we returned Gibraltar to Spain — before putting on a cast. Next Monday morning, making a shame-faced entry to the committee on crutches, I was greeted with laughter and cheers.

In 1968, prior to the Geneva session, I was required to attend ten days of meetings in Vienna. We drove all the way from London and, at weekends, could explore Carinthia and visit Dürnstein where Richard I was imprisoned and eventually rescued by Blondel. Evenings when there were no official functions we spent at the opera, depending upon the advice of the lady concierge of our apartment block who, like most Viennese, knew exactly what was on and who was singing.

Vienna had the charm of a set from an old film: one would hardly have been surprised to encounter Johann Strauss on the street. Youngsters sped about on mopeds with violin cases instead of football boots slung across their shoulders. Modern cars seemed out of place. At a pedestrian crossing I halted the car rather late when an old man started to cross. Half way over he stopped, turned to face me, raised a gnarled and twisted stick, and shook it at me.

'*Verdammtes Auto* — *Weg von der Strasse*,' he exclaimed. 'Damned car — get off the road.'

I could only bow to him in respect. Steeped in this atmosphere, we broke the long drive back to Geneva to spend an idyllic night at Die Blaue Gans in Salzburg.

The next year the entire committee flew to Bucharest for a series of meetings. Looking round the plane, I saw Lord Caradon, his American opposite number Paul Hoffman, Secretary General U Thant, Sadruddin Khan and other notables. The thought occurred to me that if we crashed there would be a lot of job vacancies. But the Romanian pilot of our Ilyushin turboprop made an impeccable landing. When I went up to the flight deck to thank him, he grinned.

'I flew in the RAF,' he said.

This was my first visit to a communist country and I was struck by the drabness of the city and of life under Ceausescu's brutal rule. The shops bore numbers instead of names and had little to offer. A car sale room showed a few ageing photographs of bygone models, but only one Skoda vehicle. The modern architecture was in soulless concrete: little of the old glamorous Bucharest remained. Our stay was relieved by a weekend trip to the Carpathian mountains but even the out of season ski resort seemed dispirited.

One may ask why it was necessary to hold these meetings in so many different places; and what, if anything, they achieved. Apart from Geneva, other countries were often anxious for a slice of the cake and to host UN meetings in their capitals, partly for the domestic prestige of the ruler, as in the case of Romania, or just to enhance their international repute. Against such considerations arguments of economy carried little weight.

The value of the meetings themselves had to be measured more in political than practical terms. Each member country's delegation had its own hobbyhorse to ride and wanted to be heard on the international stage, to canvass support and to concert strategies for the future with those of like mind. The results of international gatherings are by their nature slow to be felt and, when they are, they are often less than perfect compromises, but they are better than having no international cooperation at all.

It has taken humans several thousand years to devise a system of government for themselves, their tribes and their countries. Even at that level the imperfections are only too evident. Government of nations is only in its infancy and will take centuries to develop. As with all governments it will depend on the consent and support of the governed, not only financial support but in the last resort also physical power to enforce its decisions. These are mountainous problems for the comity of nations but in less than a century they have made a creditable start.

Anguilla

In July 1969 we were getting ready after ECOSOC to return to America where we planned to spend two weeks leave with friends on the coast of Maine before the onset of the General Assembly. One morning I had a summons from Lord Caradon. Would I be ready to go to Anguilla for a couple of months to act as commissioner while the new incumbent took overdue leave? I was taken by surprise but, after a few moments to collect my thoughts I realized that it was more important than leave. It was agreed that I should spend a week in Maine, then leave my family in New York while I travelled to the Caribbean.

Anguilla is an island in the Leeward group of the Lesser Antilles, less than a third the size of the Isle of Wight, about 15 miles long and two to three miles wide: hence its name which is Spanish for 'eel'. Sighted by Columbus in 1496, it was not until 1609 that British seamen under one Captain Harcourt first landed. Some years later it was invaded by Caribs who abducted most of the women and children, and in 1688 by Irish brigands whose brogue, and some of whose names, survive to this day. The French attacked it three times in the eighteenth century but HMS *Lapwing* eventually destroyed their ships and drove them off. The strangest invasion of all was in March 1969 when a force of British paratroops and 60 London bobbies (policemen) landed 'to restore order'.

Under British administration Anguilla had been attached to St Kitts which is 60 miles off. Since recent moves towards self-rule in the West Indies the Anguillans had become increasingly restive at the prospect of being governed from St Kitts whose Chief Minister Bradshaw was a notoriously abrasive character. Eventually the St Kitts police were thrown off the island which declared itself independent and issued its own stamps which delighted philatelists.

A visit to Anguilla by a British minister designed to allay their fears had been badly handled and a shot had been fired — at a bird I was told later — but the British party made an undignified exit.

Then followed the ridiculous invasion by paratroops and bobbies. Lee, the commissioner, had become so unpopular (undeservedly) that he had to be relieved. His replacement Thompson was overdue for leave. Hence the need for me to fill the gap.

In Anguilla I quickly got to know Ronald Webster, an alleged rabble rouser who led what London described as the rebellious faction. He was a simple character and anxious to be understood and I made a point of meeting him most days for a chat in an attempt to lower the political temperature. After a while he started to call me his 'chum'. On discovering that he was a keen if not accomplished cricketer, I challenged him to a match.

At first he did not realize that I myself would play and found it out of keeping with the traditional posture of the commissioner; but, once convinced, he entered into the spirit of things and selected a local team. My team included locals, paratroopers and policemen. In the event a good time was had by all: I hit a six, Ronald made two catches, and his side won by two runs — a perfect result for my purposes. For days afterwards, the match was the talk of the island and I was welcomed everywhere.

'You de man hit de sixer!'

After that administration was easy. I asked for the paratroopers to be withdrawn and the number of policemen to be halved. This caused some dismay among the islanders for their presence had provided both a useful injection of finance to the economy and a few romances.

Finding it difficult to sustain myself with no domestic staff I sent a signal to New York asking for my wife to join me. Caradon reacted swiftly and well: three days later Shirley stepped off an aircraft at Anguilla's little airstrip. I had taken over an isolated pink villa overlooking a sandy bay on the south shore and there, looking across to the island of St Martin, we set up house, supplied with lobster by a local fisherman. It was a romantic setting. We explored the glorious empty beaches and Ronald invited us to breakfast, a sign of favour. We also paid a visit to the Governor of the Dutch sector of St Martin and spent a night there. Later he returned our visit for a jolly lobster lunch party in our villa.

My relations with Ronald were now so cordial that I was keen for some of my anti-colonial colleagues at the UN to see things at first hand. Sadly, the Tanzanian ambassador, Malecela, was unable to come but I did entice Billner of Sweden to come for a few days. He found it all very strange and I am not sure that his visit bore any material fruit.

Bradshaw in St Kitts was adamantly opposed to letting go of Anguilla. But, having got to know the Anguillans, I was sure that they would never consent to that link remaining and that any attempt to force the issue would be forcibly resisted. London feared for Anguilla's economic viability but I suspected that officials there also preferred to bundle up territories in convenient units before sending them off to independence. Since my experience in the Pacific I had come to realize that small islands could survive on their own with boats and fishing nets. Anguilla also had glorious unused beaches to tempt tourists. Although the resident population was only about 7000, there were at least as many Anguillans working abroad in New Jersey, in England, and at sea in merchant ships; they were excellent seamen and some of them had risen to ranks of responsibility. Remittances sent to their families provided a valuable additional resource. I had no doubt that Anguilla could manage by itself and advised the FCO accordingly. This is one of those happy, though uncommon, instances of advice being accepted — and proved right.

Back at the General Assembly in New York we found the usual press of diplomats scurrying self-importantly about — a huge contrast with Anguilla. Sometimes the Security Council would meet in the evening to cope with a new crisis, an outbreak of fighting or a threat to the peace. I would take Shirley to watch history being made: it was more riveting theatre than any play and could be amusing, especially when Lord Caradon was in action. By comparison, the General Assembly in plenary session was cumbersome, but it was enlivened occasionally by eminent visitors, notably when Khrushchev came and banged his shoe on the desk.

But my time was up. In January 1970 I was to return to the FCO as assistant to the head of a department dealing with Pacific affairs. Still a first secretary at the age of 50 I was disappointed and thought of giving up the Diplomatic Service. However, the wise counsel of Leslie Glass, Lord Caradon's deputy, persuaded me to soldier on in the expectation that it would lead to better things. And it did.

15

Belize

Four years at the UN had given us a taste of the life diplomats enjoy in the field. It is comfortable, luxurious even, protected, insulated from some of the rough edges of life as we had known it in Uganda, but stimulating in the sharp, sometimes vibrant, company of diplomats from other countries and their spouses. Returning to London and the daily commute from Surrey to Waterloo brought me down to earth.

An awkward year followed, as difficult I expect for the nice lady head of department as it was for me. However, my first contact with the impressive leaders of the islands was given to me by the constitutional conference that preceded Fiji's independence. I also became acquainted with the Rev. Tebuke, the leader of the Banabans of Ocean Island with whom I was later to become more closely involved. And in June our second son, Jonathan, was born.

Then, at the end of 1970, I was given charge of the West Indian department. My first concern, obvious to any Colonial Service officer, was to visit the territories for which I was now responsible. This later evoked a complaint from the FCO administration that my department had spent more on travel than almost any other. I took this as a compliment. I was struck first by the sheer multiplicity of islands. The larger ones like Jamaica, Trinidad and Barbados, were already independent. Then came a group of 'associated states' which occupied a kind of half-way house with internal self-government but leaving

Britain responsible for defence and external affairs. These included St Lucia, St Kitts, St Vincent, Grenada, Dominica, and Antigua: they sounded like a squadron of battleships passing in review. Then came a flotilla of dependencies for which my department was responsible — Montserrat, the Bahamas, the Turks and Caicos, the Cayman Islands and the British Virgin Islands — and these were just the British islands. There were also French and Dutch islands, some curious hybrids like St Martin which was half French and half Dutch, some associated with the USA and a few independent ones like Cuba, Haiti and the Dominican Republic. It was difficult to remember each island's position, its problems and the names and faces of its leading politicians. After my experience in Anguilla I was anxious to listen to the men on the spot and I found that the various Governors welcomed my visits.

In addition to the islands, we had a dependent territory on the mainland of Central America, namely British Honduras which had earlier been known as the Honduras or Bay Settlement. (The name Honduras stems from the Spanish *hondo* meaning deep water.) In about 1650 the first British arrivals had settled at the mouth of a river that became known, like the settlement itself, as Belize, said to be a Spanish adaptation of Wallace, the name of one of the first settlers. (In 1973 the name of the territory was changed to Belize and the town became Belize City.)

I spent three days there with Sir John Paul, the Governor of the territory. I also met George Price, the Premier, and his ministers. Sir John was due to complete his tour of duty in less than a year's time and on my return to London I asked those concerned in the FCO to start making arrangements for a successor. I heard no more for several months until one day David Scott, the under-secretary, sent for me and asked if I would accept the Governorship. It took my breath away. I had not aspired to this position and it was hard to collect my thoughts. I saw that it was going to create problems with the children's education. Seeing me hesitate, David asked if I would like time to think about it, but I knew the answer and needed no second bidding. I felt very fortunate.

John Paul was due to depart in November 1970. The financial secretary, a very able Belizean civil servant named Rafael Fonseca, would hold the fort until I arrived early in the new year. I arranged to spend two weeks' holiday in the Alps over Christmas before we left for Belize, but early in December we received intelligence that the Guatemalans were preparing to invade the territory which they had long claimed to be part of Guatemala. Ministers had to decide what to do and it was put to me in jocular fashion:

'Shall we send a warship or send Posnett?'

I thought that a sudden change of plan and an early arrival might look like a panic measure and could jeopardize our source of intelligence in Guatemala. It was a risk but I decided to stick to my plans.

These were then nearly scuppered by a summons to Buckingham Palace on a day when we expected to be in the Alps. A private audience with the Queen took precedence over everything else and we changed our plans. Our taxi driver to the palace was almost as nervous as we were, but Her Majesty at once put us at our ease and sat us down to chat about the problems of small dependencies. When she turned to ask about the domestic arrangements in Government House, Shirley was, for once in her life, tongue-tied.

In due course, leaving Nina and Dickon at boarding school, we took Jonathan, aged 18 months, and flew to Jamaica where we spent two days with Nick Larmour, the British High Commissioner. On the morning of our flight to Belize I called at the High Commission where a telegram from the FCO was awaiting me:

'We have reason to believe that invasion of British Honduras by the Guatemalans may be imminent. Good luck. Douglas Home.'

After we were airborne I asked to see the captain and showed him the telegram. I told him the risk was slight but he should be alert to the possible danger and make sure that the airport was in British hands before landing.

In due course we landed, to face a long receiving line led by the acting Governor and including the Chief Justice, Premier, Bishop, Commanding Officer of the British garrison and on down the line. We then left for the 50 mile drive to the new capital of Belmopan where the swearing-in ceremony took place. Only then could we begin to unwind. Shirley took a look round her new home while I had a serious talk with Colonel John Shipster, the garrison commander.

In the event, an invasion did not materialize on that occasion, but it became an ever-present threat with which we had to live. Meanwhile, I had to get to know the country.

✳ ✳ ✳

Belize is roughly the size of Wales and runs for more than 200 miles down the eastern coast of Central America, protected from the Caribbean Sea by a barrier reef which has played an important part in its history. It is bounded by the Rio Hondo and the Yucatan peninsula of Mexico on the north: the western border is an almost straight north–south line dividing it from Guatemala which also forms its southern boundary on the Sarstoon River. The country is about 70 miles across at its widest point and, apart from the hilly areas in the south and west which are sparsely inhabited, it is fairly low lying. Much of it is covered by thick forest which has proved to be its most important natural resource.

The first human inhabitants of the area are thought to have been the Maya whose antecedents arrived from the north-west and whose earliest known settlements date from around 2500 BC. This remarkable civilization, with its skill in mathematics, astronomy, architecture and administration, reached its apogee in about AD 800, after which it collapsed for reasons that are still debated. It left behind fabulous monuments in (Spanish) Honduras, Belize, Guatemala, and southeastern Mexico. Mayan people still occupy settlements in many parts of the area including the forests of southern Belize, and they speak their own old languages.

The Spanish invasions of the sixteenth century by-passed Belize and landed further north in the Gulf of Mexico. It was the middle of the seventeenth century when British buccaneers first anchored at the mouth of the Belize River making use of the protection provided by the barrier reef from storms and from attack. Later discovery of the value of logwood for its dye which commanded good prices in Europe led to exploration up the river and settlement at its mouth and on the cays of the reef, as well as expansion to the north and south. Access to the great hardwood forests of the interior led in turn to the establishment of the industry that was to become the mainstay of the Belize economy for three centuries.

Map of Belize

The arrival of so-called black Carib refugees from St Vincent, the import of African slaves from the West Indies and a drift of Spanish mestizo refugees from the caste wars of the Yucatan added new elements to the racial mix that has contributed to the country's wonderfully colour-blind society. Belize is said to have one of the worst climates and the nicest inhabitants. That was certainly our experience.

The Guatemalan Claim

The settlement had a turbulent history. As it grew, organs of government were set up and a code of laws adopted, known as the Burnaby code after Admiral Burnaby who helped to draw it up. But the exact legal position of the settlement was often in dispute with Spain, as were its precise boundaries. This led to endless controversy, treaties, ambiguities, threats, conventions, and occasional violent confrontations, a story punctuated by wars between the metropolitan powers. The pattern is well illustrated by the list of the main events that affected Belize during the eighteenth century alone:

1670	Godolphin Treaty acknowledges de facto position
1713	Treaty of Utrecht confirms settlers' rights
1718	Outbreak of Anglo–Spanish War
1729	Treaty of Seville appoints commissioners
1724	Spanish attack on Belize
1733	Spanish attack on Belize
1739	War of Jenkins' Ear
1747	Spanish attack on Belize
1751	Spanish attack on Belize
1754	Spanish attack disavowed by Madrid
1756	Outbreak of Seven Years' War
1763	Treaty of Paris recognizes settlers' right to cut logwood
1779	Anglo–Spanish War
1783	Treaty of Versailles
1786	Convention of London
1796	Outbreak of new war
1798	Battle of St George's Cay

On this last occasion a fleet of 30 Spanish ships carrying more than 2000 armed men commanded by the Governor-General of Yucatan was defeated by a small force of Belizeans whose knowledge of the reefs and skilful tactics enabled them to drive off the invaders with, it is said, heavy casualties while suffering not a single fatality themselves. This action has acquired legendary status in the Belize folk memory.

In 1802 the Treaty of Amiens seems to have caused more problems than it solved and war broke out again in 1804. The Treaty of London in 1809 sought to put an end to the recurring hostilities between Britain and Spain. It was followed by additional provisions in the Treaty of Madrid of 1814, but argument about the boundaries of the settlement continued until effective Spanish sovereignty in Central America was swept away in 1821.

The continuing Guatemalan claim to the territory has its origins in the year 1483 when Pope Alexander VI, presumably on divine authority, divided the New World, recently discovered by Columbus, between the kings of Spain and Portugal. It is hardly surprising that this decision was not accepted by other countries which became interested in the area, notably France, the Netherlands, Britain and even Denmark. Indeed, the dividing line had soon to be amended by treaty when more accurate geographic information became available. Nevertheless, the Spanish claim to sovereignty over Central America was never seriously contested.

When in 1821 Spanish rule was overthrown, Mexico became independent while the United Provinces of Central America became a federated state. The latter did not survive for long before it disintegrated into the several states of Guatemala, Honduras, El Salvador, Nicaragua and Costa Rica. Guatemala's claim to Belize is founded on its purported 'inheritance', through these upheavals, of Spain's sovereignty over the area now forming Belize, on the doctrine of *uti possidetis*. That doctrine has not been generally accepted as a principle of international law; but there are other flaws in the Guatemalan case.

(1) Under Spanish rule, Belize had never been wholly, or perhaps even partially, within the province of Guatemala (as opposed to Mexico).

(2) Neither Spain nor Guatemala had ever physically occupied the area to give substance to the claim of possession (the Palmerston doctrine).
(3) The continuous occupation sustained over three centuries by British settlers gave rise to a prescriptive right that supersedes any earlier title to sovereignty.
(4) The wishes of the present inhabitants must now prevail over any purely historical claim.

This succinct summary of the issues fails to convey the ocean of complex arguments into which scholars of international law have been plunging happily for years, thereby filling yards of bookshelves in law libraries around Latin America and elsewhere.

Because of the dispute Britain had no diplomatic relations with Guatemala. It did, however, have an able consul-general in Guatemala City, John Weymes, who helped me to establish informal and confidential contact with a senior officer in the Guatemalan government. As soon as possible I took an opportunity to pay a visit there with Shirley: this seemed to me an important preliminary step towards reducing tensions as well as contributing to my own education.

A person like me, without experience of Latin America, found it difficult to understand the Guatemalan government's rigid and militant attitude to the Belize question. I had still to learn how the history of the region had created and hardened its claim, how the *machismo* of the hot-blooded Guatemalan officer corps with an under-employed army impelled the government to an aggressive stance. Even then I found it hard to credit that they would seriously contemplate force of arms against us. That I was to learn later.

With John Weymes we explored some of the country's beauty spots and visited the famous market at Chichicastenango where the colours of the fabrics stunned the eyes and the scent of burning copal filled the nostrils as we peeped into the church. From the people we met I could sense that there was still a colour bar: the Indians were in effect second class citizens, exhibits for tourists and excluded from the political leadership. I began to understand why the prospect of living under that sort of regime was so noxious to the people of Belize's egalitarian society and hence why they attached so much importance to continued British protection.

District Officer on tour: West Nile

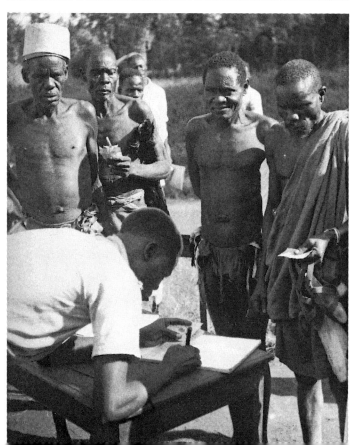

Clerk at work in Alur country

3. LEFT. Alur Drummers

4. BELOW. District Officer's house at Moyo

5. ABOVE. Empire flying boat on the Nile at Laropi

6. BELOW. Mount Elgon: Jackson's summit

7. ABOVE. Uganda
Independence: Prime
Minister Obote and the
Duke of Kent

8. LEFT. Kabaka of Bugan
dancing with Duchess of
Kent at State Ball

9. ABOVE. UN Mission to Pacific: meeting an old man on Yap island

10. BELOW. With Premier George Price at parade in Belize

11. ABOVE. With James E.
Jones filming 'The Cay' in
Belize

SCOUTS OF BELIZE

12. LEFT. With Belize Sco
at Queen's Birthday Parad

13.ABOVE. Prince Philip in Belize with Premier Price and Governor

14. BELOW. Government House, Bermuda, with President Amoral of the Azores

15. ABOVE. State Drive in Bermuda

16. BELOW. 1979: Welcome back to Uganda from an old friend

16

Mr Price's Country

George Price, the Premier of Belize, was a remarkable character. Unlike Ronald Webster in Anguilla, he was difficult to get to know. Having trained for the priesthood in a Roman Catholic seminary he realized that he was miscast and entered politics with a singleness of purpose that won him repeated elections thanks to his political skill and energy. But from the Governor he liked to keep at arm's length. Though I would have been happy to be on first name terms with him, he always called me 'H.E.' and did not like to be addressed by anything more familiar than 'Mr Premier'. I sometimes found it difficult to remember this and at times slipped into calling him 'my friend' or 'Mr Price'. 'George' would have been unthinkable.

He never wore anything other than a simple white *guayabera* — a loose fitting Mexican style shirt. For him this was formal dress suitable for a cabinet meeting, for an evening function or for visiting royalty. He was particularly sensitive to anything suggestive of colonial dependency: hence he abhorred the Governor wearing uniform. I was glad enough in that humid climate to fall in with his style and I only wore full uniform (which was a novelty for me anyway) once a year for the Queen's Birthday parade.

He lived an abstemious monastic life in a small bungalow in Belmopan and spent a lot of his time touring the country, mending political fences and keeping his ear to the ground. I would have liked to be able to draw on his unrivalled local knowledge, but it was not to be.

For him, local politics were not in the Governor's department. On some things he was inordinately prickly. When Belize House was repainted in a delicate shade of coral pink, Mr Price was angry that we had chosen a colour he described as being that of the opposition party (whose flag was actually maroon) and it had to be repainted to his satisfaction.

The flag of Mr Price's own People's United Party was blue, a colour also predominant in the flag of Guatemala. Some of his political opponents were not above accusing him of being ready to sell out to the Guatemalans. This was definitely not on Mr Price's agenda: he had no wish to exchange British protection for Guatemalan hegemony. For years his aim had been to lead Belize to independence, but the Guatemalans had made it clear that they would not recognize or tolerate an independent state of Belize. The threat of invasion was very real to the people of Belize and Mr Price was far too astute a politician not to realize that popular support for independence would depend upon his being able to ensure continued future security for Belize against just that eventuality. This meant, in effect, that Britain must continue to provide for its defence. That, however, was something against which the British government had resolutely turned its face. I saw my task as being to try to find a way to reconcile these contradictions.

First, however, Mr Price wanted to change the name of the territory from British Honduras to Belize. For him this was symbolic: it would remove the implication of colonial dependency. I saw no good reason to object. Spanish speakers had always called it 'Belice' and confusion with the Republic of Honduras was a continual irritant. In the FCO there was apprehension about a Guatemalan reaction, but they were eventually persuaded to agree. The change was made. The Guatemalans protested. And that was that.

The problem of defence was more difficult. Britain maintained a guard battalion which was deployed at Airport Camp near Belize City on the coast. The regiments changed over every six months and they treated this as a good opportunity for training. The army's main task in case of an invasion was to secure the airport so that reinforcements could be flown in. The capital Belmopan, lying only about 20 miles from the border, was virtually undefended.

The Belize government also maintained a defence force which, except for a small nucleus of permanent staff, was run on a part-time volunteer basis. Training camps were held regularly, using instructors from the British garrison. But this small force would obviously not be able to defend the country in the event of an invasion. That left Mr Price in a quandary: independence was his declared aim, but he well knew that, without the presence of the British garrison, Guatemala would instantly swallow up Belize. And the government in London was adamant that it could not keep a garrison there after independence.

I was never happy with the logic of that policy. The anti-colonial tone at the UN, particularly in the General Assembly's fourth committee, had created a strong impression in London that the UK could not expect international sympathy or support in the face of what its experts predicted would be solid Latin American backing for Guatemala's claim. My own experience in the fourth committee led me to doubt this. I suspected that even among some Latin American countries the Guatemalan claim might not attract support and that Mexico in particular would question its authenticity. The battle of St George's Cay had, after all, been fought against a Mexican, not a Guatemalan, squadron. I thought it would be possible to obtain support from other parts of the third world, led by the West Indians, particularly if Mr Price or some of his ministers were to appear in person as petitioners. As the elected representatives of the people they would be strongly placed to stigmatize the Guatemalans as neocolonialists seeking to obstruct their move to independence. However it was not until our hands were forced by the Guatemalans themselves that this could be put to the test in New York.

A New Capital and Old Trees

The building of the new capital at Belmopan was prompted by the appalling damage inflicted on Belize City in 1961 by hurricane Hattie and the ensuing tidal wave which engulfed the low-lying coastal areas. A temporary housing estate named Hattieville was hurriedly built to accommodate the homeless, but the longer-term solution was to move the capital to higher ground 50 miles inland. This project, largely funded by British aid, was dear to the heart of George Price who was one of the first to take up residence in Belmopan and was personally involved in the choice of a name — an amalgam of 'Belize' with the Mayan name of a nearby river 'Mopan'.

For the Governor a single-storey house was built on a rise near the state buildings and named Belize House. It had no mosquito protection and was likened by one visitor to a 'prefab in Dagenham'. John Paul had taken the first steps towards landscaping the surrounding area, but it was still little more than a field of rubble left by the bulldozers. I got it grassed over and planted trees, including a fruit orchard, an avenue of royal palms and later on some mahogany.

When the seat of government moved inland to Belmopan in 1970, the old Government House in Belize City was retained on its lovely site overlooking the harbour. (Belize is non-tidal and only two feet above sea level.) It provided us with an attractive weekend residence from which to meet the city dwellers — businessmen, church leaders, fishermen, boat builders and soldiers from the garrison at Airport Camp — they all comprised the beating heart of the country.

The climate in Belmopan was a little less oppressive than on the coast where the humidity would hover near 100 per cent. But the midday temperature was usually in the high eighties and Belmopan lacked the sea breeze that prevailed on the coast. More annoying than the climate were the legions of biting insects — mosquitoes, sandflies, ticks and, worst of all *botlass*, a small black fly whose painful bites would draw blood and would irritate for days afterwards. Before a game of tennis, one needed to daub repellent over arms and legs.

In Belize I could indulge my interest in trees. Visiting the majestic hardwood forests we saw how the scouts employed by the timber company sought out and identified trees whose girth met the rigorous standards laid down and below which felling was not permitted. The younger trees were left to mature and thus the canopy was preserved. The felling and logging of these giants was an impressive operation. Some of the trees were of varieties whose wood is so dense that it is heavier than water and so could only be floated down the river by shackling them in rafts between the relatively lighter logs of cedar and mahogany. Navigating these rafts downstream, and then along the coast to the sawmill, required a high degree of skill by the pilots of tugs and the raftmen on the logs. Meanwhile replanting, mainly of mahogany, went on continually under the forest canopy. I was told that these trees could not be grown in open ground but was not convinced of this dogma without trial. I planted two dozen young saplings in the grounds of Belize House. On my last visit, eight years later, they were flourishing and 20 feet high.

Over the last half-century agriculture had developed to become the country's economic mainstay. In the north sugar cane was grown and refined by a local subsidiary of Tate & Lyle. South of Belmopan luxurious groves of citrus clothed the Stann Creek valley. The best grapefruit we ever tasted had an ugly mottled skin, too unattractive to sell as whole fruit in British or American supermarkets so they could only be used for canning. Oranges were processed locally and it was fascinating to watch a lorry load of freshly picked fruit quickly reduced to a stream of juice, then concentrated by steaming off the lighter oils, packed in barrels and finally frozen for shipment. Surprisingly their destination was often Florida where Belize juice was used to cover local shortages and mixed for sale as 'Florida Orange Juice'.

Mangoes were exported to the USA and used, I was told, to provide thickening for Campbell's soups. Bananas were being developed as an export crop with the help of British aid funds. In the central areas of Belize tobacco was a profitable crop, largely in American hands. Lobster and crayfish found a ready market in North America, but the quantity had to be limited to avoid depleting stocks. Tourism was not yet a major industry although the wonderful coral reefs were a great attraction for divers. Jacques Cousteau on his yacht *Calypso* was one of our visitors.

A valuable contribution to the agricultural economy was made by the Mennonites. They are descendants of the Anabaptists who were so bitterly persecuted in the sixteenth century in Switzerland and southern Germany and had migrated first to the Ukraine, then to the Low Countries and finally to America. They adhered devoutly to the scriptures and liked to live within their own communities although over the years their rules have become less rigid. Their farming was exemplary.

One cannot live for long in Belize without becoming interested in Mayan archaeology. Norman Hammond from Cambridge and David

Pendergast from Canada were both at work on digs and fascinated us with their didactic explanations. We were allowed to see and handle the magnificent jade head discovered at Altun Ha and we visited the work going on at the impressive temple high on the hill at Xunan-tunich. This conveniently overlooks the Guatemalan border and provided the army with a useful observation post when invasion threatened. There were other sites hidden in the forests that were more difficult to reach: it was eerie in dense forest to find elaborate stonework through and over which tree roots had grown. One could only marvel at the skill of the masons and wonder what had happened to the civilization they represented.

In Belmopan we met two young American women 'spelunkers' — or speleologists to give them their formal title — who were engaged in mapping underground rivers formed by the caverns that had been excavated over the centuries by the action of the water on the limestone of the hills. The hills near Belmopan, they said, resembled a Gruyère cheese. They took me with two children on an expedition up one of these river caves which ran for half a mile underground. The experience aroused my admiration for the skill and nerve their occupation required.

Hurricanes and an Earthquake

Hurricanes were a perennial threat to Belize during the late summer months. The shallow water between the shoreline and the reef about eight miles out would be sucked out to sea by the low pressure of the approaching storm only to be hurled back later in a devastating tidal wave as the storm centre passed inland. Belize City is only a few feet above sea level and it was almost destroyed by hurricane Hattie in 1961.

When the possibility of a hurricane loomed a special committee would convene and hole up in a stronghold in Belize City to oversee emergency arrangements if required. We were in touch with the hurricane centre in Miami from which we could keep track of the storm's movements. Regular local broadcasts would inform the people of Belize about the progress of an approaching storm, warn them of danger, and give advice about what precautions to take. During my term in Belize I was only once required to camp overnight in Belize

City while a hurricane approached. It was heading straight for the coast of Belize and things looked ominous until about 2 a.m. when the storm centre veered suddenly northwards and struck the Yucatan peninsula in Mexico, sparing Belize of its worst effects.

The next morning I flew with the OC Troops in one of his helicopters to examine the situation further north. We crossed into Mexico and landed at Chetumal in the southern Yucatan to find buildings seriously damaged, the control tower knocked askew, and the airport buildings missing much of their glass. The eye of the hurricane had passed just to the north. The local Mexican army commander drove us round the town which had suffered quite badly. We offered to give them whatever help we could once they had assessed the situation. I reported to London and Mexico City what we had seen of the situation there.

✳ ✳ ✳

A geological fault line between two tectonic plates runs down the western side of Central America; it is marked by a string of volcanoes, of which several are still active. Earth tremors are commonplace and interspersed now and again with more serious quakes. In Belize we were far enough removed from the main line of geological activity to avoid the worst effects of these upheavals, though they could sometimes be felt.

One morning in 1975 the telephone rang while we were having breakfast. It was the *Daily Express* in London asking how the earthquake had affected us.

'What earthquake?' I asked.

They said that Guatemala had been badly hit a few hours previously and that they had been unable to get through to the British consulate. This was all news to me. I had sensed nothing, but a guest staying with us at the time appeared from his bedroom to say that a tremor had woken him in the night and that he had seen the ceiling fan swaying.

Realizing that the consulate in Guatemala City would have been closed for the night if the *Daily Express* had rung, I immediately tried to telephone the residence of Bill McQuillan who had recently replaced John Weymes. I was relieved to hear him answer. He had not yet ventured out and could only say that his own residence seemed to be intact. He had thought that the telephone connections were down and was glad to find that I could get through to his house. We agreed that I would call him again later by which time he hoped to have a better idea of the situation and about the safety of British citizens there. I would meanwhile inform the FCO that he was safe and that I could act as a link until direct contact was re-established. For the next few days our telephone to his house became his channel of communication to the FCO.

It turned out to have been a severe shock, but the epicentre had been some distance from Guatemala City, where damage had been limited. It was several days before the full extent of the disaster in the countryside became known. There, buildings were less substantial and had collapsed during the night while their occupants slept. There had been heavy loss of life. Once again Belize had been spared.

17

A Governor's Life

Governor, Commander-in-Chief, and Vice-Admiral of Belize. With such a resounding title it was perhaps appropriate to have the use of a launch, the *Patricia*, with which to visit the cays (islands on the reef) and explore the coast. *Patricia* was a lovely old craft on which we could live for several days, sleeping on deck and catching fish to augment our diet. She had a permanent crew of four who were on the strength of the Customs department and were familiar with all the reefs and islets, the best anchorages and the best fishing grounds. They took us on many splendid trips, sometimes with visiting dignitaries, sometimes with our children and sometimes by ourselves. Once a year we would sail down south to Punta Gorda and then up the Sarstoon River. On these trips we usually took with us the OC Troops and the Commissioner of Police because the river Sarstoon was the Guatemalan border. The army maintained an observation post on a hilltop near the point where the road from Guatemala City passed close by the river on its way north to Flores and eventually up to our frontier. This OP was to prove its worth later.

Another time we cruised north past St George's Cay up to Corozal and to the Rio Hondo which forms the border with Mexico. Where the river became too shallow we transferred to a canoe with an outboard engine to probe further upstream. Suddenly we were surprised to see dolphins playing: these were a rare variety that had adapted to life in fresh water.

Map of Central America

Central America

After we had been in Belize for two years I was invited to attend a meeting of heads of missions in Central America. It would be held in Costa Rica under the chairmanship of the Minister of State at the FCO. This seemed a perfect opportunity for me to visit the Central American states and get to know the area better as well as to meet the various British Ambassadors, all of whom were concerned indirectly about our dispute with Guatemala. I was authorized to travel by car, visiting Guatemala, Honduras, El Salvador and Nicaragua *en route* to San José. The Governor's car had crowns in place of number plates but for this trip I had them removed and a number substituted to avoid difficulty at customs posts. We took no staff: Shirley and I travelled alone as 'tourists'.

After a night at a small hotel at Zacapa in southern Guatemala, we took a rough track across the hills to the border of Honduras where I found two frontier guards reading pornographic magazines with their feet on the table. After a long, slow, bumpy ride we reached the village of Copan, famous for one of the great Mayan sites, and spent a blissful afternoon there with the whole wonderful place to ourselves. Copan had an atmosphere and magic no other site possessed. We could almost feel the Mayans looking over our shoulders as we examined the fabulous staircase, each step carved with hieroglyphs.

The next day we drove up the long mountainous road to Tegucigalpa where Ambassador David Pearson and his attractive French wife Camille-Henriette welcomed us. They told us about the infamous 'football war' between Honduras and El Salvador when a long-standing boundary dispute erupted into war after a Honduras team visiting San Salvador beat the home side. When not discussing the politics of Central America, they regaled us with blood chilling stories of life in the resistance in wartime France when she had been a resistance fighter and he was parachuted in by SOE. So well did he play his cover role as a pro-Nazi foreign worker in an arms factory under German control that the French resistance suspected him of being a double agent until he was fully cleared from London. Mrs Pearson had later been betrayed and arrested by the Gestapo, but escaped. Her betrayer was identified and duly 'executed' — she did not say by whom, but we drew our own conclusions. A remarkable woman.

We arrived in Nicaragua only a few days after the severe earthquake of 1974. The ambassador had tents in his garden to accommodate British people whose houses had been destroyed. He drove us round the city of Managua where the devastation was appalling: every building had collapsed or been seriously damaged — debris littered the streets, cars were squashed beneath collapsed canopies and church steeples had toppled. The human casualties were still being counted.

We drove on south past the great Lake of Nicaragua in which are said to live the only fresh-water sharks in the world. Out of the middle of the lake springs the impressive volcano of Concepción to more than 5000 feet. Arriving next day at our hotel in San José we were greeted at lunch by an earthquake which rocked the tables and made the chandeliers swing violently for ten seconds.

The Minister of Agriculture, who had visited Belize, invited us to spend a weekend at his hacienda on the Pacific coast. His hospitality was lavish, flying us down from San José, putting us up in a shore-side chalet, and having his daughter show us round the estate on horseback. He also arranged for me to pay a call on the President of Costa Rica, the charismatic José Figueres.

At the presidential palace I was shown in with minimal formality. I had expected only a brief formal salutation, but was left alone with the President who sat me down and engaged at once in serious discussion in English about the problems of the region. Costa Rica is an oddity in Latin America: it has no army and has been relatively free from the kind of political violence that seems to be endemic elsewhere. I was kept there talking for half an hour. When I got up to leave the President insisted on accompanying me out of the room, down the stairs, out of a side door and on to the street. Some passing girls immediately recognized him, rushed over calling him by his familiar name 'Don Pépé' and engaged him in animated and affectionate conversation. He was an exemplary democrat, I thought, and a striking contrast to many other Latin American leaders.

Before leaving Costa Rica I took the chance to drive up the amazing road that climbs to the top of the volcano Irazu at 11,260 feet. Our car felt the altitude and we felt no desire to run about as we looked down from the rim into the steaming sulphurous green liquid in the crater.

On our return journey we stopped for a night in the hilly region of

Nicaragua near León. I was surprised to hear the black clerk at the hotel desk speak perfect English with no American accent. He explained that he came from the Mosquito Coast where English, which they had inherited from their West Indian forbears, was their native tongue.

Thence we drove on to San Salvador, where the Ambassador took me to meet the Foreign Minister, a charming man who was brutally gunned down a year later. He took us down to the port of La Libertad on the Pacific coast where I was surprised, in those cold war days, to see a Russian freighter unloading grain.

During the two-day drive home through Guatemala I had time to digest all these experiences. After seeing for myself the different parts of this wild and beautiful region, after meeting some of its leaders and learning from our ambassadors about some of its mysteries, I felt better equipped to see the problems of Belize in their wider context.

The Death Penalty

The policy of advancing its dependent territories towards independence required the government in London to relinquish to the territory an increasing degree of control over its domestic affairs. This sometimes led to a conflict between the policy the territory government adopted and the one London advocated. A case in point arose when, following a free vote in the House of Commons, capital punishment was abolished in Britain. That move reflected a change in the social morality of British society since the war. No such change had taken place in the dependencies and certainly not in the West Indies; so, when the FCO asked Governors to invite their ministers to introduce parallel legislation, Mr Price and his ministers would have none of it.

Wilful murder was rare in Belize: only twice during the four years I spent there were convictions recorded that led to a sentence of death being passed. Whether this was cause and effect, I doubt: the low murder rate may simply have reflected the law-abiding nature of the populace. But the attitude of ministers certainly reflected public opinion and was in line with the stance adopted in neighbouring territories. The independent Commonwealth states in the West Indies all retained the death penalty for murder. I could see no grounds for trying to press Mr Price further.

As a young man in Uganda, I had faced the difficult problem of passing a mandatory sentence of death upon persons convicted of murder. On those occasions I had been able to make representations to the Governor upon whom responsibility rested for deciding whether or not to exercise the royal prerogative of mercy and commute the sentence to imprisonment. My recommendations had invariably been for commutation, not because of my personal dislike for capital punishment but because in each case I thought there were mitigating circumstances. Now in Belize I found myself in the more fearful position of having to make that final decision myself. To advise me in such matters I had a small committee comprising the Premier, the Minister of Home Affairs Lindy Rogers, and the Attorney General Harry Courtenay. My own personal views about capital punishment were beside the point: my duty was to apply the law taking account of the views of society in Belize, not Britain, and of their elected ministers.

The first case that came before me was of the deliberate killing of a policeman by a criminal he was trying to arrest. The advisory committee observed that this was not only a cold blooded crime but also a deliberate challenge to the forces of law and order. There were no mitigating circumstances and public opinion would never understand or accept commutation of the sentence. I could see no reason to disagree and, after some anxious thought, decided accordingly.

The second case was more difficult. Two white Americans living near Stann Creek had been involved in some dubious financial dealings and had quarrelled. During a furious row, one of them had pulled out a gun and, thinking himself unobserved, had shot his compatriot dead. A Belizean passing nearby with her baby had seen what had happened and, when the killer realized this, he turned his gun on the fleeing woman, left her for dead and departed to look for an alibi. By amazing good fortune, the woman survived to tell the tale and her baby was unharmed.

The murderer was convicted and sentenced to death. The judge's report to the Governor sought by laboured and unconvincing argument to support a recommendation for mercy. I discovered later that he was morally opposed to capital punishment and I think he had probably allowed his personal feelings to influence his judgement — a luxury the Governor could not afford.

The case caused outrage in Belize, not so much on account of the murder itself but because of the subsequent ruthless and brutal attempt to kill the Belizean woman who had witnessed the crime. The advisory committee was unanimous that the law should take its course and, despite the advice of the judge, I could see no reason for acting against the committee's advice. I refused to commute.

A week later I received an urgent telegram from the FCO. The US Ambassador in London had called on Mr Callaghan, the Foreign Secretary, to intercede to prevent the hanging of the American murderer. To support his argument, the Ambassador quoted the US Consul-General in Belize who had reported that the judge had recommended mercy. I was asked for particulars of the case and the reasons for my decision.

For the judge to reveal to the Consul-General — or anybody — the contents of his report to the Governor was a serious breach of confidence, but the damage was done. I was asked to reconsider my decision. It was explained to me that, in the last resort, ministers in London might feel obliged, in view of Parliament's attitude to capital punishment, to advise the Queen to exercise the prerogative of mercy herself.

I replied that I was not minded to go against my ministers' advice which was soundly based and with which I concurred. We thought the judge's recommendation was unconvincing and out of touch with Belize public opinion which was outraged by this crime. However, I agreed to put the arguments raised by the Foreign Secretary to my ministers and to report further after discussing it with them. Meanwhile the sentence would not be carried out.

I then had a talk with Mr Price and his colleagues and explained what had happened. I said that I was not prepared to alter my decision unless it was on their advice. But I pointed out the likely embarrassment if the Queen were advised to overrule our decision; and I reminded them of the importance to Belize in the longer term of the continued political and financial support of both the UK and the US governments. They quickly saw the point and decided that it was not in the political interests of Belize to make this a sticking point. They warned me that I might be pilloried for a racist decision in favour of a white man, but agreed that I should commute the sentence to life imprisonment. I conveyed this decision to London, commuted the sentence and, as Mr Price had predicted, was attacked in the local press for racism.

The interesting sequel to this was that the prisoner later escaped and fled back to Texas where he then committed another murder for which he was sent to the electric chair.

Naval Occasions

To provide cover for British territories in the Caribbean against a military emergency or natural disaster the Royal Navy maintained a ship under the control of a senior naval officer stationed in Bermuda and known by his acronym SNOWI. This guard ship, usually a tribal-class frigate, called twice a year at Belize to show the flag and to liaise with the OC Troops at Airport Camp on defence matters. These ships carried helicopters which the captain would use either to fly up to call on the Governor at Belmopan or to fly him out to his ship for the navy's legendary hospitality. On one such visit Neil Blair, who was in command, took me in his ship 100 miles down the coast to Punta Gorda, keeping inside the reef all the way, a passage fraught with hazards from shallows and lurking coral heads. I had to admire the navigating officer who was kept intensely occupied for many hours on end.

I had no experience of naval protocol and during these visits I learned some of the arcane niceties, such as how to respond when one is piped aboard ship, which end is the quarterdeck, and how should an officer acknowledge a salute when not wearing headgear.

One year Shirley and I were invited by Tom Russell, the Governor of the Cayman Islands, to attend some official celebration there. It so happened that HMS *Gurkha* was to sail to the Caymans for this function immediately following a visit to Belize, so I signalled SNOWI to ask if we could take passage on *Gurkha*. He replied that I could certainly do so but that for Shirley he would need to obtain permission from their Lordships of the Admiralty. This was duly forthcoming and we were embarked by helicopter, feeling guilty for usurping Captain Fox's cabin. A screened area had thoughtfully been set up on a small deck area where Shirley could sunbathe unobserved, though I noticed later that the area was visible from the bridge above. Sadly she was too seasick to take advantage of this facility.

Flying back from the Caymans on this occasion, the immigration officer at Miami airport politely pointed out that my US visa had expired — it was not the first time I had been guilty of that oversight.

During our third year in Belize SNOWI himself was embarked on the guard ship during a routine visit and came to stay at Belize House. During dinner a phone call came through for him from London. When he returned to the table he seemed somewhat distraught. He told us that the guard ship was to be withdrawn as a result of recent cuts in the naval establishment and that his own post was to be abolished. This was bad news not only for him but for Belize. We spent a sombre evening.

A Royal Visit

The people of Belize had always hankered after a visit by royalty, partly perhaps as a reassurance that they would not be abandoned to the Guatemalans, but mainly because of their long-standing attachment to Britain (whence came the first settlers) and to the British monarchy. A visit by the Queen under the shadow of the Guatemalan threat was thought to raise too many dangers. But after Her Majesty's state visit to Mexico it was arranged that, while the Queen returned to London, Prince Philip would sail with the royal yacht down the coast to stay for a few days in Belize as the first stage of an official tour of Central America.

Britannia anchored in the roads off Belize City and His Royal Highness came ashore by launch. The Premier and I welcomed him at the dockside and I took him for a drive round the city in an open car so that he could see and be seen. I asked him to take the seat of honour on the right side, but he demurred.

'No! You are the Queen's representative: I am just her husband.'

Travelling round the country with the Prince, we had to stay alert to try and answer his flow of questions. What is that tree, that bird, that crop, that building? How is this done here? Why that way? It is done differently in Mauritius (or New Guinea or Indonesia or Ethiopia). I tried to make sure that Mr Price and Eric King our chief agricultural officer, were always alongside to offer information. Even Mr Price was stumped when the Prince asked him about land tenure and the relative advantages of farming cooperatives.

'An interesting suggestion,' was all he could say in response.

After a convivial evening at Belize House with a few interesting non-political Belizeans, we moved down the next day through the citrus growing areas to Stann Creek where the *Britannia* had meantime been repositioned. Shirley and I were invited to join the royal party on the yacht for the overnight passage up the coast to Belize City, where an investiture was to be held the next morning. We were given splendid cabins, offered a dip in the miniature pool on deck which we declined, and after dinner we all watched a film.

An investiture on board ship was an exciting novelty for Belize and vastly savoured by the lucky ones who came on board with their spouses to receive their honours. When that was over we went ashore and took the Prince for a drive up north to the sugar refinery, where he met a number of local people and we were given a splendid barbecue. It was then back to Belize City and to the airport, where an aircraft of the Queen's Flight was waiting to take the Prince to El Salvador for the next stage of his tour. HRH took the controls and waved farewell from the flight deck.

During the tour, the Prince and I had discussed the threat from Guatemala and he had found it difficult, as I did, to credit that the threat of invasion was real. A week later I received a letter in which he said that, after his visits in Central America, he now recognized why the threat from Guatemala was taken seriously in Belize.

Showdown with Guatemala

Towards the end of 1974 I went with Mr Price to London for consultations at the FCO. My three year term as Governor was due to expire early in 1975 and the matter of my successor came up. Mr Price surprised me by asking whether I could stay on for another year: our relationship had not always been smooth, but I suppose he may have preferred to retain the devil he knew. Shirley's health had been a problem, but we both loved Belize and when Ted Rowlands, the FCO minister, asked me to stay on I agreed.

Our two elder children used to fly out to spend school holidays with us. This involved their staying overnight in Miami under the care of British Airways and then flying on to Belize with one of the Central American airlines. They soon became adept travellers and familiar with all the shops at Miami airport. On one occasion they arrived without their passports, health documents or return tickets which had somehow disappeared *en route*.

When the summer holidays came round in 1975 we took ten days' leave in which to enjoy the sights and beauty of Guatemala. We drove first to Flores on its lovely lake and then into the forest for our first encounter with the fabled Mayan centre of Tikal. Here, hiding in the forests of the Peten, astounding temples reach up well above the 100 foot forest canopy. Wandering round this forsaken city was an unforgettable experience. Who had built all these massive structures and carved the intriguing stelae? What was their motive? How had they lived? Where had they gone? Tikal baffled us with these mysteries.

We drove on through the jungle of the Peten, up through the highlands to Guatemala City, and down to the ancient capital city of Antigua. An earthquake had devastated Antigua 200 years before, but some striking ruins remained to give echoes of its past grandeur in the midst of what was now a busy country town. Looking out from the spacious gardens of our hotel, I was attracted by the symmetrical volcano called Agua that towered above us: it looked an interesting climb which Dickon, aged 12, and I decided to attempt.

Leaving the road at 6000 feet, we followed a rocky path up through woodland and, after two hours, realized that Agua belied its name: there was no water, no stream, to be seen. Suddenly, we heard the sound of an engine and a motorbike came up the path behind us. The rider halted to greet us: he explained that he worked for the radio relay station at the top of the mountain and discouraged us by saying that we were not yet half way up.

As we gained height our progress slowed. Dickon was as much affected by the altitude as I was. Pauses for breath became more frequent and the number of steps we could take between them got fewer and fewer — 30 steps — 20 — 10 — each step up had become a burden. When we finally reached the top we had been climbing for six hours. There, at the small radio hut, we found our motor cyclist and two other cheery technicians. They offered us a welcome mug of tea. We asked them the altitude: 3776 metres or 12,385 feet. No wonder we felt exhausted!

Tree cover on the summit allowed little outlook over the surrounding country. Soon we set off down again, glad of the relief to our lungs but beginning to feel the strain of pounding down a 30-degree slope. After three hours our knees were like aching jellies. It was 6 p.m. when we walked back into the hotel feeling the need for rest, refreshment and comfort. But we were greeted with the news that we were expected at a reception and must hurry to change.

Next day, on the long drive back to Belize, we had just crossed by ferry into the Peten forest when we had a puncture. As I was changing the wheel a Guatemalan army lorry drove by in a cloud of dust with soldiers leaning out of the back, and towing a trailer with a bulging tarpaulin cover. Halting later for a picnic, another truck with soldiers and a trailer. With barely 30 miles to go to the border of Belize, we had a second puncture — and I had no second spare tyre. We were 15 miles beyond Flores, the nearest town. A lorry coming in the opposite direction stopped and an obliging lorry driver, seeing our plight, offered to take me there. I heaved the two punctured tyres into the back and climbed in. Shirley and the children were left to wait by the roadside in the wilderness. Almost two hours had passed before I got back with two serviceable tyres. My family was relieved to see me. By now it was late and, as soon as I had fitted one of the tyres, I turned the car round and drove back to Flores for a night in the comfort of an hotel.

Discussing the day's adventures over supper, the children told me that more trucks had passed while I was getting the tyres mended: they had counted up to six trucks during the day. I resolved to tell this to the garrison commander when I got back to Belize.

Two days later, on a Saturday morning in Belize City, I met Colonel Duncan Green at Government House and was startled by what he had to tell me. From his observation post on the hill at the head of the Sarstoon River, ten armoured personnel carriers had been seen passing up the road the previous day in the direction of Belize. He had also learned from other sources that Guatemalan gunboats had passed through the Panama Canal in transit from the Pacific to the Caribbean Sea and that some Guatemalan training aircraft had been adapted for use in an offensive capacity.

Duncan observed that our defence strategy was based on the assumption that we would have at least 24 hours' notice of troop movements from Guatemala City towards the frontier and that this would allow time for reinforcements to be flown in. Now that we had Guatemalan troops and transport right on the border, the 'lead time' had disappeared. Their ground forces could cross into Belize at a moment's notice and be in Belmopan within the hour. If this happened our own troops could hold the airport in Belize City but little else. He advised me to alert London to this unexpected change in the situation. We discussed possible alternative explanations for the evidence before us but could find no reasonable assessment other than preparations for an invasion. Much against my instinct I had to agree; and we drafted an immediate signal to the FCO and Ministry of Defence accordingly.

Meanwhile, Duncan had placed an observer with a radio on top of the old Mayan temple at Xunantunich which overlooks the only road that crosses the frontier. I drove back to Belmopan wondering whether our weekend was to be rudely disturbed by the arrival of Guatemalan soldiers. Locating Mr Price, I warned him of the situation and promised to keep him informed of developments.

On Sunday morning I was brought an urgent signal from the FCO. The Cabinet in London had authorized the immediate dispatch of reinforcements. A second message gave details: a battalion of infantry would be leaving by air within 48 hours and a half squadron of RAF Harriers would be flying out as soon as the necessary logistical arrangements could be made. I was stunned by the speed of Mr Callaghan's response and awed by the effect my telegram had created. I felt like someone who has lit a match and finds he has started a forest fire — it felt like our own miniature version of the Cuban missile crisis.

Two days later I was sitting in my office when a deafening roar drove me out to see what caused it: a couple of Harriers were flying low overhead. The populace was as yet unaware of what had been going on and initial alarm was only alleviated when the aeroplanes were recognized as British. I gave a short radio talk to explain what was happening and to reassure the public that there was no need for alarm.

The sequel to this was a complaint by Guatemala to the Security Council in New York about the aggressive actions of the United Kingdom in Belize. This gave us the opportunity I had hoped for to present the Belize position in that forum. Thanks to Duncan Green's foresight we were able to produce pictures taken from our observation post of armoured vehicles passing along the road to Belize. The Guatemalan accusation was rejected. Later, when the General Assembly convened, we arranged for two Belizean ministers to appear before the fourth committee as complainants, in effect accusing Guatemala of blocking the independence to which Belize aspired. To my relief, only a very few of the Latin Americans supported Guatemala; some abstained and some courageously supported the Belize case which won by a large majority.

   From that day on the future of Belize was assured. The unanimous support of the Commonwealth persuaded London in due course to offer a defence agreement which helped Mr Price to win popular support for a move to independence. But that still lay in the future. In Belize, the Harriers with their amazing capacity to hover and move backwards, forwards, sideways, up, down and round along with their deafening speed were creating a huge impression. In case the Guatemalans were watching, we made sure that their presence was highly visible. My office was daily receiving letters from young Belizeans asking to join the RAF.

✳ ✳ ✳

The time came for us to depart. We planned a leisurely road trip through Mexico and the USA to Canada in a camper van I had purchased from American visitors who wanted to dispose of it. Then, with just ten days to go, Shirley was struck down with a severe abdominal haemorrhage. The Belmopan doctor was away. A call to Duncan Green brought a helicopter, complete with medical team, and we were flown to Belize City, Shirley in tears at the dashing of her hopes for our holiday trip. Copious blood transfusions and major surgery by a skilful Indian surgeon Sunil Roy with a Belizean anaesthetist Lennox Pike saved her life. But ten days later, when an RAF VC10 had come to fly her home, she relapsed with peritonitis. RAF surgeon John King assisted at a further operation, after which she lay on the danger list for a week. Beto Espat in Belmopan obtained essential drugs from San Salvador.

Meanwhile, I handed the government over to Fonseca until the new Governor arrived. I went with Jonathan, now aged five, to stay with the ever helpful Vera and Duncan Green until Shirley was fit enough to be flown home.

Landing at Brize Norton, the station commander appeared with a bouquet of flowers for Shirley on her stretcher. She was to spend the next two months in and out of the RAF hospital at Wroughton, followed by three weeks at the John Radcliffe Hospital in Oxford before she was able to resume something approximating normal life at a cottage rented from friends near Harlow. We owed her life to the RAF and to many skilful doctors.

18

Ocean Island

January 1977. Some old friends ask me to join them for two weeks' skiing in the Arlberg, based at St Anton: Ashley Greenwood, an old lawyer friend from Uganda days, with his wife Horry and her sister Jennifer, a former ski racer from the Howard stable. Shirley, at home in the cottage at Chilton, is fighting her way back to health after her long and grievous illness in hospitals from Belize to the John Radcliffe, but she is adamant that I should go and the FCO has no reason to keep me in London.

I had not been to St Anton for 15 years and it was a joy to rediscover the glorious runs from the Valluga and to ski behind Jennifer, trying to keep up with her as she took the steepest line with carefree abandon. After six days working our way back into form we were gathered for the evening in a smoke-filled *stübli*.

A waitress in traditional *dirndl* came by.

'Herr Posnett?' I heard her enquire at a nearby table.

I froze. Only Shirley knew where I was. I got up and was shown to the telephone. It was the resident clerk at the FCO.

'We didn't know you were away. You should have left a contact address.'

I said nothing.

'The Minister wants you to come in tomorrow to see him. He has an urgent assignment for you.'

'Oh! Where?'

'In the Pacific I believe. Can you be here at 4.00 p.m.?'

'Well, I am in the middle of a package holiday and my return flight from Innsbruck is not till next week. If it's really important, I could try to catch a train from here to Zürich tomorrow, but I'd need a flight reservation from there. If you ring back in half an hour, I'll find out about train times.'

The others were sympathetic with my discomfiture: I was less than amused at the prospect of interrupting a glorious holiday. I discovered that the earliest train was the international Pullman from Bratislava and Vienna which was due to halt at St Anton at 8.15 in the morning and to reach Zürich at about 1.00 p.m. When the telephone call came through I passed this information on and asked for the consul in Zürich to meet me at the station with an air ticket and to get me to the airport for the next available flight.

'We've already spoken to the consul,' he replied.

'He's booking you on the 2.00 p.m. flight from Zürich to Heathrow. We'll expect you in the office at 4.00 p.m.' Click.

I was stunned. One final beer with the Greenwoods who wished me luck and lent me a rucksack; then I stepped out into the cold starlit night, crunching the snow under my boots down the road to my lodging. There I had to tell my landlady and pack up — skis, sticks, boots and all.

Next morning I was up early and lugged my bag and skis half a mile to the station. It was snowing hard: I thought how good the skiing would be the next day. At the station I bought a ticket to Zürich and was told that the train would be late on account of the bad weather. On the platform a single woman with two suitcases was waiting for the same train. She was American and it turned out that she too had a plane to catch. A stewardess with Pan Am, she was returning from leave and needed to be in New York that evening, as she was to be on duty the next day.

Time dragged on and we waited with increasing frustration till the train eventually pulled in, covered with snow and nearly two hours late. At last we were off. Crossing into Liechtenstein and Switzerland the blizzard continued. The train was going to be very late and there was nothing we could do about it. At last the Lake of Zürich appeared through the driving snow. By now it was well past 3 p.m.

My flight would have left. I told the Pan Am stewardess that I was being met and offered her a lift to the airport.

Zürich Hauptbahnhof. A man held up a card with my name on it. I introduced myself and explained the delay. To our surprise and relief he told us that the blizzard had halted all flights including mine. We would still be able to catch it if we hurried.

In London it was 4.30 p.m. local time when I finally arrived at Heathrow. I went over to the enquiries desk where a woman in uniform was speaking on the telephone. After a moment, she picked up a pen and started to write slowly as a name was spelled out to her. Reading upside down I saw her spell out the letters P O S N.

I gesticulated to attract her attention, pointed to her paper and to myself. She spoke into the phone and held it aside.

'I am Posnett,' I said.

After a moment of surprise she spoke again into the receiver and handed it to me.

'Why aren't you here?'

I explained about the blizzard.

'Get here as quickly as possible and come straight to the office of the Minister of State, Lord Goronwy Roberts.'

'But I'm still in ski clothes!'

'Can't be helped. Come as you are.'

An hour later, having deposited my skis and bags, I arrived at the FCO and found my way to the Minister's office. The Private Secretary was unperturbed by my dishevelment, apologized for the inconvenience to my holiday and ushered me in to the Minister. I apologized for my lateness and my garb. Goronwy waved me to a seat and started to explain why he had sent for me.

The British government had been involved in a long running dispute with the inhabitants of Ocean Island in the western Pacific. (They were called Banabans after the Melanesian name for the island, *Banaba* meaning rock.) The dispute concerned compensation for the phosphate rock that had been dug from their island, leaving it virtually uninhabitable. They had been offered a new home on an island in the Fiji archipelago but they were still dissatisfied and had launched an action against the British government in the High Court in London. In giving judgement for the Crown, the Vice-Chancellor (a senior judge in the Chancery division) had voiced criticism of how the Banabans had been treated; now a parliamentary question had been put down in the House of Lords to which the Minister had to reply the next day.

He had decided that an independent enquiry was needed to go into the whole matter, find out the facts on the ground and make recommendations about the course of action that the government should now pursue. Goronwy wanted to be able to announce in the Lords tomorrow that he was appointing me to undertake this. As a former colonial Governor with some knowledge of the Pacific, he thought I had the requisite standing and experience to make a credible independent assessment. Was I prepared to do it?

I realized wryly that my holiday had been aborted simply to get the Minister off the hook over a question in Parliament. My only previous acquaintance with the Pacific region had been on the UN mission to the US Trust Territory of Micronesia; and that was ten years ago and not directly relevant to the Ocean Island dispute. Nevertheless I was intrigued. I needed a challenge and I accepted the assignment. We had a general talk about the problem and I agreed to start work the next day.

Back in the outer office I made a telephone call to Shirley. I had not had a chance to tell her of these events and she thought I was still in Austria when she answered the telephone.

'Guess who's coming to dinner!' I said.

✳ ✳ ✳

Ocean Island is a speck of rock rising from the empty wastes of the Pacific Ocean. It grew from the tip of an extinct submarine volcano on which, over aeons of time while the sea covered it, coral grew and gradually built great castles and pinnacles. Then the sea receded slightly and, for many millions of years, migrant birds paused on their transoceanic journeys to rest and feed and to deposit layer upon layer of guano which, as ages passed, became phosphate rock. These simple geological and zoological processes created an island, with a cap of phosphate covering the coral.

Much more recently, in the last millennium or two, a different kind of migrant reached the island, not by air this time but by sea. They came in outrigger canoes, usually by accident because the island's existence was unknown elsewhere. And, when some of these drift-aways contained females, the first colony of human Banabans was established. First noticed and visited by a British ship in 1804, the island was formally annexed to Britain in 1900 and became part of the Gilbert and Ellice Islands Colony immortalized by Arthur Grimble in *A Pattern of Islands.*

When German possessions in the Pacific, notably Nauru, came into allied hands after the First World War, the governments of Britain, Australia and New Zealand set up a consortium of three commis-sioners which came to be known as the BPC, or British Phosphate Commissioners. It was charged with managing the mining of phos-phate on islands in the region, including Nauru and Ocean Island. This remained the situation, apart from the years during the Second World War when Japanese forces occupied the islands and a number of the inhabitants were taken away to work elsewhere.

To get to Ocean Island, I flew via New York and Los Angeles to Fiji. Thence I took a small plane to Tarawa, capital of the Gilbert Islands, landing on the way at Tuvalu in the Ellice Islands. The Japanese had occupied Tarawa in 1942 and it was the scene of bitter fighting before the Americans recaptured it in 1944. Now, 33 years later, atoll life seemed much as one had imagined it — nowhere more than a few feet above sea level and with a lagoon fringed with coco-nut palms to supply food and building materials. The people looked well nourished and content. But nourishment, I discovered, often comprised imported cans of food and drink, not just the fish and coconut of earlier times. I soon began to see how complex was the administration of these island peoples who had sounded, from Grimble's book, to lead so peaceful and idyllic a life.

I knew that the Banabans were demanding separation from the Gilbert Islands. The Ellice Islands had also voted to secede from the Gilberts and to go separately to an independent state. Demands like this were frequently a problem in colonial territories moving towards self-government and posed a difficulty that had often puzzled the United Nations. As Ocean Island was part of the territory of the Gilbert Islands, any change in its status would be of concern to all the islands in the group. The Gilbertese had acquiesced in the splitting off of the Ellice Islands. So I hoped for a conciliatory attitude from them in the case of Ocean Island too.

The Governor, John Smith, warned me that it would not be that simple. And when I met the Chief Minister Ieremia Tabai, he soon disabused me of the idea that the people or his Ministers might agree.

The royalties paid by the BPC for their phosphate mining were divided 85 per cent to the government of the Colony and 15 per cent to the Banabans' own council. I could see that some financial juggling would be necessary and thought, at first, that this might be the main problem. But I found that Gilbertese objections to any separation were more deep rooted. All Banabans were of the same stock, spoke the same language, and shared the same beliefs and tribal divinities: Banaba, they claimed, had always been part of this homogeneous group. Separation was unthinkable and was only being demanded, according to the Gilbertese, because of the phosphate royalties which the Banabans wanted all for themselves. The case of the Ellice Islanders was quite different: they were a distinct people with a different language and had little in common with the Gilbertese.

Shades of Katanga I thought. How many times in other parts of the world had the discovery of oil or of mineral deposits led to demands for separation and poisoned relations between one part of a country and the rest? I asked the Governor to arrange a public meeting and suggested that he should not attend lest there be any suggestion of undue influence.

The public meeting opened my eyes. I was harangued and cross-examined for more than four hours. It was a warm day and after three hours the official interpreter collapsed and had to be relieved by a substitute. At the end I told the gathering of a few hundred that I felt as though I had been through 15 rounds with Muhammad Ali. This at least raised a laugh.

The next day I boarded a small tramp steamer bound for Ocean Island 240 miles away. The island is not much more than a mile across and too small for an airstrip. The captain was a tubby Gilbert Islander clad in tattered khaki shorts. Equipment on the bridge comprised a wheel, an engine-room telegraph, a compass, and a case of beer. I could see we were in safe hands. I discovered that my fellow passengers included Professor Ron Crocombe from the Institute of Pacific Studies in Hawaii. He was able to give me invaluable help and advice from his wide experience and examined for me the areas of agriculture on the island.

I awoke next day to a warm clear Pacific dawn and in time to see Ocean Island heave over the horizon. It looked green and pleasant, not the desolate moonscape some of the wilder reports in London had led me to expect. We had to go ashore by boat for there is no harbour. The seabed shelves so steeply down from the coast that ships cannot anchor and have to tie up to buoys. Once ashore I found that much of the island consisted of sharp coral rocks and pinnacles from which the phosphate cover had been removed. Surprisingly, trees and shrubs managed to grow in some parts and give a cover of greenery, but there was little fertile soil and hardly any agriculture. Most of the few hundred residents were not Banabans but Gilbertese from other islands working for the BPC. The true Banabans comprised about fifty souls, a rather aimless group who turned out to be squatters sent from the settlement in Fiji and paid to stay for six-monthly tours of 'duty' so as to maintain a Banaban presence on the island.

From Ocean Island I found my way back by stages to Fiji, where I spent some time with the displaced Banabans at their settlement on the island of Rabi. The island was fertile and uncrowded but the Banabans made a rather sad impression, not because they had been ill-treated but because they seemed to have lost their spirit and purpose, what is sometimes vaguely called 'moral fibre'. They had depended for so long on the revenues from phosphate royalties which, even their 15 per cent share, provided a large income for a small community, that their ancestral skills as sailors and fishermen had fallen into desuetude. They had become a tribe of *rentier*s who had lost the ambition to improve their own lot, had developed expensive tastes, and had laid nothing aside for the future. I could see that when the phosphate on Ocean Island ran out and the royalties dried up in a few years' time, the Banabans would come down to earth with a bump. The only recommendation I could usefully make was to set up a trust fund to help cushion their fall. But I was not sanguine that it would cure their spiritual malaise.

Trying to understand these problems I was lucky to be able to draw on the knowledge of Stanley Arthur, the British High Commissioner in Fiji. Himself an Orcadian (from the Orkney Islands) he was well equipped to understand the minds and problems of people from a small remote island. On one trip with him our motorboat engine gave out and we drifted helplessly for half an hour until another boat hove in sight. When it drew near to offer help it turned out to be the Prime Minister's official launch with Ratu (Lord) Mara himself on board. He enjoyed the idea of rescuing us and welcomed us aboard. I had worked across the table with him during the Fiji constitutional conference in London five years before and now we had a fascinating hour or more of talk with him on the way back to harbour in Suva.

The Ocean Island mission gave me my first opportunity to visit Australia and New Zealand. Besides ministers and officials, I met members of the BPC organization which is based in Melbourne, but perhaps the most interesting meeting of all was with Harry Maude, Professor of Anthropology at the Australian National University and renowned for his knowledge of the peoples of the Pacific. I could only mop up the drops of wisdom overflowing from his vast reservoir of learning.

Back in London I worked on my report. The constitutional demand for separation of Ocean Island from the Gilberts was not difficult to refute, but the matter of financial compensation for an island made uninhabitable was not so easy. In the end I came up with a sum of seven million Australian dollars to be put into a trust fund. Lord Goronwy presented the report in the House of Lords and the Secretary of State, Dr David Owen, presented it in the Commons. I sat in the gallery as he made complimentary remarks about the report* and announced the government's acceptance of my recommendations with the sum of money increased to ten million dollars. He dealt courteously with the earnest questions raised by members from both sides:

---

* Hansard reported: *Dr Owen*: 'I am most grateful to Mr Posnett for his valuable report on this longstanding and difficult problem. ... I would urge honourable gentlemen before forming a final judgement to read the Posnett Report. It is a very valuable and balanced account of the complex problems that we are dealing with.'

as none of them had yet read the report (which ran to 60 pages) Dr Owen had no difficulty handling their sometimes misinformed allegations.

It had been an interesting exercise. I had less than three years to go before reaching the compulsory retiring age of 60 and, hoping for a pleasant final post, I wondered where I might be sent. I was offered the position of Consul-General in Cape Town, a post the personnel department had considerately chosen partly because of the excellent medical facilities that would be available for Shirley, who was still recovering strength after her dreadful and protracted illness. A consular post is not concerned with policies of the government of the country or their effect upon the lives of its people. In those days of apartheid I could foresee awful difficulty living in the white dominated community in South Africa after my years in Uganda. I wrote to David Scott, then our ambassador in South Africa, for advice and he agreed that it was not a post which I would fit. I rang personnel department and explained why I must turn it down. Two hours later the phone rang on the desk of Jim Hennessy with whom I was sharing an office at the time. He listened, then looked at me and smiled before promising to ring back.

'They've offered me Cape Town,' he said. We both laughed.

Jim had been our man in Kampala at the time when Amin's behaviour was at its worst and the British High Commission had to be closed. For him, there was nothing much to choose between Uganda and South Africa and he accepted the Cape Town post. He was a true professional who knew that his job was to serve wherever he was sent, however distasteful the regime in the country might be. I, on the other hand, with my colonial background, had been trained to get close to the people of the country rather than to distance myself from them in the way diplomacy often demanded. Jim and I were to meet again: he became the last Governor of Belize and was my host at their independence celebrations.

As a result I became type cast as a kind of colonial troubleshooter dealing with the problems of small island dependencies as they ploughed their erratic courses towards self-government. A new post was created for me as adviser on dependent territories but it carried no promotion. I took on a number of missions to trouble spots in the

West Indies and the Pacific where ministers needed a quick fix. One of these was to Dominica, not to be confused with the Dominican Republic. (Both were first sighted on a Sunday: early navigators were not always imaginative in the names they gave to newly discovered islands. In the Pacific there are several Christman Islands as well as Easter Island.) In Dominica the elected government led by Patrick John had sought British agreement for a move from associated statehood to full independence. The opposition led by the dynamic Eugenia Charles objected to the terms of the proposed constitution concerning matters such as the method of electing the President and appointments to the electoral commission. They feared it would allow John to override any opposition, using his control of the island's only radio station.

Under the West Indies Act of 1967 an Associated State could terminate that relationship and move to independence by passing legislation approved by a two-thirds majority in the state House of Assembly and endorsed by a two-thirds majority in a popular referendum. Not surprisingly none of the states had sought to fulfil these stringent conditions. Instead they preferred to ask the British government to proceed by way of an Order in Council. This required approval by each House of Parliament, and to obtain this Ministers in London needed to be able to show that this change was the will of the people in the territory.

In Dominica Patrick John's party had been elected with a clear majority but because of the strong challenge of Eugenia Charles on the constitutional issues I was asked to visit the island to see if agreement could be reached between the parties and also to assess the general state of public opinion there. After a series of meetings I found that, despite their differences, both parties wanted independence; but, apart from the political leaders, few members of the public understood, or cared about, the niceties of constitutional procedures. The real divide was a personal one between those who supported John, mainly in the capital town of Roseau, and those who distrusted or even detested him, particularly in rural areas. The issues were not straightforward and David Cockerham, who was assisting me, entertained serious doubts. However, I knew that, if my report was to be of help to Parliament, it must conclude with a definite recommendation. I argued that Patrick John had won a clear majority in the last election on a platform of independence. He had also accepted a number, though not all, of the amendments to the proposed constitution which the Opposition had asked for. I recommended that Britain should agree to his request to move to independence under the constitution embodying the amendments that had been agreed.

My report* was presented to Parliament in July 1978 and its recommendations approved. The main debate took place in the House of Lords and I was surprised to read later in Hansard the glowing remarks of several speakers on what Lord McNair described, in a moment of hyperbole, as 'the famous Posnett report'. Since then it has been gratifying to see that the electoral system works, and in fact enabled Eugenia Charles to win the next election and become Prime Minister.

My next trip was to the Solomon Islands where the problems were of quite a different kind. It gave me the chance to see the site of the bloody battle for Guadalcanal where, in 1942/3, the Americans under General MacArthur eventually defeated the Japanese. Since that time the inhabitants had developed to a stage where they were well able to manage their own affairs, but the far-flung archipelago was riven by sharp inter-island suspicions exacerbated by language differences. My task in looking for a way forward was greatly helped by the presence, as constitutional adviser to the local ministers, of Yash Ghai. An astute lawyer, he had studied originally at Makerere in Uganda where we shared many recollections and friends. His company for part of the way on the journey home gave us time for much interesting discussion. We were to meet again in London at the constitutional conference which led to the territory's independence.

Meantime, Sir Alexander (Nick) Waddell, the British commissioner on the BPC, was retiring and I was consulted about a replacement. As it was only a part-time job, the post might easily be combined with my other duties, thereby saving the government an additional salary. Thus it fell out that for a short period of my life I became a kind of businessman but without the stresses which I am told are the normal

---

* Miscellaneous No. 20 (1978). Cmnd 7279.

lot of busy executives. I acquired a splendid office in New Zealand House and enjoyed trips to the antipodes every year. It was on one of these flights that I found myself sitting next to a handsome African. It was Emeka Anyaoku from Nigeria and we became friends. He was later to fill with distinction the post of Secretary General of the Commonwealth.

One of the BPC's main operations was on Nauru. To visit that island I found the best route lay via Japan. This involved a transpolar flight from London to Anchorage in Alaska which gave fantastic views of the polar icecap and a close look at Mount McKinley, the highest point in North America, as we flew past.

In Tokyo I was surprised how few people spoke English. Since Air Nauru flights departed only from Kagoshima in the south island I had to take a local flight from Tokyo and even the stewardesses spoke no English. Arriving at the airport I looked for a taxi to take me to the hotel into which I had been booked. Fortunately, a friend in Tokyo had given me the name written in Japanese script on a piece of paper. This elicited a grunt from the driver. We set off across pleasant countryside and drove for a considerable distance as the yen meter whirled into huge numbers. Since the road signs were all in Japanese characters I had no idea where we were or where we were going. The driver knew no English. I have never felt so helpless and lost. At last, much to my relief, we arrived at the right hotel and my supply of dollars proved adequate.

The Air Nauru flight the next day was not full and the captain allowed me to sit up on the flight deck for our approach to the island. It is a bit bigger than Ocean Island, about three miles across, and actually has a few miles of tarmac road. Like the Banabans, the islanders suffer from the diseases of affluence. These include obesity and diabetes which are widespread because of their diet and their sad human problems. The head of the police force had just returned from a holiday in Italy during which he had bought himself a Lamborghini sports car capable of almost 200 miles per hour — but not on Nauru!

In the FCO I was appointed Adviser on Dependent Territories and deputized for ministers presiding over conferences preparing constitutions for dependent territories that were moving to independence. These were generally held in London, but in the case of Bermuda the conference was held on the island under the chairmanship of the Governor. Since my last visit in 1971 there had been three changes of Governor. Richard Sharples, who succeeded Lord Martonmere, was brutally shot down one evening in front of Government House by a local wild man who was probably high on drugs. Ted Leather took over and eventually retired to settle on the island. He was replaced by Peter Ramsbotham who had been ambassador in Washington until he was brusquely moved to make way for Prime Minister Callaghan's son-in-law Peter Jay. It was Peter Ramsbotham who presided at the conference and I quickly learned to admire his skill and to like him personally.

The five days of the conference gave me time to learn a good deal about the problems of the island (strictly islands though they are mostly joined together) and, perhaps more important, to get to know the leading personalities. Pleasant as they were, many of them held deeply entrenched views from which it was difficult to elicit any compromise, notably on the vexed question of immigration with its heavy racial undertones. Of all the places I had served Bermuda, despite the cloak of modernity, was still backward in some of its attitudes. In the end a report was patched together leaving one crucial difficulty for the Foreign Secretary to resolve after further consideration. Peter wrote a despatch which I only saw later, containing extremely generous remarks about my part in getting agreement on various contentious issues. This was to have a bearing on future events.

When the post of under-secretary for the dependent territories fell vacant in the FCO I expected to be considered. However a mainline diplomat was appointed. Between our responsibilities there were obvious areas of overlap which might have occasioned friction had we not been good friends who both realized the absurdity of the arrangement.

Retirement approached. I had achieved little of importance in the Diplomatic Service, but I had enjoyed it, learned a great deal, and made many enduring friendships. I expected no more. But fate was to take a hand.

19

Uganda: A Tyrant Overthrown

Autocratic systems reinforce, while discouraging attempts to puncture, whatever illusions may exist at the top (and) provide few safeguards against incompetence.

(John L. Gaddis, *We Now Know*)

Idi Amin Dada came on his mother's side from the Kakwa tribe in the far northwest of Uganda on the borders of the Sudan and the Congo. Since his father was a Nubi, Amin naturally followed him into the army where his imposing physique and prowess at boxing and rugby attracted the notice of his British officers. He was promoted to corporal, then sergeant and finally to commissioned rank when the army was being prepared for independence. He had his first taste of blood in operations on the Kenya border against marauding Turkana tribesmen several of whom he was later accused of unlawfully killing. His extradition to Kenya to stand trial was avoided at the instance of Obote who already had Amin in mind as his future army commander.

Amin became Obote's loyal henchman, acting for him in a number of extra-legal strong-arm operations. These included an attack on the Kabaka Mutesa, then the constitutional President of Uganda, the summary arrest of a number of ministers during a cabinet meeting, and a foray into the Congo to seize gold from the Kilo Moto mine. But mutual distrust grew. Amin suspected Obote of planning to get rid of him and took the opportunity, while Obote was away at a Commonwealth conference, to seize power for himself.

Amin then proceeded to run the government as if it were an infantry company of which he was the sergeant major. He was ill equipped to handle affairs of state on any higher plane. Brutality came naturally to him and he maintained his position by terrifying subordinates and enemies alike. He was imbued with a farcical romanticism which led him to express love for the Queen and a wish to marry President Julius Nyerere of Tanzania. He was surrounded by yes-men and subject to no constitutional or advisory restraints.

He decided to invade Tanzania — much as Hitler had invaded Russia — against all military logic and common sense, with no realizable objective and with the same inevitable result. After marching down the western shore of Lake Victoria his troops were extended and eventually hurled back by the Tanzanian army. They struggled north: no longer victorious bullies who could pillage at will, they retreated before a better prepared and better commanded force. The Tanzanians chased them across the border into Uganda, advancing into the wide cattle plains of Ankole where the longhorns provided meat for the soldiers. Amin's motorized troops were running out of fuel for their vehicles and they left personnel carriers and tanks abandoned by the roadside. The soldiers, untrained for foot warfare, took to the bush for the long trek north.

Terrified villagers fled from their homes and allowed the soldiers to take what they wanted. Close behind them came the Tanzanians in fighting mood. It was a bad time for the people. The towns of Mbarara and Masaka were deserted when the Tanzanians arrived and sacked them. The Tanzanians took over Amin's western military headquarters at Mbarara.

Now was the moment for decision. Soldiers and political leaders back in Dar es Salaam had to decide whether to push on eastward round the north shore of Lake Victoria to the capital, Kampala. This would involve eliminating Amin and replacing his government. But the rout of Amin's western army was decisive and the Tanzanians were confident of their strategy of war on foot. The long march continued until the troops, led by General 'Black Mamba', came to the five mile wide Katonga swamp 20 miles east of Masaka. The single road to Kampala runs across the swamp on a bank ten feet high and Amin's tanks held the road at its eastern end. The Tanzanian commanders considered their options. Their compatriots marching north from Masaka to Mubende could not hope to outflank Amin for several weeks. Lack of boats ruled out a waterborne crossing over the lake to the south. Scouts reported that recent rainless months had caused the water level to fall. The swamp had dried out in places and they believed that it could be crossed on foot away from the road.

The crossing began on both flanks. A force of Uganda irregular 'freedom fighters' shared the advance with their Tanzanian allies. They moved at night, ignoring the swarms of mosquitoes, stumbling, sweating, falling and cursing, occasionally giggling at each other's troubles, sometimes up to their armpits in water. The long foot safari that had started from Bukoba two months before began to roll forward again.

It was March 1979.

* * *

I was late down for breakfast. An advisory job in the FCO made few demands and, with retirement approaching, I no longer rushed to catch the early train from Godalming station. My wife was listening to the radio news in the kitchen.

'Lule's in Dar es Salaam,' she said.

'He's formed a government in exile.'

I was surprised. Yusuf Lule was an old friend. He was an intellectual who had served as Minister of Education in Uganda under the British Protectorate administration, had become Vice-Chancellor of Makerere University and had been ousted by Amin. He then came to work at the Commonwealth Secretariat in London and I had met him recently in Whitehall. He was not a political animal.

'What about Obote?' I asked.

The former Prime Minister whom Amin had deposed was known to be friendly with Nyerere in Dar es Salaam.

'Not included,' said Shirley.

'But he seems to be involved somehow behind the scenes. Several other names were mentioned that you would probably remember.'

'Any news of Amin?'

'Still in Kampala apparently, but the Tanzanians have captured a place called Mpigi. Where's that?'

'About 20 miles west of Kampala on the road from Masaka. It's where that minor road branches off to Kisubi and Entebbe. I wonder if they'll try to cut off the airport.'

'Do you suppose the FCO know who they are, the men with Lule?'

'I doubt it.'

'Why don't you tell them?'

I smiled. Shirley was convinced that the FCO needed to be saved from their own ignorance — and that it was for me to do it.

'It's never prudent to know more than the department responsible,' I said.

'Why ever not? I thought you were retiring anyway so what have you got to lose?'

This pattern of conversation had become familiar. I had left Uganda 16 years before and had never been back. I had been so depressed by the horrors of the Amin years that I tried to put it out of my mind. But 23 years of my life were sunk in Uganda and Shirley knew that she only had to scratch the surface to find a lode of interest and anxiety — and excitement. Too many of my friends and too much of my early working life were locked up there: they were not buried deep enough to be easily forgotten. And she herself had long ago fallen in love with the country where we had first made our home and where our children had been born.

I caught the 8.40 train with its usual group of commuters. With the City men having mostly left on earlier trains, there was a preponderance of civil servants, lawyers and people whose business did not demand their presence before ten o'clock. It was Thursday and I was lucky to find a corner seat. I looked through the paper, but by the time we had passed Woking I had ceased reading and fallen to thinking. I could not put Uganda out of my mind. We had talked before about the possibility of Amin's overthrow, but attempts to assassinate him had failed and that very failure had lent him an aura of invincibility which many Africans, I knew, attributed to supernatural powers. His army was thought to be well-equipped and trained with Libyan help. It was difficult to accept at face value the reports of their successive defeats by the Tanzanians whose martial abilities were unknown and discounted. But if Mpigi had fallen they were within striking distance of Kampala and Entebbe. And, if Lule were setting up a provisional government in Dar es Salaam they must be thinking that Amin's expulsion from his capital and eventual defeat were in sight.

I was so cheered by these thoughts that I resolved to ignore my own advice, or at least to see if the East African department at the FCO could give me more news. Then I remembered that a friend of mine, Derek Day, had recently returned to London after a tour abroad as an ambassador and, to my surprise, had been assigned as under-secretary responsible for Africa. It had never failed to surprise me how the FCO regarded Africa as a continent for which special knowledge of the different countries or their languages was not important in deciding postings. I myself, after 23 years in Africa, had, with one brief exception, been assigned invariably to other areas. The skill and intelligence of the mainline diplomats were unrivalled and they were always careful to tap the special knowledge of others when needed. But few within the hierarchy had had the opportunity to live in 'black' Africa, to know its sights and sounds and smells, learn its languages and understand its peoples. These deeper aspects were sometimes thought to be unnecessary for the day-to-day business of diplomacy, but I thought this wrong. I knew of cases where ignorance of local beliefs, customs or sensibilities had led British diplomats unwittingly into positions that provoked local hostility, harmed British interests and even sometimes led to their expulsion. As these thoughts ran through my mind, I decided to pay a call on Derek Day and to offer him such background information about the Ugandans now coming to the fore as I could provide.

It was not long after I had reached my office in Great George Street that I had occasion to cross the road to the main Foreign Office building. I then found my way to Derek's office. It was some years since we had met and he seemed as pleased to see me as I was to see him. He immediately started to ask me about Uganda. He told me that the Foreign Secretary, Dr David Owen, had sought advice on how to establish links with Lule if and when his new group became a real government on the ground, once Amin had been pushed out of Kampala. Since the British had, like the Americans, broken off all diplomatic relations with Amin's government two or three years before and had closed the High Commission in Kampala, we had no direct means of getting information about the situation on the ground. Derek intended to advise that a first secretary from the department should fly to Nairobi to keep in touch with developments across the border in Uganda. He welcomed my offer to put my local knowledge at his disposal.

I spent the rest of the day disposing of unimportant paperwork, consulting about arrangements for my retirement, presiding over the twilight of my career. For 39 years I had worked in Africa and other lands, usually in a government capacity. I had no regrets and felt I had been lucky to enjoy so many fascinating years and make so many cherished friendships in different continents. The prospect of retirement at 60 was depressing, but I resigned myself to having to find new fields of activity. At 5.30 p.m. I put away my papers, picked up my coat and walked along the corridor to the entrance hall. Regulations required me to show my security pass on leaving as well as when entering the building, but dipping my hand into my pocket I found it empty of the small folder containing the pass.

'Damn!' I turned round and retraced my steps. As I opened the door of my office, the telephone was ringing. I picked it up.

'Posnett,' I said curtly.

'Dick, it's Derek Day here.'

Interest stirred.

'Oh yes?'

'Dick, I hope I've not let you in for something, but you remember our conversation this morning?'

'Yes,' uncertainly.

'Well, when I was putting our proposals about Uganda to the Secretary of State, I mentioned in passing that your know-how about Uganda and the emerging personalities would be available to us here. Owen asked why, instead of sending someone from the department to Nairobi, we didn't send somebody who knew the country and the people and could speak the language. I had to say that we had nobody in that category except you, and that you were in fact an old friend of

Lule's. And, in brief, he wants you to go out immediately and report on the situation.'

I took a few breaths.

'Dick, are you still there? I'm sorry if I've let you in for it.'

'Derek, I just can't believe it. It's what I'd love to do. How soon do you want me to leave?'

'Could you go tomorrow?'

I thought quickly. I would need to brief myself at the department and get myself organized. I doubted if things in Uganda were going to move all that quickly. It was now Thursday. I suggested I should take Saturday evening's flight to Nairobi. Would he ask the department to book me a seat and warn our High Commission in Nairobi to meet me?

I made a quick telephone call to Shirley, whose surprise was mingled with some concern. Then I went for a short visit to a farewell drinks party for Evan Luard, a junior minister whose seat at the forthcoming election was unsafe. He was an old friend who had stayed with us in Belize and had played piano duets with Shirley. We had recently travelled in the Pacific together. I wished him well and left for home. Though my emotions were in turmoil my mind was busily working through all the things that needed to be done in the next 36 hours — plans, lists of things to be done, calls to make, clothes to pack, friends to tell.

Shirley and I sat up late talking. While my mind was occupied with a thousand practical and professional details, I was elated at the prospect of a possible homecoming after so many years. It seemed like a dream coming true. My euphoria spilled over and swamped her apprehensions. She was anyway so pleased for me that she was careful to conceal her anxiety. We expected I would be away for a few weeks but realized it was impossible to calculate. We did not even know how long it would be before Amin would be driven from the capital and before I could get into the country, or even if it would be possible to get in at all. Reports of the fighting were uncertain and Uganda was evidently likely to be in turmoil. None of this was comforting to Shirley.

The next day passed in a rush. I tidied up my affairs in the FCO and picked the brains of the department to find out all that was known about the situation in Uganda. It was not a great deal, for the

Tanzanian forces issued no communiqués and there were no media reporters on the ground. I could only make such arrangements as seemed prudent for finance in the field: Uganda currency was unobtainable. Local transport, accommodation and other details would have to be arranged on the spot. Nobody knew who would be in control in Kampala over the coming days and we had not 'recognized' any new government. I had no papers of accreditation.

I went home to pack a few clothes and make more phone calls. I had done all I could do: now to be off.

✳ ✳ ✳

The deputy High Commissioner met me in Nairobi on Sunday morning and took me to his home at Muthaiga where all was peaceful among the bougainvillaea and hibiscus. I was impatient to get on with my job, but he told me that nothing could be done on a Sunday: the High Commissioner would see me tomorrow. Meanwhile he and his wife did their best to make me comfortable.

Next day the High Commissioner took me to see the head of the Kenya Office of External Affairs. I explained my mission and agreed to keep him informed. Meanwhile, I tried to find out all I could about the situation in Uganda, where the two armies were, what were Lule's movements, how might I get to Kampala? The Tanzanians gave out no news. The High Commission had little information, but I was fortunate to find an old Uganda friend Charles Harrison, a newspaperman who was always a mine of information, reliable or otherwise. I discovered that Martin Aliker, an Acholi dentist friend of mine now settled in Nairobi, was away in Dar es Salaam and I thought it would be good news if he were to be part of a possible Lule regime in Uganda.

Relations between Kenya and Tanzania were strained at that time and the border was closed. But the phone lines were open and, with the help of a kindly operator I managed eventually to get through to Lule's headquarters in Dar es Salaam and was able to speak to him. I greeted him and told him of my mission which he was pleased to hear about. I asked him his plans, but he carefully refrained from saying anything specific. He suggested I listen to Saturday's radio news. The implication was obvious. It was now Wednesday and I determined to try and get into Uganda on my own.

The High Commission could not help with transport and I had some difficulty finding a car to hire. Eventually I made contact with a helpful Indian who was prepared to hire me a dubious looking old Japanese car. I did not tell him where I proposed to take it lest he should change his mind.

After stocking up with a few comestibles for survival I set off on the road up to the edge of the Rift Valley where I had to stop to take in the breathtaking view before driving down the escarpment and on to Naivasha. After beer and a sandwich, I pressed on to Gilgil where I had to make a call on David and Brenda Opie, the parents of one of my son's contemporaries at boarding school in England. I guessed that they would welcome news of their boy and asked the way to Pembroke School where David was the headmaster. I had never met them before but they gave me a typically warm East African welcome. Hearing that I had no definite night stop in view they offered me dinner and a bed for the night which I was glad to accept.

I set off early the next morning for the longish drive over Mau Summit and past Eldoret to the Uganda border. I was happy to be on my own, feeling at home again in familiar country and wondering what I would find. What I met when I arrived at the Malaba border post was a scene of great confusion. Many lorries were parked along the roadside and nothing was moving. A stream of people was coming from the Uganda side. Many of them were Asians and I spoke to a number of them. They told me that they were fleeing to escape from Amin's soldiery who were pillaging the area around Tororo and Mbale. The soldiers were out of control and rampant. Nobody was safe. They said that there was no way I would be able to get through to Kampala and it would be very dangerous to try. The Kenya border officers confirmed these depressing reports.

The last thing HMG — or I — wanted was for me to get caught by Amin's forces, so I decided to try a different route further south where the situation might possibly be quieter. The map showed a minor road leading south along the Kenya side of the border to meet the road from Kisumu near the border post at Busia. I had forgotten that 'minor road' in Kenya might mean a very muddy track over black cotton soil and, with my car's worn tyres, I was soon stuck. As usual, a crowd of *totos* — youngsters — emerged from nowhere and, with a bit of financial encouragement, helped to push me out. One of them asked if he could come with me to Busia and this gave me some welcome company and a source of local knowledge. He also helped to push when we inevitably got stuck again and it took us almost two hours to cover the 20-odd miles to Busia.

There the tale was the same. Refugees were pouring across from the Uganda side of the border and there was no prospect of my getting through. Whatever the situation was in Kampala it was cut off from the Kenya border by the remnants of Amin's army.

By now it was getting late in the day, too late to contemplate driving the hundreds of miles back to Nairobi. I decided to make for Kisumu, about 100 miles to the south, where it should be possible to find some kind of accommodation for the night. This took me across the lovely country of the Luhya and the Jaluo, past Kakamega and down to the shores of Lake Victoria. In a hotel, new since my last visit 16 years before, I was given a room and a late dinner. Although I had not achieved my objective I now knew a good deal more about the situation in eastern Uganda and could begin to make alternative plans.

The next morning I phoned the High Commission in Nairobi to make known my whereabouts and to report. The High Commissioner told me that he had received a signal from London to say that the Secretary of State wanted to know why I was not in Kampala. I told the High Commissioner what I had learned on the border and asked him to report it to London. I added that the only way to get into Uganda now would be to fly. Since all air services were at a standstill because of the fighting I asked if the High Commission could explore the possibility of finding a light plane that I could charter to get me to Entebbe. Meanwhile I would get back to Nairobi with all best speed.

Then I hit the road. I was able to give a lift to a highly educated (at Makerere in Uganda) African lady who regaled me with fascinating gossip about university life and intrigue in Kampala and Nairobi.

Back in Nairobi I immediately set about finding a private plane that might get me to Entebbe. The war had put a stop to all commercial flights. Uganda was a 'war zone', the tower at Entebbe was off the air and nobody knew anything about the situation there, or whether

Amin's MiG fighters were still operational. I tried to telephone Dar again but this time without success. Then I tried, rather hopefully, to phone Kampala. To my surprise, I found myself talking to a Muganda telephone operator in Kampala. He was unable to get me through to any of the few Britons thought to be still in the country or to any government office in Entebbe, but he was happy to tell me all he knew about the situation in Kampala. There had been gunfire, but he thought the Tanzanians had not yet entered the city which was relatively undamaged except for some looting. He did not know about the airport but a friend had just told him that he had seen three black Mercedes-Benz limousines driving through the city in the direction of Jinja. He thought that Amin was probably in one of them. I told him I was hoping to come to Kampala and asked him if there was anything I could bring him.

'Oh yes Sir. I need a pair of trousers — medium size.'

Sadly, I was never able to trace him later to give him his trousers.

If Amin had in fact left Kampala it seemed to offer some hope that his forces were abandoning Entebbe airport and I was mildly encouraged. I passed on to the head of the Kenya Foreign Office all the information I had collected, thereby displeasing the High Commissioner who said that I had no business dealing directly with 'his' government. But a helpful and efficient lady at the High Commission had tracked down an ex-RAF pilot who had a Cessna and was prepared to try and fly me to Entebbe. I was to be at Wilson airfield at 7 a.m. next morning and my friend promised to pick me up in her Land Rover at 6 a.m. It was now Saturday afternoon and all that remained was to assemble some provisions to take with me on the assumption, borne out when I got there, that survival in Kampala might be difficult. A sally round the *duka*s of Nairobi procured me a few cans of food, sugar, coffee, biscuits, butter, a loaf of bread and two bottles of whisky. I was ready.

That evening the BBC carried news that Lule and his team had flown from Dar es Salaam to Entebbe. This confirmed that the airport there must be in Tanzanian hands: my timing seemed to be lucky.

Reflecting upon the week's events revealed some puzzling features. First, there was the stark contrast between the urgency attached to my mission in London ('can you leave tomorrow?') and the lack of it in

Nairobi ('the High Commissioner will see you tomorrow'). Had there been some failure in communication? It seemed unlikely that the FCO would have failed to convey David Owen's concern.

At that time the High Commission in Nairobi was Britain's listening post for events in Uganda, where we had no representation and where there was a war in progress. Yet I sensed in the office an air of detachment from affairs in Uganda. No visit had been paid recently to western Kenya to pick up first hand news from refugees. Procuring transport and provisioning for my trips was left to me. When I planned to drive across Kenya to the Ugandan frontier, nobody offered or was assigned, to accompany me. As a result, the High Commission was in ignorance of the latest situation, and of my whereabouts, when the FCO enquired on Thursday.

There was also a difference in style. It was strange to me, brought up perhaps in a different school, never to have been invited to the High Commissioner's residence for a meal or a drink. I would have valued a relaxed discussion with him.

None of these matters materially affected my mission: indeed, they may have hardened my resolve. Looking back, I wonder if they were early symptoms of Cradock's first law of diplomacy:

'It is not the other side you need to worry about, but your own.'*

In any event I slept soundly.

At the airfield next morning I met my pilot and we discussed plans. We agreed that it would be best to approach Entebbe across Lake Victoria without infringing Ugandan airspace until the airport was in sight. The control tower was still not on the air and we had no idea whether our arrival would be acceptable, even if the Tanzanians were in control.

Then he showed me a group of people standing nearby and said they wanted to speak to me. One of them introduced himself as the counsellor at the German embassy in Nairobi. He explained that a German newspaperman called Stiens, being barred from official access to Uganda, had tried, along with a Swedish journalist, to get into Uganda by boat across Lake Victoria. There had been no further news

---

* Percy Cradock, *Experiences of China*.

of them beyond unconfirmed reports that they had been caught on landing in Uganda and had been killed, allegedly on the orders of Bob Astles, a Briton they understood to be working for Amin. Stiens' wife Rita was desperately anxious to get to Uganda to find out what had become of her husband. Would I agree to let her come in my plane?

Standing silently against the wall was a young woman and I went over to speak to her. She explained that she needed to get to Kampala to find out about her husband, that she had spoken on the phone to the German embassy there and that they had promised to help, but my plane was her only hope of getting there. I told her that, much as I sympathized with her, I could not possibly take an unknown woman with me into a situation that was quite unpredictable and probably dangerous. I explained that I had no accreditation, no transport, no accommodation and no Uganda currency. I would have to live by my wits; and having to look after somebody else would create added and incalculable difficulties. If we got in at all, I did not know how she would be received.

She looked at me and said quietly that she would not ask or expect any help from me on arrival, merely a seat on the plane. Of course I knew that if we arrived together there would be no way I could disassociate myself from her in local eyes. The discussion spluttered on and I tried to think clearly about the possible problems if I agreed. It was a harrowing story and eventually I decided that to leave her behind would be a cruelty which I would find it hard to live with. The whole adventure was crazy and I might as well take her and hope for the best. I ought to have known better, but the decision turned out to be one that I did not regret.

Once on the plane and airborne I thought through the possible problems to be faced on arrival. I concluded that Rita might be in danger if her identity were discovered, at least if Astles and company were still about. That would impair the chances of my own bona fides being accepted. So I told her that she should pose as my secretary, that she should answer no questions, and should stay out of the limelight as far as possible. She agreed.

Meanwhile, as we flew across the Rift and the Masai country beyond, our pilot had been listening to radio traffic. He told me that there was still no contact with the tower at Entebbe but that there was another plane from Nairobi in the air on its way to Entebbe. The pilot was a woman friend of his. I asked who the passengers were. He put this on the air and got the reply: it was a BBC television crew. Good, I thought. As they were five minutes ahead of us I advised our pilot to come in from the south across the lake and to watch the other plane's landing. If they appeared to run into any trouble he was to stay clear.

Soon we were past Narok and heading out over Lake Victoria. Then we swung northwards and I could soon make out Buvuma and the Sesse islands. Then the Entebbe peninsula came into view. It gave me an extraordinary feeling to be returning after so long and in such a curious way to a country I knew so well. We could see the BBC plane on the runway and watched it park. There were no signs of fighting round the airport, so we followed them in. Near the runway lay a burnt out Libyan transport plane and, further on, a parked Boeing 707 with flat tyres and a Jetstream in Uganda Airways colours. There were no MiGs that I could see. I noticed that the tower was quite badly damaged and the apron littered with broken glass. A few knots of men were standing about in army fatigues, but I could only assume that they were Tanzanians.

We climbed out and collected our bags, including the cardboard box containing my precious provisions. Our pilot was anxious to get air-borne again without delay and I agreed. We were now committed. Some soldiers came up to me and told me that the airport was closed and we were not allowed in. I was relieved to hear him speak Swahili; he was obviously a Tanzanian. I launched into what I hoped was a convincing explanation. I said that I was a friend of the new President Lule, that he knew I was coming, that I was a great admirer of President Nyerere's, that I was delighted the Tanzanian army had beaten Amin and was now in charge — and more in that vein. I expressed admiration for their long march from Bukoba, was sure they deserved higher pay, but hoped they would enjoy their stay in Uganda where the bananas were excellent. I asked the senior NCO which district he came from, how the rains had been, had he news from his family — the normal chatter of a district officer on tour.

I noticed that the BBC team was having some difficulty and went over to see if I could help. I spoke to the Tanzanian in charge in

Swahili. I explained that the BBC had come to record the glorious Tanzanian victory and so to spread their fame in England and other countries. This seemed to ease their problems and the BBC men were allowed to go. John Osman was their senior reporter and I struck up a useful acquaintance with him.

I realized with some surprise that I had been using Swahili without more than a few moments' hesitation over vocabulary, although it was 16 years since I had spoken the language. It was certainly a valuable passport with the Tanzanians and I wondered wryly how an FCO department man would have managed.

Looking back across the tarmac I saw that Rita was still standing by our bags trying to keep out of the way, but that a white photographer was pestering her. I went over and shoved him off. I found he was German and had recognized Rita, but we stuck to our story.

We then had to sit on the tarmac to await events. The terminal buildings were uninhabitable because of all the shattered glass. I asked a Tanzanian soldier about possible transport. He told me what was obvious — there was none. Nor were there any telephones working that might have enabled me to contact the Lule government. Some while later a decrepit bus arrived bringing a relief contingent of soldiers. I asked if the outgoing contingent would give me a lift. By this time we were on good terms and they agreed. The bus would be going to Kampala and I said that would suit me fine. In we piled and the bus set off. The driver was having difficulty as the gear lever kept coming out, but we ground slowly along.

I revelled in the familiar sights. Driving through Entebbe I recognized houses where I had lived, the hotel where Shirley and I had first met, the golf course now abandoned. A helicopter stood silently near the old Entebbe Club. It was like a dream sequence. As we drove out towards Kisubi I saw groups of young Baganda girls in their Sunday best — white blouses and neat blue skirts. Then I remembered: it was Easter Sunday. I had told Shirley that I would like to be in Kampala for Easter and now I would be, though too late for the service at Namirembe Cathedral.

Further on, an old tank and a burned out troop carrier lay by the roadside. The Tanzanians told me that this was where a company of Libyans had been ambushed and had fled into the banana groves. The

Tanzanians thought it a great joke that the Libyans did not know how to fight in the plantations, only in the desert.

Finally we entered Kampala which was much as I remembered it but with several new buildings. Windows were shattered and the streets were littered with broken glass, the detritus of battle and looting. A few people were wandering about. The bus stopped at the Milton Hotel, new since my day and named after Obote. We went in with our bags and found the foyer swarming with people. At the desk I asked about rooms. No chance, they said: the hotel was full with soldiers and others. I told Rita to sit with our bags while I investigated. Looking around in the other rooms I spotted a familiar pattern of four lines of tribal cicatrices across the forehead of a nicely dressed and well built young man in the background. He must be a Lugbara from the West Nile district in the far northwest of Uganda where I had spent six years in former times. The young man was surprised and pleased to be addressed in his own language and we talked for a few minutes about familiar names and places near his home. He claimed to remember my name from the old days which was not inconceivable as the Lugbara used to give nicknames to British district officers who worked there. He told me he was the assistant manager of the hotel and said he could find me a room on the thirteenth floor. The snags were that there was not enough water pressure to reach that height and that the previous occupant had gone off with the only key.

I suggested to Rita that we should take the room for the time being, for at least it would give us somewhere to leave our bags while she made contact with her embassy. The lift was full of gun-toting soldiers and sweating girls, all in high spirits. The room, when we found it, was not too clean and the beds had not been touched since the previous occupants left. But it was useful to have a base and, amazingly, a telephone that worked. We set out to look for food in the dining room. All they could offer was tea and biscuits which we took before setting off on foot to find the German embassy.

Walking through the town, we could see the results of the fighting. More damage seemed to have caused by looting than by shooting. Not a single shop window remained intact. People were piling loot on bicycles and a 20-gallon drum was leaking paint onto the road as it was being pushed along. It was difficult to recognize the law-abiding Baganda I had known. They had obviously suffered terrifying moral oppression. Law and order had been destroyed and the people were fending for themselves.

The German embassy, when we found it, was closed. We had wrongly assumed that there would be somebody waiting for Rita. Back at the hotel she managed to telephone the ambassador. He told her he could do nothing for her till next day and offered no help or accommodation. Fortunately, among the newspaper reporters who had somehow found their way to the hotel, Rita discovered a friendly German who had known her husband and who made himself responsible for looking after her. It was a relief for me now to be able to concentrate on my own job.

First, I started phoning round to see if I could make contact with any of the remaining British residents. I was able to track down Dr Carswell, a surgeon who was shown on my list as the representative of the British community. I learned that he had stayed at his post throughout the war. He was immensely useful with information about the war, about the situation in Kampala and about the British community. He came round to the hotel in his car and offered to transport me wherever I wanted to go. This was a tremendous help.

My first need was to establish contact with Lule's government. The ministers were all said to be housed in Nile Mansions, a large new complex I had not seen before. I discovered on the phone that the Foreign Minister was Otema Allimadi whom I remembered as a rebellious Acholi (from the north) who had a taste for liquor. I set off to Nile Mansions with one of my precious bottles of whisky. Otema seemed glad to see me. I was not only an old acquaintance but also the first diplomatic representative to call on him. He was quick to open the bottle of whisky. He asked if my visit denoted British recognition of the new regime. I said that could only come from London and that my recommendation would take a little time to reach them for I had, as yet, no radio arrangements. He agreed that I should call on President Lule as soon as possible and undertook to make the necessary arrangements.

By a happy coincidence, the BBC next day carried the news that HMG had recognized the Lule regime. Strictly speaking this was premature because the area they controlled comprised barely a quarter of the country; but it suited my book. Otema was sure it was my doing and asked me where my radio was situated. In fact all I had been able to do after leaving him was to visit the official telegraph office, surprisingly still open on Sunday evening, and send a telegram to the Secretary of State in London saying simply that I had arrived and was in place. Whether it ever reached him I never discovered.

Communication was my next problem. To start with I became friendly with John Osman, head of the BBC team that was flying out television material daily. He agreed to carry letters for me to the British High Commission in Nairobi which could then transmit their gist to London by radio. That would have to do for the time being.

Next I needed money. Carswell took me round to the house of the manager of Barclays Bank, the only bank manager to remain at his post during the war. (The others had all left for Kenya as the fighting approached.) Neil had a house on Nakasero Hill, not far from where we used to live, and proved very hospitable. As to money, he explained that the banks had all been looted by, he thought, the Tanzanians and all the money taken. But he told me to wait and disappeared upstairs. A few minutes later he came down with a thick wad of notes — about 3000 shillings he thought. I asked whether a signature or receipt was required, but he merely smiled and said that he would be quite happy if the British High Commission would place its account with Barclays.

I told Neil that I had a problem about transport. He produced from his desk a set of keys for a car left behind by one of his British clients who had fled the war.

'I'm sure he would wish HMG's representative to have the use of his car,' he said.

Carswell and I then set off to try and locate the vehicle at the owner's residence. When we tracked it down at a house on Kololo hill the loyal gardener was suspicious and reluctant to allow us into the garage, but finally succumbed to my blandishments. Now I had a nice Audi saloon. All I needed was a flag to protect me from marauding soldiers who were known to stop and hijack any vehicle they could. We managed to trace a British judge, Allen, who had also stayed on through the Amin regime and through the war. He made a hobby of collecting Union Jacks. He remembered me from olden days when he had been a police officer and readily gave me a small flag which I fixed to the car's radio aerial.

Petrol was very scarce in Kampala, but I made contact with the local Shell manager and set up an arrangement whereby he would see me provided with what I required.

These were great steps forward and I now felt ready to start serious operations and to pay a few visits. These were great steps forward and I now felt ready to start serious operations and pay a few visits. The hotel was providing a useful rendezvous with local people and with press representatives who were always worth talking to for the information they were picking up. But after a day or two I began to find life at the hotel something of a strain. I could put up with the lack of a key and the lack of water to wash in, but there was still no food worth eating in the dining room. When I mentioned this to my banker friend, he at once asked me to stay with him at his house. He had eggs from his own hens, a good cook, and ample supplies of beer. And he welcomed company. In due course, I moved in with him and enjoyed the relative comfort he provided.

❉ ❉ ❉

After the fall of Kampala the Tanzanian army advanced eastward to Jinja where the Nile starts its long journey from Lake Victoria. They gave out little news and I wondered whether Amin's retreating forces would try to blow up the Owen Falls power station and cut our electricity supply. I asked one of the new ministers who assured me.

'Our men are in control at the Owen Falls,' he said.

(Years later, I read in a book by an American journalist, who had been accredited to the Tanzanians, that Jinja at that time was still in Amin's hands and that a BBC broadcast based on what I had been told had led to reprisals against the civilian population there. Amin's soldiers were certainly guilty of terrible atrocities against the local inhabitants as they retreated, as I knew from my previous attempt to cross the border from Kenya, but I doubt if any BBC broadcast was instrumental in this.) In any case there was no interruption of power supplies and the Uganda Electricity Board, still under the careful management of Mr Povey, kept things going despite all the difficulties.

Meanwhile, behind the Tanzanian advance, there remained a good deal of apparently wanton violence around Kampala. Gunfire was audible most evenings, with automatic fire punctuated from time to time by the thud of a heavier weapon. One morning I came across a dead body on the road near the hotel. But it was difficult to find out who was shooting at whom. I knew that 4000 prisoners had been released from Luzira Prison to add to the general lawlessness. The police force had suffered terribly under the boot of Amin's soldiers and was a demoralized, disorganized and decimated relic of its former self. To this unstable situation were added a lot of deserters from Amin's retreating army who had taken off their boots but retained their Kalashnikovs.

Wanting to find out what things were like outside the city, I used my liberated car to visit some of the suburbs. The first place had to be Katwe where in the old days the inhabitants, who were thought to comprise a high proportion of petty crooks, shady dealers and prostitutes, did not greatly welcome British officers. On this occasion I took with me a couple of lady journalists, an American from *TIME* Magazine and a South African. With the press corps largely confined to the hotel and dependent on official news handouts, they welcomed the opportunity to see something of the country at first hand. I hoped it might be instructive for them as well as for me.

I drove slowly into the township, keeping my eyes peeled for signs of trouble. I noticed a sound, a roaring noise like a distant football crowd. It gathered strength and my passengers, looking out of the car windows, cried out that people were running out of their houses and shops towards the car. Instead of speeding up as they expected, I slowed down and stopped. Within seconds, a crowd of shouting and, I noticed, grinning Baganda surrounded us. I got out — another surprise for the lady journalists — and was immediately engulfed in the crowd which had grown to several hundred. They were all talking at once, wanting to shake my hand, showing unmistakably their welcome for the return of the Union Jack which they had seen on my car. Some of them tried to lift me up like a football hero. It was a moving experience and I was glad that there were independent witnesses to this unsolicited testimonial to Britain's colonial past. It was ten minutes before I could climb back into the car and drive on to other parts of the city. In the days that followed, I experienced many similar, if not quite so overwhelming, demonstrations of welcome wherever I stopped.

Having missed the Easter Sunday service on the day of my arrival, I made a point, during the first week, of paying a call on the Archbishop of the Church of Uganda at Namirembe. He turned our to be a Kakwa from Koboko in the West Nile near the Sudan border, a rather backward area I knew from the old days when I had picked up a few phrases of their language. He cut a rather forlorn figure, patently out of his depth in the current political turmoil, unable to give me much information about the state of the country and, not surprisingly, out of touch with affairs in Buganda. He could offer no comment on Amin's murder of his predecessor. The reason for his appointment was obvious: he was of Amin's tribe.

The Roman Catholic Bishop at Rubaga was altogether more businesslike, intelligent and well informed. A Muganda, he had his finger on the public pulse and was able to tell me a good deal about the miseries of life under Amin. One effect of the breakdown of law and order had been to double church attendance — a refuge perhaps from the brutality of the regime. But there had also been, in the absence of the old authorities of tribe and clan, a breakdown in public morale and morality. Black markets and private violence were unrestrained.

On Sunday a week after my arrival, I drove up to Namirembe. Crowds of churchgoers were climbing the hill and I looked for somewhere to park the car, but was waved to the top of the hill. There, outside the main door of the cathedral, the whole of the Church establishment was lined up in full dress robes. The dean advanced and took me to be introduced to each of his colleagues. We then formed a procession and I was led into the cathedral. The whole congregation rose as I was conducted up the long aisle to a place at the front, where I was shown to a solitary prie-dieu draped with the Union Jack. It was another moment of deep emotion. Across the aisle was another prie-dieu draped with a Uganda flag, but it remained unoccupied. I never discovered for whom it was intended — the President perhaps?

The service was conducted in Luganda, but the dean thoughtfully interjected sentences in English so that I could follow the prayers and his sermon. When, at one point, I could not find my place in the Luganda hymn-book somebody crept up from behind and discreetly showed me the right page. When I turned to thank him I saw that it was none other than Dr Lumu, the former Minister of Health. At the end of the service it was some time before I was allowed to go back to my car after shaking a hundred hands and receiving the warm good wishes of all the assembled clergy.

Thus ended my first week back in Uganda. It was 16 years since I had been at Namirembe for the baptism of my son by the then Archbishop Leslie Brown. By a happy chance, Leslie himself was to visit us in Kampala two months later. But by then there had been other developments.

20

High Commission

A High Commission is much the same as an embassy. But, whereas an ambassador is formally accredited to a foreign monarch or head of state, this would be inappropriate between countries in the Commonwealth, some of which share the same head of state, the Queen. Instead, High Commissioners are exchanged directly between Commonwealth governments.

My next task was to reopen the British High Commission. I did not even know where it was, but the French ambassador, with whom our keys had been left during recent events, helpfully steered me in the right direction.

The BBC was anxious to film the re-entry into the High Commission so we arranged a time. The government had provided me with a soldier bodyguard and we had to use his bayonet to undo the securely fastened outer door. When we eventually got into the main foyer we were greeted with the sight of a teacup and saucer that had stood unwashed on the table for three years since the last High Commissioner had departed. Everything was inches deep in accumulated dust, but this in itself bore witness to the fact that nobody had tampered with the building. In the inner courtyard the bougainvillaea had grown out of control. Long spiky tendrils had pushed though the window louvres and created an unearthly scene inside: great for TV.

I found a flag and we all trooped out to the courtyard for a flag-raising ceremony. For this ITV had installed its cameraman on the

roof. I had obtained from the government information office the services of an attractive Muganda woman and we used her to what I
hoped was dramatic effect by getting her to help raise the flag as a
symbol of the re-establishing of friendly relations between the two
countries after the tyranny of Amin. I was told that this went down
well at home. Unfortunately Shirley was not watching the television
news in England and only heard from a friend that I had been seen in
Kampala.

To set the High Commission building to rights I needed local staff
and here I had a stroke of luck. My arrival in Kampala had been
reported with acclaim by the local newspaper and this brought a
number of old friends and acquaintances round to seek me out.
Usually they would come to the hotel lobby which I frequented and it
was there that I was greeted by Eriver Kiggundu, the former private
secretary of the Kabaka Mutesa of Buganda. He was just the person I
needed and he willingly undertook to get the High Commission
cleaned up, with only the vaguest assurance of getting paid. Even
more valuable to me were his wider ranging contacts in the town.

Another time I saw in the hotel lobby the back of a familiar bald
square head which could belong to nobody other than Godfrey
Binaisa. He was an old lawyer friend who had at one time been a
thorn in the flesh of the British administration and been rusticated to
Karamoja for his pains. He became Attorney General under Obote,
but was forced to flee during the Amin regime. Later he had been to
stay with us in England. It was a delightful reunion: he was as full of
fun and laughter as ever.

Meanwhile, I had learned on the telephone from Nairobi that I had
been appointed acting High Commissioner and, the same day, I was
asked to call on President Lule in Entebbe. When I got to what used
to be Government House, I was greeted by Martin Aliker, who had
been given ill-defined duties in the field of foreign affairs. But Otema
Allimadi, who was also present, insisted that he, as Foreign Minister,
should usher me in to see the President.

On going in to greet Lule, we embraced and were able to talk on
first name terms as old colleagues. We were both deeply moved, swept
along on the tide by the sudden transition from tyranny to freedom,
from exile to government.

✻ ✻ ✻

To set up the High Commission on a proper basis required staff and they now began to arrive. First came two wireless technicians to establish a radio link with London, then an administrative officer who relieved me of the chores of administration and security. I felt a slight nostalgia for those first few days when I had been running solo with only myself to consult or look after. Now I needed to concern myself with the safety and accommodation of new staff.

It is a requirement of diplomatic protocol that an embassy should notify the host government when establishing its own direct radio link. Accordingly, as soon as we made contact with London, I called on Otema to let him know. He took me aside in a slightly conspiratorial manner and asked if I would do him a favour.

'Would you be able to transmit Uganda government messages to our posts abroad over British channels just until we can re-establish our own radio net?'

'Of course I'd be glad to help; and I'm pretty sure that the FCO would raise no objection.'

'Well thank you. In that case may we send some messages over to your office for transmission?'

When the messages started to arrive I had expected them to be in code but, to my surprise, they were *en clair*. We derived wry amusement from transmitting messages to ambassadors appointed by Amin telling them of their dismissal and immediate recall.

I was something of an oddball in the Diplomatic Service, never having served in a normal embassy or high commission. So I was delighted when I was offered as my deputy Justin Nason with whom I had worked before in London. He was able to see that the office was run on the right lines and that we followed correct procedures. He also did his best to restrain my more extravagant impulses. The honour he later received was well deserved.

We needed proper accommodation for the staff, visitors as well as for myself. The former High Commissioner's residence was occupied by some UN Technical Assistance personnel who had surprisingly stayed on under Amin and through the war. They were persuaded to move elsewhere and vacate the house for us. After taking on a cook and a house boy I bade a grateful farewell to my banker friend and moved down the road. To start with, while Justin set about finding more permanent quarters, we used the house as a communal mess for all the High Commission staff. It was an advantage to have all the staff under one roof as security was still uncertain and none of them spoke any local language. Once staff moved out to their own separate houses they would be at greater risk and this was a problem that was to grow more serious. Meanwhile we had difficulty coping with the normal housekeeping and, as the number of visitors began to increase, I saw that, if I were to stay on, Shirley would have to join me.

Most members of the diplomatic corps had left the country before the fighting reached Kampala, but the East German Ambassador left it too late. He and his family were killed during the battle when they tried to flee to Kenya but were caught in crossfire near the Kampala Golf Club where the road from Kololo joins the Kitante road. Their burnt-out car still lay there behind the first tee. The few members of the corps who had remained at their posts during the war had become used to keeping their heads down and they rarely ventured abroad beyond their residences and offices. I was able to help them by providing such information as I could gather about the situation outside the capital. At a small French drinks party I was approached by the West German ambassador bearing a large envelope which, knowing that I was shortly to see Lule again, he asked me to deliver to the President. I asked what it contained and was told that it was a formal protest at the government's failure to protect German diplomatic property from marauders. Observing this exchange the French Ambassador took me aside and apologized for his colleague's bad manners. It was not *protocolaire*.

We all knew that the new ministers had only been in office for a few days, that they had no effective civil service in place and no viable police force. Yet they were doing their best to provide a modicum of security for foreign diplomats and we were all provided with personal bodyguards. In this situation the present protest seemed faintly ridiculous. I remembered moreover that the Ambassador had failed to provide support for his countrywoman Rita Stiens when we arrived. I felt little compunction about quietly dropping his envelope into my waste paper basket.

The French Ambassador told me how he had had to endure fearful screams from the building next door. This housed the State Research Bureau, a house of infamy where Amin's thugs, trained by East German secret police, used to beat, starve, torture and kill anybody they chose to suspect of hostility to the regime. When I passed by I noticed that the entrance was unguarded and decided I must force myself to go and look.

It happened that Rita Stiens had made contact with me that day to tell me that, with the help of the Minister of Defence, they had found the place where her husband and his Swedish colleague had been captured, killed and buried. His body was being exhumed and she would be flying with it back to Nairobi the next day. She thanked me for my help. In the course of our talk I mentioned the State Research Bureau and she at once asked to come with me. I warned her that it might be unpleasant but she was determined to come.

The first thing we noticed was the sickening stench, explained once we were inside by the dried blood and excreta on the cell walls. I quickly escaped to an office where files and papers lay about in confusion. I searched for anything that might be important and came across some papers about West German diplomats — an obvious target for the East Germans. But most of the files contained statements by or about prisoners, often written in juvenile and illiterate style, purporting to record admissions and accusations that were patently forced and false. I put a bundle of the more interesting papers I could find under my arm and, thankfully, we emerged, Rita in tears at man's inhumanity to man.

I went to see the Minister of Defence Yoweri Museveni, who later was to lead the guerrilla war against Obote and emerge as President. Being a Muhima from Ankole (a tribe kin to the Tutsi of Rwanda), his mother had named him 'Museveni', 'Soldier of the Seventh', because his birth had coincided with a visit by a team recruiting for the seventh battalion of the KAR. He had married the sister of an old lawyer friend of mine, John Kazzora. During the Amin years, Museveni had been abroad fighting with Frelimo in Mozambique, where he had acquired an understanding of guerrilla warfare and a belief in discipline and self-help, albeit with a faintly communist tinge. I liked him and found him easy to get on with. He already had agents behind Amin's lines and he allowed me to listen in to a telephone conversation with one of his men in Mbale which was still under Amin's occupation. He handed me the phone to let me hear for myself how Amin's troops were moving north in disarray, their transport running out of fuel, plundering as they went and terrorizing the local populace. Museveni was confident that the war was won but he had no news of Amin's whereabouts.

We now received our first visitors from London, two officers from the ODA (Overseas Development Administration). They were a splendidly practical pair who quickly sized up the situation and were unruffled by the lack of facilities. They announced an immediate grant-in-aid of £1 million which was a valuable boost both to our position and to the confidence of the ministers. During an evening tour with them we came across an abandoned tank near St John's Church on Nakasero. I climbed in and found belts of live ammunition still in the breech which I removed for safe keeping and left in my office cupboard. The tank was still there months later.

One day a neatly dressed gentleman in suit and tie walked into my office and asked if I would take his car. He explained that his home-stead was 15 miles from the city in an area where his new car was a sitting target for marauding robbers. If I had it, the Union Jack would protect it from hijack. I went down to the street and saw a gleaming white Mercedes-Benz. It was time to return my borrowed Audi and it would be a month or two before we could import official cars. The owner wanted just to hand it over as a loan but I insisted on a proper rental agreement which was then arranged. We also recruited a driver, selected from a number of applicants, and told him to get himself a uniform. Our mobility was thus improved and had a better look about it.

This story did not have a happy ending. Two months later, after driving us to Entebbe for a flight to Nairobi the driver, very properly but unwisely, removed the flag from the bonnet. Neither car nor driver was heard of again. Our first suspicions were proved false when a disfigured body pulled from a swamp was identified by his wife, from marks on his feet, as that of our driver. By then the car was probably in Dar es Salaam.

On another day I received a message to say that Beetle Collins, a well known planter and prospector who lived in a remote area of Ankole, had been attacked by soldiers of unknown persuasion and his sister, with whom he lived, was reported killed. There was no way of communicating. For security reasons diplomats were not yet allowed to go more than a limited distance outside Kampala, not an unreasonable requirement in wartime. But I decided that I must go nevertheless. I reckoned that there was little danger in the west and that my trip was unlikely to be noticed. By a lucky chance, the Ministry of Foreign Affairs had just assigned as my new bodyguard a Munyankole soldier.

'How would you like to go down to Ankole for a day or two?'

Of course he jumped at the chance to visit his home district. Getting petrol was still problem and I knew none would be available outside Kampala but my Shell contact agreed to help and gave me two five-gallon jerry cans. With a topped up tank I reckoned this would just about suffice for the round trip.

My bodyguard had served with the Uganda brigade, marching alongside the Tanzanians, and he was able, as we drove along, to give me a first hand account of the way the fighting had gone. Masaka, when we reached it, was coming back to life but many of the buildings had been severely damaged or burned out. We pressed on across the lovely Ankole savannah to Mbarara. Near the town, a teenager waving a gun stopped us at a roadblock. My escort jumped out and gave the boy a severe wigging. I was glad to see that he took his job seriously.

Nearby we met an officer who explained courteously and in good English that this was a training ground for new army recruits. He took me to see a parade ground where 100 or more young men and women were drilling with sticks in lieu of rifles. Only later did I realize that these were the youngsters who were going to form the nucleus of Museveni's National Resistance Movement. He had seen from the outset the danger of the armed forces continuing to be dominated by northern tribes and quietly set in hand his own training scheme in Ankole as a precaution against what he feared might happen, for example if Obote were to return. Three years later his foresight was to play a vital part in liberating the country after Obote's second coming.

The hotel in Mbarara had been sacked so we had to find somewhere else to sleep and eat. The officer suggested the RC mission which is a mile out of town. There the father in charge welcomed me warmly, allocated a small room that had been a nun's cell, and took me to the refectory for dinner with a group of priests and lay brothers from various countries. They were a cheerful lot, having survived the horrors of Amin and the attack by the Tanzanians which had left the town partly in ruins. The mission had escaped serious damage and the Tanzanians had behaved with propriety when they arrived. They had taken over Amin's military base on the eastern side of the town and their soldiers were under good, sometimes severe, discipline. They told me that one soldier, convicted of some crime, had been executed out of hand. They had no firm news about Beetle Collins and his sister, but explained how to get to his place which was about 50 miles to the southwest along a bush road. I slept soundly with my bodyguard lying across my door outside.

After breakfast next morning we set off across the Ankole hills and, after a couple of hours, spied a low house on the top of a rise a mile away. Beetle welcomed us warmly and showed me round his place, introducing his tame crested cranes. I had brought him a bottle of whisky which he badly needed for he had been confined to his house since the attack ten days before. He told me the sad story of how a gang in battledress, whether Ugandan or Tanzanian he did not know, had driven up, ransacked the house, tied him and his sister up and taking his watch and her jewellery, then dragged her away into the long grass where she was afterwards found dead. He was left injured and lame.

We had a long talk. I told him that it would be impossible for either us or, I thought, the government to provide protection for him there with so many armed deserters about. I urged him to move to Kenya where he could stay with his brother in Eldoret. His loyal staff supported my plea and begged him to move: they were also at risk, of course. But Beetle was adamant that he would stay in his own place where he had all his books and belongings.

After a few hours with him and bearing numerous messages, I set off back to Mbarara where I stopped at the mission to give them his news and to arrange for communication with Beetle through mission channels. Then I pressed on to Masaka and Kampala where I arrived, to the relief of the staff, well after dark.

The next day I wrote to George Duntze in London telling him the story and asking if he could arrange for the replacement of Beetle's watch which had been a present from an old sporting association, the Uganda Kobs. In due course a new watch arrived which I was able to deliver safely to Beetle.

Soon after this trip Museveni sent for me and reminded me that diplomats were not permitted to move beyond a limited radius from Kampala. He had seen me in Mbarara. Somewhat taken aback, I explained that the reason for my trip had been to succour a British subject attacked and severely wounded by soldiers who had killed his sister. Museveni was unimpressed.

'I could have shot you,' he said.

'That would not have helped you to get British aid,' I responded.

I went on to praise the officer in Mbarara who had been so helpful and behaved so courteously to me. We parted amicably and I thought that that was the end of the affair. I was wrong.

❋ ❋ ❋

My assignment had been to get into Uganda, to make contact with the new government and to report on the situation. After two and a half weeks I had achieved those objectives and felt it was necessary to return to London. I needed to report in person more fully than was possible by telegram and to discuss future dispositions. With Justin now installed in the High Commission I could safely leave things in his hands. So three weeks after my arrival I found myself once more on the plane, this time back to London to talk to the FCO, ODA, Commonwealth Secretariat and various aid agencies. I had a lot to tell my wife, who had missed my brief appearance on the BBC news.

One interview was with Antony Duff, then deputy under-secretary but later to become HMG's intelligence coordinator. After a general discussion, he told me that he had been instructed to reprimand me for breaking the rules about movement of diplomats in Uganda. I realized that Otema must have reported my Mbarara adventure and I explained the reasons why I could not in good conscience have failed to make some attempt to contact and succour a distressed and injured British subject whose sister had been killed. I had been unable to get reliable information or assistance from the government or any other quarter. He made no comment and I guessed that he understood my attitude though he could not say so.

I was asked to return to Uganda as High Commissioner for the time being. I was due for retirement in mid July, but they proposed to extend my service by a few months. I agreed and said that I would be glad to return, but only if my wife could accompany me. I was told that this could not be approved for such a limited posting. I explained that this was not simply for personal reasons but was essential to the running of the High Commission. I was the only person with knowledge of local languages and able to communicate with domestic staff. The residence was being used as a mess for staff and there was a growing incidence of official and other visitors who needed to be catered for. A housekeeper was essential; Shirley's presence would solve that problem while her previous nursing experience in Kampala would be an asset. Eventually it was accepted that 'in the special circumstances of the case' Shirley could join me.

We spent an exciting evening at home making all the hurried plans that would be necessary to let the house and arrange for our faithful dog 'Askari' to be cared for. The children were not an immediate problem. The boys were at boarding school and we could decide later about their summer holidays. Nina, rising 18, was employed as an assistant keeper at the London Zoo and was living in a nearby hostel. (We underestimated her resourcefulness: within six weeks she was in Uganda, having flown out as a supernumerary stewardess on a cargo flight to Entebbe.)

A day or two later I was on the plane to Nairobi and found myself sitting near old friends — Martin Aliker, Michael Macoun (coming to advise on police rehabilitation) and George Kanyehamba, a Mukiga law lecturer at Cardiff who had just been appointed Attorney General of Uganda. Our minds were too full to sleep.

* * *

A week later Shirley arrived at Entebbe. The drive past the Lake

Victoria Hotel and on to Kampala was reminiscent of the first day we met in 1957. She was then an air stewardess with BOAC and I had driven her to Kampala for dinner at the Kampala Club: but on this occasion it ended differently. After dark Kampala exploded with gunfire. As we could not sleep we sat on the balcony drinking tea and watching the fireworks.

'Is it always like this?' Shirley asked.

In the morning we learned that the newly formed National Council had overthrown Lule in a 'palace coup'. It was not prepared to accept his authoritarian methods and wanted such things as appointments of ministers or ambassadors to be subject to its consent which Lule would not accept.

Having ousted Lule the Council faced the problem of finding a successor acceptable both to it and to the general public. Consisting of a self-appointed group of *émigrés* — rather like de Gaulle's circle in London during the war — few National Council members were known locally or could command popular support. Their choice eventually fell on the slightly improbable figure of Godfrey Binaisa. He was asleep in his bed, as he told me later, when they woke him with the startling announcement:

'Wake up! You are to be President.'

Faintly bemused and completely unprepared, he was rushed to Entebbe. A born survivor, he made a fair hand of winning the support of the National Council and, importantly, the army. The problem lay with public opinion. In Buganda he had never been forgiven for siding with the National Congress Party against Kabaka Yekka, the royalist party. He had served for a time as Obote's Attorney General and the Baganda suspected him of being Obote's stalking horse, so his name was anathema.

Kampala erupted in violent demonstrations and strikes. The Makerere students marched into town and a big crowd gathered on the open ground in front of the High Court. A nervous army contingent opened fire. There were numerous casualties, including Paulo Kavuma, former Katikkoro and mayor of Kampala, who was wounded in the leg. The honeymoon period was over and the task of uniting the country now looked seriously difficult.

Support for the government waned and disorder increased. The noise of nocturnal firing became incessant and a number of well-known figures were murdered. One morning I was summoned to a house just down the road where an Acholi Bahai teacher and his family lived. When I got there I found the man, his wife and their two children lying dead in pools of blood in front of the house. A day or two later a German diplomat's residence was attacked.

Nobody was safe and I thought we should take precautions in case of an attack on our residence, where we still had some staff members living. We devised an escape route which we planned to follow in the event of a frontal attack on the house. It involved climbing out of an upstairs window onto the roof of the annex, down a ladder at the end and up another ladder we had leaned against a high thorn hedge. From there we would have to jump down onto the adjoining field — and doubtless break our legs. We used to train visitors over this obstacle course. Happily we never had to use it but our guests were certainly impressed.

The next step I thought was to arm myself and I asked the FCO for permission to get a shotgun which would be some deterrent without being lethal except at close range. The response was to refuse me a weapon but to send out a pair of SAS security guards and they arrived two days later. To start with they lived with us, sleeping by day and prowling round the staff houses at night dressed all in black. This gave a useful boost to staff morale.

About this time I had my first game of golf. Some weeks earlier I had been to look at our old house on Nakasero Hill and found it deserted, papers and rubbish lying about, the garden unkempt. Looking across the hedge to the next door house I saw a tall African who came towards me. Suddenly I recognized the familiar grin of my old friend Alfred Omara, a civil servant from Lango. He had been a keen sportsman and he told me that he and others were trying to put the Kampala Golf Club back in order. They were short of mowing machines: maybe I could help. He asked if I would join the Greens Committee!

Now, having found some clubs for me to borrow, he took me down to play. It was fun to walk the familiar course. The fairways were a bit rough and the greens uneven, but still playable after a fashion. The rough though was to be avoided: the grass was four feet tall and full of discarded boots left behind by deserters from Amin's army.

The caddies were delighted to have some custom again. I was told that the Italian ambassador was the only golfer among the diplomatic corps. A very short-sighted man, he was popular with the caddies. He had a remarkable record of holes-in-one thanks to helpful fore-caddies who would drop his ball into the hole and then pretend to find it there when the ambassador walked up. He was known to give generous tips, especially for holes-in-one.

On another afternoon I was playing with Martin Aliker and the Minister of Finance, who both teased me about Africans being allowed to play on the *bwana*s' golf course. Half way round a boy ran up and engaged Martin in animated conversation. He was then dismissed and we played on. Martin walked alongside me and asked whether it would be convenient for him to stay the night with us at our residence. I was puzzled but agreed at once, waiting for him to explain. When an opportunity arose he told me that he had received a message from friends in the army that he was number one on the hit list of a group of soldiers based in Mubende who knew where he was living.

Shirley was delighted when I brought Martin home and told her that he would be staying to dinner and wanted a bed for the night. We gave her a bland explanation and she asked no questions. We had a convivial evening together: as he retired Martin told Shirley that he would be leaving early so he would say goodbye now. The next day I told Shirley the full story. She confessed that she had guessed something like that and had spent an anxious night.

✳ ✳ ✳

The Tanzanian forces had been sweeping up the eastern province by-passing Karamoja. Now we heard that they had captured Gulu in the Acholi district which adjoins the southern Sudan. There was no news of Amin himself: it was only later that we knew he had crossed the border and, doubtless with the help of his Libyan allies, gone on to Saudi Arabia where he was given asylum.

As soon as possible, I set off with Shirley to see how the Acholi had fared. Gulu was virtually undamaged as it had not been defended, Amin's forces having disintegrated before reaching there. The hotel was operational and found us a room. As luck would have it Otema turned up to stay there too but he was friendly and raised no objection to my presence. Shadows of the past kept intruding — an Arua versus Gulu cricket match in 1949; another much later with Andrew Cohen playing for Entebbe; and the royal visit by the Duke of Kent in 1962 when John Twining was the DC and had upset Obote for reasons I have long forgotten.

We went out to the CMS mission and there, imperturbable as ever, was Phoebe Cave-Brown-Cave. She ordered tea which was brought by a neatly dressed maid and she poured out into fine china cups while we chatted as if we were on the vicarage lawn discussing parish affairs. She was the picture of a self reliant, self controlled Edwardian lady. I thought how well she would have got on with my mother who had spent most of her life presiding over a mission station in India.

We were short of petrol for the return journey but a kindly Tanzanian officer arranged for us to have five gallons of fuel, sufficient to get us back to Kampala. On the way home we spent a night at the lodge in the park overlooking the Nile rapids at Karuma. It was hereabouts that, 115 years before, Sir Samuel Baker had crossed the river on his way to find Lake Albert — and had declined an offer by the *Mukama* of Bunyoro of six head of cattle for his wife. How much history had been crammed into that century.

The Uganda government had been asked for its formal *agrément* (diplomat-speak for agreement) to my appointment as High Commissioner and this was forthcoming despite my transgressions. In due course the formal letters arrived and the day came for me to present them to the President. An official car came to collect Shirley and me. Justin and other staff followed in a second car. At State House we were ushered through to the front verandah. On the lawn overlooking the lake a guard of honour was drawn up with a band: we were to get the full treatment.

After the two anthems had been played I was asked to inspect the guard. I remember thinking that this was a strange turn up for the book and not what I had expected when I left Uganda in 1963.

We were then ushered indoors and, after a few moments, President Binaisa entered with Otema and several other Ministers. The normal procedure on these occasions is for the incoming ambassador to present his predecessor's letter of recall, something I obviously could not do as there had been no British High Commissioner for the past three years. I simply presented my own letter of appointment and, in a brief formal address to the President, I spoke of HMG's satisfaction at the restoration of diplomatic (and friendly) relations and of my personal pleasure at being able to return to the country that had so long been my home. Binaisa replied in kind and called for champagne and a toast.

Once the formalities had been completed Binaisa came over and embraced Shirley, explaining to everybody that the last time they had met was at our house in England where he had done the washing up.

'I was the *toto jikoni*,' he laughed.

By chance the Commonwealth Secretary General, Sonny Ramphal, was present on a visit. We had known each other for some time in connection with West Indian and Pacific island affairs and he took the opportunity to tease me.

'I never know whether Dick is the British High Commissioner here or the Uganda High Commissioner in London.'

He obviously sensed my sympathies with Uganda, but I wondered what the FCO would have thought. I recalled one official's quizzical remark after reading my report of Lule's replacement by Binaisa:

'How is it that the presidency of Uganda seems to be reserved for Posnett's personal friends?'

* * *

The school holidays were now approaching and we decided that the two boys should come out to Uganda. This started another argument with the FCO which found our decision accorded ill with my recent request for a firearm. We were prepared, if necessary, to bring the boys out at our own expense since we knew they would never forgive us if they were not allowed to come and share the adventure. Eventually the FCO relented and the boys duly arrived, flying from Nairobi in a chartered light plane on which they were the only passengers.

At the time I was still, by a strange twist, a member of the British Phosphate Commissioners and needed to attend a board meeting in Melbourne. On the way back, passing through Nairobi I got to know the Australian High Commissioner Hugh Dunn who was also accredited to Uganda but had not yet visited the country or presented his credentials. I urged him to come with his wife and stay with us in Kampala; and I suggested that we should make a grand tour together of western Uganda. He liked the idea and in due course they arrived. Hugh was an expert on China and Margie an anthropologist specializing in the Pacific islanders. So it was interesting to pick their brains.

When Hugh had completed his official business in Kampala we set off for Kabale in two vehicles. The plan was to halt somewhere for a picnic lunch. Nina and the boys took spells to ride with the Dunns in their Range Rover. After lunch the Dunns carried on to Kabale where the White Horse Inn had been warned of our coming. Meanwhile, we diverted to visit Beetle Collins to see how he was getting on. It was an enthralling experience for the children and they at once took to Beetle in his remote hideout with his crested cranes. He was still unwilling to contemplate moving and claimed that the security situation in the area was now much calmer.

We rejoined the road to Kabale and climbed the long hill up to the district border. At the top a huge banner was displayed across the road.

'WELCOME TO YOUR EXCELLENCY'

I was puzzled how news of our arrival had reached this place and why we should be so honoured. We drove on through the lovely Kigezi hills to Kabale, seemingly untouched by recent events. Up the hill at the White Horse Inn we saw a lot of vehicles parked outside and uniformed men standing about. At the desk the clerk told me that the President and his party had taken over the whole hotel for the night. The Dunns, however, had arrived safely and had got a room — the last one available. The banner on the road was now explained.

Recalling something the bishop at Rubaga had said to me, I decided to go across the valley to the RC mission. There we were welcomed with some hesitation, but after we explained our plight they took us in. The bishop here had only that day got back from a conference in southern Africa, but despite his weariness he soon had his staff seeing to our needs and insisted on offering us dinner. We had to sit talking for an hour while the meal was being prepared, the children finding it hard to stay awake. But at last, well fed, we collapsed wearily into our strange beds.

The next morning we bade a grateful farewell to the bishop and his staff and drove back to the hotel to rejoin the Dunns. They were in audience with the President. As soon as they emerged, an ebullient Binaisa came out to greet us. He wanted to chat with us informally and to retell, for the benefit of his entourage, the story of washing up for us in England. He laughed to hear that he had unwittingly compelled us 'to sleep with the Romans'. (His father was an Anglican clergyman.) As the presidential cavalcade drove off, Binaisa leant out and gave Shirley a cheery wink.

We then set off with the Dunns for a day trip to Kanaba Gap. After about 25 miles, the road passes near the end of Lake Bunyoni and turns sharply to the right. Just beyond that a flourishing local market was in progress and we spent half an hour picking up some handicrafts and buying bananas. Our son Dickon bought a walking stick for 50 cents which he still uses and treasures. On and up we went through the bamboo forest to 8000 feet and the sudden glorious revelation of the Virunga volcanoes from Kanaba Gap. The Dunns and our children were spellbound. It was too hazy to see the more distant mountains but Muhavura's 12,000 feet reminded me of my first ascent with James Hunter in 1943 when we consumed a can of peaches by the crater lake on the summit.

Back at the White Horse Inn, we dined under the stars and played cards with the children by candlelight.

The next day we drove north-east up to Lake George, across the Kazinga Channel and to Mweya. The Safari Lodge was open for business though food was limited. Some of the staff had been there since the early days, including one who had served Rennie Bere when he was the warden. They were glad of our news from the outside world. On a drive round the park we saw very few animals compared with earlier days. A trip on the launch next morning revealed the reason: bloated carcasses of dead hippo were floating in the channel. They had been machine-gunned by soldiers, whether Ugandan or Tanzanian nobody knew: they all looked alike in battledress. Nina, fresh from London Zoo, was horrified.

From Mweya the Dunns returned directly to Kampala where they

would spend a couple of days in our residence before going back to
Nairobi. But we turned north up the eastern flank of the Ruwenzori
mountains which were decked in cloud as usual. Crossing the
Mobuku River I remembered my first expedition in 1942 with Rennie
Bere, during which I collected my first dose of malaria at 13,000 feet.

Fort Portal had escaped the war almost unscathed and seemed little
changed. Groups of schoolboys in uniform were chattering near the
college at Nyakasura founded by a former naval officer.

I had hoped to show my family some pygmies in Bwamba but was
told that the road over the mountains was impassable. So next day
we drove instead down the zigzag road to the Semliki flats south of
Lake Albert. At the Park Lodge the staff had seen no visitors for a
long time but were anxious to help. Loud squawks from the back
announced the capture and demise of our lunchtime *kuku* which,
when it came, had its revenge on us by being uneatably tough. While
waiting for lunch we took a drive round an area in the park where
we were told lions had been seen recently. There was no track but
the ground was dry and firm enough for our car. Alas, no game was
to be seen.

'*Askari wamepiga yote.*'

The story was the same as at Mweya: soldiers had shot them all.
Later we discovered what a deep impression all this had made on our
daughter who wanted to return one day to get the lodge going.

On the road back to Kampala we could see that the tea gardens of
Toro had been sadly neglected, as had the road. At Mubende we
drove up the hill for a picnic under the same wide spreading acacia
where we had camped on safari nearly twenty years before. A car
drove up and a smartly uniformed officer approached and asked who
we were. When we explained, he was polite and helpful. He was an
instructor at the army training base at the foot of the hill and told us
how recruitment policy aimed to keep a balance between the different
tribes. On the drive to Kampala, the road grew steadily worse and it
was a relief to get home.

News had arrived in the office of an impending visit by the British
Minister of Overseas Development, Neil Marten. Uganda Ministers responded positively to this first visit by a minister from another country
and showed how much importance they attached to it by ensuring that

his three-day programme was full and hectic. We enjoyed having him to stay at our house and getting to know him off duty. At one memorable lunch party, as well as Museveni we had invited Ndahendikire, a fellow Munyankole but one who had served as a senior officer in the army under before taking over the management of the Kilembe copper mine. Inevitably he and Museveni crossed swords, arguing the relative merits of trying to combat Amin's excesses from within the system or going into exile. Marten listened attentively, putting the occasional question. Afterwards he told me that he had served with the SOE in France during the war and found the controversy at our table strangely reminiscent of the mutual hostility in France after the liberation between the underground resistance fighters and de Gaulle's returning exiles.

Kampala continued to be plagued by incidents of violence. The Uganda soldiery in particular, mostly very young and inadequately trained, were febrile and trigger happy. One evening on Nakasero, passing the same abandoned tank with its hatch open, I halted the car to let the children see it. When a soldier walked up I asked him about it; but just then son Dickon lifted his camera. The soldier turned on him, raised his gun and shouted 'Stop that or I'll shoot you!'

Our next trip was to Mbale where many of the shops were empty although the buildings were relatively undamaged. We found that both missions, Protestant and Roman Catholic, had survived fairly well. Over supper at the White Fathers' mission, we heard news from missionaries who had come in from different parts of the district to see me. One had come from Kapchorwa up on the northern slopes of Mount Elgon and reported continuing violence and lawlessness in Sebei and Karamoja. Soldiers had come home with guns, or sold them to locals, and these were being put to fatal use in Karamoja and Turkana. It was this kindly teacher whose murder I had to report a few weeks later.

Jonathan, aged nine, was with us on that trip and I was able to drive him up the road, new since my day, to the top of Nkokonjeru, 'White Cockerel' mountain which looms over Mbale. This was better, I thought, than the slog of several hours on foot of former days.

On the way home to Kampala we had a scare. Coming unexpectedly upon a roadblock, I overshot the mark by a few feet. We heard a shout and saw a soldier run to a shelter and pick up his gun. I reversed to the exact stopping line and waited. Jonathan piped up.

'Daddy. Is he going to shoot us?'

I sincerely hoped not, but the soldier was angry and barely 20 years old. I did my best to calm him and eventually he waved us on.

Back in Kampala I had a call from the hotel and went round to greet an old acquaintance Gaspare Oda, a Lugbara from West Nile who had been an MP at the time of independence. I took Nina with me to meet him. He had been on a visit to Dar es Salaam and I guessed that he had been in touch there with Obote whose party he used to support. We talked for an hour about West Nile affairs, old friends and recent events. The people had suffered under Amin's soldiers, notwithstanding it being his own district. The Tanzanians had been welcomed and had behaved well. But soldiers of the new Uganda army were undisciplined and troublesome. He planned to return to Arua next day and asked us to come and visit him there as soon as possible. Two days later I had news that, on arrival in Arua, Gaspare had been shot dead outside his house. Nina, who had liked him, was appalled.

✳ ✳ ✳

The time for my departure was now approaching. The boys had already returned to school in England. As we were making plans for our homeward trip Nina sprang a surprise by saying that she would not be accompanying us. She had been doing some part time work at the office of the National Parks and had now been offered a post as assistant to a Cambridge zoologist who was coming out to make a detailed survey and enumeration of the wild life in the National Parks. That this was necessary was plain from our own visits, but we were flabbergasted at the idea of leaving our daughter there on her own. But she was confident and not to be dissuaded by all the arguments put to her, by us and by others. In the event, the following year gave her an irreplaceable experience — and us endless worries.

There was one final thing I resolved to do before our departure, namely to visit my old stamping ground in the West Nile district. Otema reluctantly agreed to my going and alerted the authorities in Arua. I set out one day with our new driver, appropriately named

Safaali. A Muganda, he was less keen than I was to visit outlandish regions.

We drove north and then west across the game plains towards Pakwach. This was uninhabited country that had been a closed area in the old days on account of sleeping sickness. Away to the south-west the mountains of the Congo loomed blue in the distance, the same mountains Baker had described when recording that most dramatic moment of African exploration when he first saw Lake Albert from the eastern escarpment. At last we came to the Nile which I had first seen from the river steamer 38 years before when arriving to take up my first appointment as an administrative cadet. The river is wide here: I had once tried to drive a golfball over it from the bluffs on the west side and it carried barely a third of the way across. Now it is spanned by a bridge.

Stopping near the shops in Pakwach village I spied a familiar face. It was Hypolito Omach, formerly a clerk and later *rwot* (county chief) of the Jonam whom I knew so well. A small group gathered, beer was offered and reminiscences flowed. This was the area of my first ever safari, where I had shot elephant and hippo to be eaten by hungry people, and had nearly been shot myself accidentally by the *rwot* Anderea Ali who was himself later murdered. It was fascinating to hear the Alur dialect again and to find words and sentences slowly coming back.

I tore myself away and we drove on past Nebbi and Okollo where a permanent structure had long since replaced the old bamboo bridge over the River Ora. At last we drove into Arua where I had lived for so many years in my youth: it was a nostalgic moment. I noticed that the main street down from the *boma* through the *duka*s was bedecked with flags strung from side to side. Had we again clashed with a presidential visit? I halted at the police station to check in. The officer in charge was expecting me. When I pointed to the flags he smiled.

'That's all in your honour, Sir! You are expected at Ombachi.'

Suitably abashed I drove out to the RC technical school where I was met by a smartly dressed group which included one or two white and Asian faces. I realized that this comprised the whole of the district establishment — DC, doctors, technical officers, chiefs, missionaries, traders. I was overwhelmed by this reception which seemed to go far beyond what would have been expected for a diplomat's first visit. Tea was served and I tried to talk to as many as possible of those present.

There were many young faces, but a scattering too of older ones that I half remembered.

'Do you remember me Sir?'

A well-built, middle-aged man grinned at me. Seeing my puzzlement he added:

'I was your golf caddy, Sir. Now I am the district sports officer.'

A grizzled Asian came up. This time my memory came to the rescue.

'Khalfan Mohamed's son,' I said.

He was delighted and launched into tales of misery and survival during Amin's regime. A smart Tanzanian officer saluted and introduced himself.

'Please let me know if I can be of any service, Sir.'

I asked him whether I would be able to get to the Sudan border. He thought I could go as far as Koboko: beyond that would be dangerous for remnants of Amin's forces were just across the frontier and liable to make raids into Uganda territory.

Next day we drove north through the rolling grasslands of the Lugbara which I had roamed almost 40 years before and knew so well. At Maracha we halted while I tracked down an old mentor and former Sultan, Maskini Adua. His handsome face was little changed, although he had suffered much deprivation since the British left. He lived now in a modest grass hut. We talked for a long time recalling old adventures shared. I vowed to myself that I would try to get for him some recognition, possibly financial assistance. Sadly this came to nothing before he died. It was a privilege to have known him.

Further north, at Koboko we were in the country of the Kakwa tribe which is divided by the international border with the Sudan. I guessed that they had some sympathy, and perhaps links, with Amin who originated there. A Tanzanian officer confirmed that Amin's men were infiltrating across the border to pillage. He described the unstable security position along the frontier from the Congo in the west to the River Nile at Nimule. It was a difficult line to protect.

Next day I was due to head home, but first made a circuit through the Alur highlands. At Vurra we stopped near a beer party and I found another former county chief relaxing with his friends. We had some cheerful talk before I pressed on to Atyak where I sought out Valente Oyoma who had been a young clerk and a star footballer 30 years before. Later promoted to succeed his father as *rwot* of the Alur he was now retired but easily recognizable as the man I had known. More talk before I had to leave if we were going to get back to Kampala that night.

It had been a moving experience to meet so many old colleagues and then to have to leave them, knowing we would not see each other again. But I had now done all that I had to do, seen the places and met the people that had made my life in Uganda so much worth while. I was ready to depart.

21

Atlantic Episode

'the still vex'd Bermoothes'

(*The Tempest*)

Having retired from the Diplomatic Service I was surprised, at the end of 1979, to be asked about possible appointment as Governor of Bermuda, a post that had often been filled by political appointments or by military or naval men.

Bermuda is the tip of an ancient submarine volcano which juts up 13,000 feet from the deep ocean bed near the Atlantic fault line. The weather is that of the mid-ocean equable but windy and subject to violent storms. The islands are protected by a reef a few miles offshore which helps to account for many wrecks including that which brought the first settlers ashore in 1609 when Admiral Sir George Somers' flagship on passage to Virginia struck rocks near St George's Island.

A population of about 60,000 tends to increase and makes for a high density in an area of barely twenty square miles. More than half the population are non-white but the economic strings are still largely in white hands. Tourism is a major provider of jobs, often two or more jobs to one person. But the hidden resource lies in the offshore insurance, investment and banking industry. At a recent count some 11,000 brass-plate companies were registered in the capital Hamilton, most of them obviously having no more presence than the plate itself, for which a good fee is levied. With stable government and no income tax and Bermuda is a tax haven for American and British money, and an important centre for global captive insurance and re-insurance business.

The colony's constitution provided for an elected parliament from which the leader of the majority party appointed a cabinet of ministers, along lines similar to those at Westminster. After the introduction of elections politics had become polarized along racial lines and the franchise had tended to favour the prosperous white community. However the governing United Bermuda Party had made serious efforts to attract support from non-whites and had brought some of them into the cabinet and into positions of leadership. The rival party was almost entirely non-white: it was led by Lois Browne-Evans, whose sharp intelligence I had come to admire during the constitutional conference.

The Governor's role under the constitution was largely formal, representing the Queen as Head of State. Although nominally responsible for defence and external affairs, these were in practice the business of Her Majesty's Government in London. In domestic affairs only internal security and the police came within the Governor's remit and on these he worked with and through a committee of local Ministers. Peter Ramsbotham, the retiring Governor whom I had known during the constitutional conference, warned me that his duties were a good deal less than a full time job. He advised me that, if I accepted the post, I should come ready with hobbies to occupy my time: his was bird watching. I was also to discover that great store was set by public show and appearances, a marked contrast with Belize and Mr Price.

Before deciding to accept the post I consulted my family. I next had a talk with David Gibbons who was then both Premier and Minister of Finance. We had met during the constitutional conference two years earlier and he assured me that my appointment had his full support.

Before leaving London I was briefed at the Bank of England and learned of its concern at the lack of a central bank to handle the large amount of foreign exchange business that was now conducted by the two big private banks, whose profits went to their shareholders. The potential conflict of interest for some ministers was, I supposed, hard to avoid in such a small tightly knit and financially oriented community. (The role of the Bermuda Monetary Authority has since been enhanced and improved.)

From my experience at the constitutional conference I knew there was pressure, mainly from the black community, for a greater degree of political emancipation. An enquiry into the pros and cons of independence from Britain had shown up a fairly negative balance of economic advantage; but I suspected that human aspirations for political autonomy might lie not far below the surface, even though the island was already self-governing in almost all practical respects. I made a point of declaring on arrival that this was a question solely for the Bermudians to decide: there would be no pressure from Britain either way.

The deputy Governor was Peter Lloyd, son of Sir Thomas Lloyd, the revered former Permanent Secretary at the Colonial Office in London. Peter was an able administrator having started his career as a district officer in Kenya. He was very well informed about Bermudian affairs and I was fortunate to have him to guide my footsteps on first arrival. Later I learned that he had applied for the Governorship himself and had been disappointed not to get the post, but he never allowed that to affect his loyal support for me. I knew he would make an excellent colonial Governor and I made my view on this clear to the FCO. I was gratified when he was appointed Governor of the Cayman Islands, although this meant losing a valued friend and adviser.

About a year after we arrived Gibbons handed over the premiership to a 'non-white' Minister, John Swan, and I took an early opportunity to talk to him about his own aspirations. I also explained that I was already retired and had only accepted the governorship with some hesitation, in the hope that I could continue to make a useful contribution. But it was not a career post for me and I would be ready to leave and make way for somebody else whenever he wished. I refrained from adding that the ceremonial and pomp attaching to the post did not much appeal to my wife or to me.

By this time agreement had been reached in Belize over a defence arrangement with Britain that would deter any recurrence of the threat from Guatemala. This made it possible for them to go forward to independence, and Swan and I were invited to attend the celebrations. It was a great pleasure for me to meet again old friends and colleagues there, while for Swan it was an opportunity to see and feel at first hand the vibrations that always accompany such major transitions. The retiring Governor of Belize was my old colleague from the FCO, Jim Hennessy, whose career had crossed with mine in Uganda. Jim and his wife very kindly put me up at Government House despite all their other commitments, not least a royal visit. George Price was also the soul of kindness, on top of the world now that he had achieved his lifetime ambition. John Swan was absorbing the atmosphere and I could feel, during our return trip to Bermuda, that he had sensed the political imperative. We gave a joint interview on Bermuda radio during which his feelings began to show. I was not surprised when, some years later, he sought public support for independence in a referendum and resigned when it was lost.

Bermuda had played a vital role as a staging post for transatlantic shipping during two world wars. It was now playing an equally important part in the cold war as a base from which the movements of Soviet submarines through the north Atlantic could be monitored by using sophisticated technology. The airport was sited on land leased to the US government as part of the wartime 'lend lease' deal for destroyers, and there the US Navy stationed a squadron of Orion surveillance aircraft. When US Admiral Harry Train (CINCLANT) paid a visit, I invited him to address a select dinner audience of leading government figures about the crucial strategic value of Bermuda as a base.

Other American visitors included Vice-President Gerald Ford, with whom I enjoyed a few holes of golf, and Vice-President (as he was then) George Bush with his wife Barbara. We had a good talk together during which he discovered in passing that I had a back problem. This led to a funny incident. At a reception that evening one of his aides buttonholed me, led me to an adjacent anteroom, took off his belt, lay down on the floor, and asked me to buckle his legs together so that he could demonstrate an exercise which he said was helpful for back problems. At this juncture who should come in but Barbara Bush: her eyes widened and she rapidly withdrew.

Bermuda's geographic location made it a convenient refuelling stop for aircraft flying between Europe and Central America. Sometimes the passengers included high dignitaries whom I would meet and, if

necessary, entertain. Margaret Thatcher made simply a dinner stop on
her way home from Mexico City. She needed to be in her office at
Downing Street the next morning but Shirley persuaded her to take
off her shoes for a brief rest after dinner. Archbishop Runcie spent a
few days accompanied by Terry Waite, a man of imposing presence
who had worked in Uganda and who was to achieve note as a hostage
in Beirut. Prince Charles and Princess Diana we took to see the old
town of St George's and showed them what is reputedly the oldest
church in the western hemisphere. The church is approached by a
long flight of steps and on the way down, knowing that Diana was
pregnant, I offered her my arm. She politely declined.

The King of Saudi Arabia spent a night in transit and, while driving
with him to the airport, I sounded him out about the presence in his
country of Amin from Uganda. The King said that they had offered
Amin sanctuary as a fellow Muslim, although deploring the harm he
had done to 'your people', meaning the British. I hastened to explain
that it was not the British who had suffered so appallingly, but the
Ugandans, many thousands of whom had died violently, some after
torture, under Amin's oppression. The King listened impassively but
gave no indication of his thoughts.

It was interesting to look over the list of previous governors; many
of them had naval or military backgrounds but several, more recently,
of a political nature. There I saw the name of Lord Burghley whose
path I had crossed twice before — when he presented prizes in
London to a schoolboy athlete and later, in Cortina, when he spon-
sored Uganda's application for admission to the Olympic Games. I
wrote to invite him to visit and was delighted when he accepted, only
to be saddened when his death intervened. Another former Governor
did, however, come and stay. Sir Julian Gascoigne was a delightful
guest who became a good friend and with whom we were to stay a
few years later at his home in Devon.

Perhaps the most intriguing visitor we had was Godfrey Binaisa
whom we had last known as President of Uganda, a position he had
lost in an election that led to the second coming of Obote. I enjoyed
introducing Binaisa to black leaders in Bermuda, especially to some
who were involved at the time in a strike over a labour dispute. He
told me that he had given them a lecture on their good fortune in

being able to live in peace in a society of plenty compared with conditions in most parts of Africa. I never heard how they received his homily.

Recounting these interesting visits may seem to imply that the Governor's substantive duties were undemanding. This was indeed the case: the specifications of the post did not include job satisfaction. The incessant social round of lunches, receptions and dinners, with the concomitant dressing-up and speech making, soon began to pall and took a particular toll of Shirley's health. We were fortunate in having an excellent doctor, Gordon Black, but eventually he decided that further abdominal surgery was unavoidable, after which she had a spell in England to recuperate. We began to see that Bermuda was not for us and I started to ponder the possibility of bringing forward the time of my departure. But before my thoughts on this had crystallized events took another turn.

A visitor from the FCO told me that I had been accused of misusing government funds. I was too shocked for words, and was even more dismayed when I learned of the petty and largely administrative nature of his complaints. For example it was alleged that

- private telephone calls from the Government House switchboard had, he claimed, not been properly accounted for, though no specific instance was mentioned. In fact, each month a list of calls was circulated to me, and to all the other personnel who used the switchboard, so that private calls could be identified and paid for;
- Shirley's Mini car which she liked to use rather than the official Daimler had been filled with petrol from the government pump by the totally trustworthy Government House chauffeur. I learned that this was the established practice: the amounts were tiny and one would think that this saved the government money;
- my entertainment allowance had been used to provide for private visitors as well as for official guests. The Governor's emoluments in fact included an element estimated to cover the cost of the entertaining that went with the job. As with ambassadors this was specified to be 'non-accountable' and did not call for any distinction to be made between different categories of guest, even if such a division of cost had been practicable. However I had arranged

for the allowance to be paid into a separate account so that I was able, at the end of the day, simply to return to the government the unused balance.

Any of these complaints could have been quickly sorted out across a table with a modicum of goodwill and common sense. Sadly, instead of that, the allegations had been made to the FCO behind my back. An FCO official who investigated absolved me of any attempt to defraud the government; but after talking with the Minister concerned he told me his impressions.

'He wants to get rid of you,' he said. 'I think he wants to throw the book at you.'

He had invited the Minister to come and meet me so that he could explain the specific nature of his complaints, but the Minister had refused to do this.

'I'm afraid you will not get a fair hearing.'

The Minister proceeded to make critical public statements without informing me. The Governor, representing the Queen, was inhibited from any public answer or rebuttal so it was a one-sided argument. But it became obviously impossible in these circumstances for me to continue to work with the government under the constitution.

I had a long, frank and friendly discussion with John Swan. It would have been perfectly possible to continue to work with him as Premier under the constitution; but he was in a somewhat uneasy position, constrained by political loyalties.

After that the leader of the Opposition asked to see me. Lois Browne-Evans was naturally highly critical of the actions of the government.

In London I went to consult my old friend Hugh Caradon, who had a wealth of experience in such difficult matters, both as a Governor and as a Minister of the Crown at the United Nations. He asked me a simple question. Could I continue to work with the present ministers in Bermuda? If not my proper course would be to resign my commission. I followed his advice and wrote to the Secretary of State thus:

Publicity has recently been given to critical statements about the handling of public monies at Government House in Bermuda. I am sorry that no direct approach was made to me about this so that any alleged irregularity could be promptly checked and, if necessary, corrected. However, I have refrained for constitutional reasons from making any public response to such allegations.

I can assure you that no public funds have been knowingly misused at Government House, either by me or by any member of my staff.

The publicity that has been generated has created an atmosphere in which it would no longer be possible for me to carry out my responsibilities as Governor; nor would I wish to do so. I must therefore ask to be released from my Commission as Governor. I have reached this conclusion with deep personal regret because of many valued friendships in Bermuda. But my hope is that by vacating office it will be made easier for you and for my successor to maintain the good relations with the Bermuda Government which are essential to the working of the territory's Constitution.

I would like to express my grateful thanks to you, Sir, as well as to your many distinguished predecessors under whom I have served in various dependent territories for the past forty odd years, for the unfailing kindness and support which I have received.

The Secretary of State replied:

Thank you for your letter of 23 February. I am extremely sorry that you have found it necessary to come to the conclusion that you should offer your resignation as Governor of Bermuda. I am particularly distressed that you have to do this in such unhappy circumstances.

I am grateful for the assurance which you have given. At the same time I appreciate the reasons why you feel that it would be best if you did not continue as Governor. I have therefore recommended to The Queen that your resignation be accepted and Her Majesty has been pleased to agree.

May I end with a word of appreciation for the service you have given to the Crown during your long career.

Yours sincerely

Francis Pym

A historian* has offered this view of these events:

> So strong was the opposition to decolonisation that several influential White Bermudians were outraged when in February 1981 the FCO's former Dependent Territories Adviser, Sir Richard Posnett — who had made a name for himself as a great decoloniser — was appointed the island's Governor. Wishing to dispense with some of the pomp of office, Posnett attempted to get closer to the Black population and to turn Government House into something of a 'people's palace'. Believing the link with Britain to be in jeopardy, in March 1983 the leading Whites made trivial allegations concerning the Governor's management of his entertainment allowance which forced Posnett to resign.

In fact I had always made clear in public statements that on the question of independence I was strictly neutral. Moreover, it is wrong to suggest that the Minister's attitude reflected a widely held view among whites. Typical of the many messages of support we received was the following letter from a much-respected former premier, Sir John Cox.

> I wish to say to you both that I am greatly distressed by and greatly deplore the scandalous things that have been said by persons in high position who have behaved in a way which would not have been tolerated during my active career in politics. My colleagues in those days would not have been party to what has been done.
>
> I am glad that Sir Richard has dared them to come out with the

---

* George M. F. Drower, *Britain's Dependent Territories: A Fistful of Islands.*

substance of their insinuations. From what I have gleaned from various sources they have nothing but trivia to relate.

So ended an unhappy chapter. We returned gratefully to our home in Surrey and were comforted to receive messages of sympathy and support from all over the world, most movingly from Uganda and from Ministers in Belize.

22

The New Romans

The evil that men do lives after them,
The good is oft interrèd with their bones;
So let it be with Caesar.

(Mark Anthony in *Julius Caesar*)

After two thousand years the works of Caesar's empire in England can be seen to this day in Roman roads, Roman baths, the ruins of Roman forts. They were ahead of their time in spreading the concept of literacy. In our society the lingering effects can be felt in the language, in the law and surely in our genes. The benefits are undeniable. Here at least is an exception to Mark Anthony's maxim.

When I was serving in the most remote part of north-western Uganda, close to the frontiers of Sudan and Congo, I used to wonder how my situation compared with that of a Roman centurion on duty at Hadrian's wall, charged with defence of that outpost against the marauders to the north and with ruling the savage Britons to the south. Emperor Hadrian actually made the long trip from Rome to north Britain, a journey which in those days might have daunted even our own much travelled monarchs. What strange motive moved the Caesars so to extend their responsibilities and their lines of communication? The imperial ambition is indeed hard to read, but it was certainly very different in Rome from London during the days of the British Empire.

'Trade follows the Flag': so ran the dogma of British imperial expansion, propounded no doubt by those wishing to see their commercial interests protected in a peaceful environment. But in practice the converse was usually true. The East India Company was the archetype of a commercial venture leading inexorably to the establishment of an empire. Surprisingly perhaps for a country that in two or three centuries established an empire on which the sun never set, Britain's parliament was a reluctant imperialist, dragged into the role by circumstance, chary of embarking upon overseas colonization that might, and often did, involve military deployment and which would almost certainly become a burden on the Exchequer. So how did it all come about?

First, the navigators of the Elizabethan era, with their Portuguese and Spanish counterparts, discovered the patterns of ocean currents and trade winds, mastered the skills and then developed the ships and rigging needed for trans-oceanic sailing. They returned home with samples of exotic tropical produce — rice and spices, tea and cane sugar, cotton and tobacco. This evoked the commercial interest necessary to finance further expeditions. The Spaniards brought home gold; but as behoved 'a nation of shopkeepers' it was trade that attracted interest in Britain, a small island that came to depend upon it.

Two other factors came to influence parliament during the nineteenth century. One was the growing liberal conscience in Britain that led to the abolition of the slave trade and which was pricked by reports of horrible brutality in India, particularly during and after the Mutiny of 1857. Then came the reports about Africa, the dark and unknown continent, from the great explorers like Stanley, Livingstone, Speke, Baker, and Mary Kingsley. These aroused the evangelical zeal of the churches to the need to bring Christian enlightenment to the heathen. Although there was little love lost between the missionaries and the traders in the field, both in their different ways brought influence to bear upon the government and parliament in London. So too did British settlers in some territories.

Once London was persuaded of the need to adopt responsibility for, and sovereignty over, an overseas territory, it soon became a matter of national prestige for this to be protected, if necessary by force. This was an important factor during the two world wars and was still a motivating influence as recently as the Guatemalan threat to Belize in 1975 and the Falklands War in 1982.

In a framework where an empire was developing by force of circumstance, territory by territory, rather than by overall design, it took time before, in 1854, a Cabinet Minister was appointed with specific responsibility for the colonies. Soon afterwards, following the Indian Mutiny, a separate department for India was created. Out of these developments arose the Indian Civil Service (the ICS) and the Colonial Administrative Service. Now, within a mere 100 years, they have gone. What did they achieve for good or ill?

Recruitment for the Colonial Service had been based largely upon principles inherited from the ICS where leadership, fair play, and self-reliance were as important as scholastic achievement — a style that tended to favour the Corinthian public school product, seeking an active outdoor life and having all-round ability on the playing field as well as in the classroom. Academic standards were probably less demanding than for the ICS. Sir Evelyn Baring, a former member of the ICS who became Governor of Kenya, once wrote with brutal frankness (and perhaps a little prejudice) that members of the Colonial Administrative Service were generally less intelligent than those of the ICS.*

That was too sweeping a generalization, but it was probably true that competition for the ICS attracted the better brains. At least in the earlier decades of the twentieth century India offered a more attractive and lucrative career than life in one of the smaller, more remote and more backward colonial territories. Although the Colonial Service provided staffing for some relatively advanced territories like Ceylon or Cyprus, it was not open to applicants to choose where they would be sent. We were invited to express a preference. In my own case, a preference for Rhodesia or Nigeria led to appointment to Uganda. (The judgement of those concerned in the Colonial Office was astute.)

This is not to say that the selections for the Colonial Service proved in practice inferior: there is something to be said for men of more modest pretensions when toiling in difficult conditions with practical problems among less educated people. Most of us did not aspire to be proconsuls.

---

* C. Chenevix Trench, *Men Who Ruled Kenya.*

Our job was to see to the welfare and development of the people, not to exploit them. Listening to some of the speeches at the UN General Assembly, one might have thought that the evils of colonialism left no room for good, yet I found it hard to recognize in those descriptions the profession to which I had devoted the previous 20 years of my life. Even with his impeccable credentials as a colonial administrator, our respected leader Hugh Caradon sometimes found it difficult to see the good for the odium.

I cannot judge the systems or successes of other colonial powers. The Belgians started badly under King Leopold, eschewed responsibility for the advancement of the people of the Congo and finally abandoned them. Of the Americans I saw and admired their efforts in the Pacific islands, which had been ravaged by successive foreign conquests and whose strategic value is paramount. Even in British territories my experience was not necessarily typical. But subject to that caveat, what did we achieve and what have we left behind?

Foremost we brought law and order which enabled people to live their lives free from fear of their fellow men and confident in the justice available to everyone. It was not always so: as recently as 1900 the Viceroy of India, Lord Curzon, reported that there was 'no justice' in cases where Europeans and Indians were concerned.* But in my own experience the impartiality and fairness of the colonial courts could never be faulted. Racial discrimination had been eliminated almost everywhere in the colonial territories by the time of the Second World War, although in Bermuda racial segregation in certain public buildings persisted even longer. In any case, the fundamental principle of the rule of law became ingrained in the rising generation of lawyers and politicians and has survived in most countries, despite being trampled on from time to time.

Education was an essential concomitant to social and economic development, of which an important element was to provide all the different tribes with a single international language. The Christian missions deserve most of the credit for developing almost universal education within a matter of two generations. To ensure high stan-

---

* Lawrence James, *Raj: The Making and Unmaking of British India*.

dards the territory governments gave them financial and supervisory support and took particular responsibility for supplying higher education. In Uganda, Makerere College became a university and Mulago Medical School trained doctors and nurses to a standard that was eventually accepted internationally. Thus the country was furnished with a growing corpus of educated professionals to run the essential services. That the present Secretaries General of the United Nations and of the Commonwealth both come from former British dependencies in Africa speaks for itself.

Communications and transport played a vital role in opening backward areas to economic development and to social enlightenment. This was especially noticeable in remote areas where I served and where the people had hitherto been isolated from the rest of the country and from the world beyond. Roads, railways and ships, posts and telegraphs, served to open the windows of civilization to the villages of the interior, to bring them unimagined tools, materials, markets, comforts and facilities, but most important, news and ideas. This had proved an explosive influence in India and its effect was similar, although on a lesser scale, in Africa and in the Pacific islands for example.

Famine is an ever-present threat in Africa when the rains fail. One of the District Officer's less glamorous duties was to make regular inspections of the famine precautions in each village — the storing of grain for next season's planting and the maintenance of adequate reserves of cassava in the ground. By these means we managed generally to counter the problem and avoid disastrous food shortages. Sadly these precautions have not lived after us and north eastern Africa has been ravaged by appalling famines during the last years of the century. The expanding population can only exacerbate this threat.

Some territories were less well favoured than Uganda in terms of climate, soil or availability of ample land. This could make it more difficult to introduce new cash crops, more enlightened farming methods or soil conservation measures, especially where nomadic customs led to overstocking of grazing land or where, as in Kenya, white settlement had occupied valuable arable land. Getting over these problems was a major concern of our later colonial governments.

Another affliction in many areas of Africa was the spread of infectious, parasitic or contagious diseases which periodically decimating the population as well as gravely impairing the physical and mental capacity of those who survived. The fight against these scourges was one of our major preoccupations. Eliminating sleeping sickness, isolating and treating leprosy, mosquito control, provision of latrines — all these figured largely in the government's efforts to improve the health of the people and so in the work of the district Officer.

These were among the means adopted by British colonial governments to improve the lot of the people in their care. But what of the foresight which I have accused the Belgians of lacking? Perhaps the most important things we could leave behind were the machinery and the human resources which would enable the countries not only to govern themselves but to survive as states in the harsh international climate of the modern world. To educate in the arts of administration and to provide a democratic constitution figured high on the list of priorities during the postwar march to independence.

Once a general level of literacy had been reached it was not difficult to introduce a democratic system of government responsible to an elected legislature. But that is just a machine: like a motorcycle it can be used to advantage — or it can be lethal. Tom Mboya in Kenya was one who quickly saw the power of the ballot box to achieve his political aims: his premature death prevented us from seeing what sort of use he would put it to. George Price in Belize was one who put it to good use. But sadly democracy by itself does not ensure good government. Hitler, Obote, Mugabe, all were elected.

As James Morris put it, 'It was apparent to nearly everyone that whatever else the subject peoples would get from independence it would not be better government.'*

Returning to Uganda after the years of tyranny under Amin's soldiers, the desire of the populace for a return to order and the rule of law which they had enjoyed under the British came across loud and clear. But even a working system of courts and honest policing cannot prevent an unscrupulous military leader like Amin or Pinochet to

---

* James Morris, *Farewell the Trumpets*.

name but two examples, from seizing power, overthrowing the constitution and imposing a dictatorship. The only known prophylaxis
against such coups lies in the hearts and minds of the people and their
leaders; and that is a part of social, political and national culture
which may take centuries of hard experience to develop.

Almost as difficult was the problem of nation building. The human
ambition to govern one's own tribe or island invites suspicion or
resentment when other tribes or islands are involved. To create an
artificial nation was especially intractable in a country like Uganda
which, although of modest size, had been the crossroads of past tribal
migrations, Nilotes and Hamites from their different distant origins
crisscrossing the Bantu homelands and leaving their mark in languages and genes so that now in almost every district of Uganda the
people speak a different language and in some, the West Nile for
instance, several languages. In such a mix no amount of constitutional
subtlety could erase tensions and suspicions between tribes. Curiously,
it was in the realm of sport that national consciousness first became
apparent.

During the period after the second World War when decolonization
became an accepted aim of policy there existed in London a preference to establish larger units on the assumption that they would be
more viable as independent entities. This was a false trail. The larger
the country the less easy it becomes to govern. In Africa, countries as
large and diverse as the Congo or Nigeria are inherently difficult to
govern. And federations inevitably create tensions between the component parts and the centre. This is not just a 'third world' condition.
Even the United Kingdom is not immune to fissiparous tendencies. In
the event our attempts to set up federations of territories in East
Africa, Central Africa, South Arabia and the West Indies all fell apart.

Despite these misconceived policies, the political record has not been
without success. The best example is India, a vast country still ruled
by democracy and due process of law half a century after independence from the British. Of course, India's traditions of government
stretch back much further, well beyond Britain's, but the record is still
impressive. Once the seeds of democracy and the rule of law are sown,
they usually take root. Among the Latin American countries, where
the gun has often been more respected than the ballot box, Belize, a

British colony for more than a century, is a shining example of a small country where the politics of violence has never been accepted and in which a democracy has flourished in contrasting surroundings. Even in Uganda, the wounds caused during Amin's misrule seem to be healing with the restoration of orderly government.

British colonial rule has not been without a saving grace. Even those who lived under it remember it fondly. But it will be for future generations to judge the long-term effects on the human condition.

23

Homecoming

'a foreigner in the country of my birth'

(Steve Biko)

After a lifetime spent abroad I now had, at the age of 64, the chance to explore my own country, a task made easier by an appointment in 1984 to the Lord Chancellor's Panel of Independent Inspectors, a grandiose title for a group of retired public servants whose task was to preside over public enquiries where the issues were contentious or where, because of the government's involvement, one of the professional inspectors employed by the department might not be seen to be impartial. I found these enquiries not unlike meetings held by a district officer on tour. They gave me a splendid opportunity to get to know England and Wales, not just the scenery but the people, their lifestyle, their history, their dialects. I was impressed by the differences between countrymen and townsfolk, between Devon and Manchester, between Norfolk and Wales, between Ealing Broadway and Hadrian's Wall.

Public rights of way are particularly sensitive to controversy: enquiries gave to all those who felt strongly about the issue the chance to put their arguments in a public but not unduly legal forum. And for me it provided the occasion to walk across the countryside with farmers and ramblers, riders and surveyors, local residents and outside pressure groups, and in this way to learn about local concerns and ways of life. I learned how the English language varies from place to place depending on which of our successive conquerors last left their mark in each area. I learned the differences between a 'green lane', a 'drift-way' and a 'county road'. I followed a 'ginnel' in Lancashire and crossed a 'syke' in Northumberland.

Wales was always a delight. Enquiries invariably attracted a full house, come to listen and occasionally to interject comments from the back-benches. A joke at one's own expense usually helped to put one onside with the audience. Once, in an area where the language is a sensitive issue, simultaneous interpretation was provided. However one witness wanted to show his independence.

'Out of courtesy to you, Sir, I shall make my statement in English.'

'That's very kind of you Mr Jones,' I said, 'but it would be a pity if all the people here were unable to understand what you have to say.'

A roar of laughter ensued.

Another time an English MP was the principal objector to an order for reclassification of a green lane across his land as a byway open to all traffic. During his speech, he tended to forget that he was neither at the hustings nor in the House of Commons.

'Is it the wish,' he said, 'of the yeomen of this great county of ours to see a quiet idyllic country walk, where birdsong and flowers now reign, transformed into a dirt track for raucous cross-country motor-cycles billowing lead fumes? Are we to allow our rural countryside to be despoiled like this? Is this the way our parish wishes its affairs to be conducted by outsiders?'

Solicitor for the Council rose to cross-examine.

'After such eloquent argument I can only think of one question I should like to put to the witness. When the Wildlife and Countryside Act of 1981, under which we are proceeding, was considered in Parliament which way did the witness vote?'

One of the purposes underlying the system of public enquiries is to see that, as far as possible, everybody goes away satisfied that they have had a fair hearing. A contumacious witness can sometimes be reduced to sweetness by a compliment on the cogency and vigour with which he has presented his case. Even when he subsequently finds his arguments rejected by the inspector's report, he may be gratified to see that they have not been ignored and he may perhaps remember with satisfaction his day in court.

A lady representing the ever-vigilant Ramblers Association argued with conviction in favour of a line for a footpath which she described as commodious and convenient for a mother with a pram. Having myself, the previous day, had to force my way through the undergrowth blocking this line, I heard the witness without comment and at the end simply asked her to accompany me on a site inspection, preferably with a pram. Regrettably she failed to show up. But a month later, during lunch with an old FCO colleague in London, he surprised me by asking how I was enjoying conducting public enquiries. Not having told him of my newfound activity, I asked him how he came to know of it.

'Oh! My wife told me. She was giving evidence before you recently and was impressed by the care and courtesy with which you listened to her arguments.'

I could only hope that her regard for me would remain as high after she read my report.

Return to India

One morning in the autumn of 1984, the post brought a surprise: an invitation to attend the celebrations in Medak of the sixtieth anniversary of the opening of the great church built by my father and now a cathedral of the Church of South India. Over the years, I had often thought of a possible return to the scenes of my youth, faintly but fondly remembered, but the occasion had never arisen. Now, without warning, here it was — as if a door had been opened to a long hidden garden.

January 1985: Bombay airport in the morning. Clamour and crowds on the streets, honking cars, incipient collisions, and people — people everywhere, bulging out of buses, hanging onto suburban trains, and marching one way down a street.

'A demo?' I ask.

No: just commuters hurrying from the station to their workplaces. Like ants in a nest where each member has his own purpose, belying the onlooker's impression of chaos, life for these masses is better organized than it appears. We had too little time to explore this vast metropolis with its five major religions, countless races, busy shipping port, and cycling *tiffin* carriers. A visit to Malabar Hill and the towers of silence where the Parsees go after death, a trip to see the cave carvings at Elephanta partially despoiled by Portuguese priests, then to Victoria Station, monument to British nineteenth-century railway architecture, where we boarded the Hyderabad express. Semi-private sleeping arrangements had Shirley sharing a compartment with a charming Hindu lady, Jivan, and her two sons returning from a *puja* with shaved heads. I had a bunk above a chemist who, like every other passenger it seemed, wanted to know where we came from, where we were going, what we thought of India and so on.

The train rolled out through industrial areas and dusty suburbs, past shanties and cricket pitches where matches were always in progress. The long slow climb up the Western Ghats with their beautifully stratified rock faces led past the weekend homes of wealthy Bombay residents and on to the spreading cantonments of Pune, formerly Poona of British army folklore. Jivan insisted on sharing with Shirley the sandwiches brought to the station by her sister in Pune: the railway food she said was unclean — whether for reasons of caste or hygiene was not clear.

Hyderabad station at 6.00 a.m. Nobody there to meet us. Jivan was met by her husband Jayant Dhanwatay and they insisted on taking us home to their house for breakfast, typical of the friendly helpfulness to strangers we encountered everywhere. A telephone call to the office of the Church of South India brought a car with the Rev. Prabhaker Rao, treasurer of the diocese. Long black hair and an ingratiating manner gave a misleading first impression of this helpful and efficient man.

The city of Hyderabad was founded by a Muslim Shahi ruler in 1591 as the new capital of his kingdom in place of Golconda, the massive fortress a few miles away. It became a model garden city. In 1685 the Moghuls overthrew the Shahis and their viceroy became the first Nizam of Hyderabad and founded a dynasty that lasted until India's independence. The walls of the Nizam's palace were cracking, my father had told me, under the weight of gold: he was the richest man in the world. The adjoining city of Secunderabad was established across the river in 1806 and it became an important British army cantonment. The two now form, in effect, a single city.

Some 60 miles to the north the little town of Medak grew up round a prominent hill on which the Shahi rulers built a fort. And it was at Medak that the Methodist mission was established in 1894. Lying right in the middle of the Indian peninsula at an altitude of about 2000 feet on the great Deccan plateau, the climate is dry and in the hot weather temperatures rise as high as 120 degrees in the shade. We set off for Medak in the bishop's car which, like most cars in India, was an Ambassador. Our driver Ananta Rao, known as Nanti, was to be our trusted guide, guard, and helper during our stay. (The name Rao attached to so many Telugu names means literally 'royal'.) Along the road much of the jungle had been replaced by vineyards, or fields of rice and sugar. Bunches of grapes, deliciously cool looking, were hanging for sale at wayside stalls. Bullock carts were carrying sugar cane to the mills, each load worth some 250 rupees. After 50 miles we caught our first glimpse of the top of the cathedral tower high above the surrounding countryside. Driving into the old mission compound all seemed familiar, down the avenue of ashoka trees,* past the church, past the staff house — and there stood the dear old 'Big Bungalow', just as I remembered it, my boyhood home.

The Bishop and his wife came down the stairs to welcome us and led us up to the living quarters on the first floor. It all felt eerily familiar, the spacious upper verandah much as I remembered it.

The Bishop's wife Daisy, a sweet and efficient woman who had trained as a nurse in England, had thoughtfully engaged a special cook to provide us with western style food. This turned out to be tasteless and, after one night, Shirley told Daisy that we would be happy to eat with them: we had not come to India to eat English food. They laughed and, from then on, we ate our meals together. We tried to eat like the rest with our fingers, but lacked their expertise. Our laughable efforts helped to break the ice and I was offered the help of a spoon. We were given a bottle of boiled water, whereas they drank simply from a jug. The Bishop explained that they were accustomed to it, but they did not want our health to suffer — another example of their solicitude for our welfare.

Bishop Victor Premasagar is a phenomenon, a shining intellect, with

---

* A nickname for the mast tree — polyalthia longifolia.

degrees from British universities and widely travelled. A language virtuoso he is at home with Sanskrit, Hindi, Tamil, German, and Hebrew (as befits an Old Testament scholar). His grandfather had been an untouchable — a term for outcastes deriving from the Hindu belief that they are unclean and that a touch from them on any person, food or utensil is spiritual poison. Victor's father, whom my father brought to school in Medak, eventually became a pastor. He was now living, a charming old man, with Victor and Daisy in the Big Bungalow and claimed to remember me there as a child. Now his son was a bishop!

✳ ✳ ✳

The Church of South India was formed in 1947 when, after more than 20 years of hard discussion, the various Protestant churches operating missions in India finally reached agreement to amalgamate. The CSI was the first successful attempt to develop practical ecumenism, setting a pattern that has since been followed by national churches in many parts of the world. The missionaries of the various denominations, including Anglican, Methodist and Congregationalist, were the prime movers, seeing as they did the futility of sectarian dispute in approaching a country where Christianity itself was a novelty. But they needed to carry with them their respective home churches, Lambeth Palace, the Methodist Conference, and so on. It was not easy to accommodate long-established doctrinal differences or to compromise on deeply entrenched dogma. The Methodists had to swallow episcopacy which Wesleyans found hard to accept and the Anglicans had to accept the title of Moderator for the primate. But, beneath matters of nomenclature, there were important theological problems to be resolved.

The rising tide of Indian Christian leaders sometimes proved more conservative than their home churches, more Methodist than the Wesleyans, more Anglican than Canterbury. A Methodist minister, Rev. Daniel Napoleon, addressing the Provincial Synod in unaccustomed English, ended his argument against union with this peroration:

'If union come, Methodism go to dog, India go to dog, world to dog!'

The long and sometimes painful gestation has borne abundant fruit, giving the CSI a lively spirit of its own as well as an important influence both locally and abroad. The record shows that, although he had left India before the work came to fruition, my father played a significant part in the negotiations.

* * *

The celebrations — Victor liked to call them the diamond jubilee which sounded strange in the plains of south India — were directed to thanksgiving and dedication in a three-day programme packed with displays, speeches, exhibitions, services, pageants and prayers: one event followed another in relentless succession. Victor paraded us like prize pigs — cutting a ribbon, unveiling a plaque, being photographed, and invariably being asked to speak to the large throngs craning their necks to see us. Some of the events were directed mainly to women and Shirley gave neat simple talks received with rapt attention and applause.

We were constantly garlanded and gifts were showered upon us. As the son and daughter-in-law of the legendary *Pedda Doragaru* (a Telugu phrase implying top authority that has become attached exclusively to my father), we were regarded as some kind of reincarnation demanding veneration, to our personal embarrassment but to the obvious joy of the assembled multitude.

The CSI compound stretches for almost a mile in each direction. With its various schools, dormitories, hospital, offices, residential quarters, vegetable gardens, football and cricket pitches, all centred on the magnificent church, it forms a village within a village. During the celebrations the whole compound became a camp, with shelters, market stalls, cooking fires and the quiet murmur of the many thousands of visitors coming from miles around to take part in the festivity. Many, perhaps half, of these were Hindus or Muslims — evidence of the eclectic nature of religious sentiment in India.

The central event was a service of thanksgiving in the cathedral. In the vestry a crowd was gathered, including the Moderator of the CSI who came from Kerala, a dozen bishops and other assorted clerics. Victor arranged us in processional order, assigning a British missionary from Bangalore, Eric Lott, to keep an eye on us and to translate the proceedings. Having made sure that everyone understood his place and role in the service Victor, like Eisenhower on D-Day, said:

'OK. Let's go!'

He led us out and round to the front entrance where a vast crowd was gathered below the wide flight of steps. Loudspeakers had been fixed so that they could follow the service. A pile of sandals on each side of the entrance showed where the congregation had shed their footwear before entering barefoot as Indian custom demands. We threw our shoes in a corner, wondering if we would ever see them again.

The floor of the cathedral (there are no pews) was packed in every corner, leaving only a narrow aisle. Everybody wanted to greet us with *namaste* (both hands together) or even to touch us if they could. The men sat on the west side of the cathedral and the women, making a striking contrast in their gorgeous many-hued saris, sat on the east side. Many more packed into a gallery that runs round three sides of the nave. I estimated a total congregation of 3000 inside and another 1000 or so outside. Victor later told me that there were many more than that and that a third of them were Hindus, many of whom brought offerings.

During the service Victor called Shirley and me out from our seats in the choir stalls onto the chancel steps. I handed over the message I had brought from the Archbishop of Canterbury and then spoke briefly, after which we were led down the aisle to 'meet the congregation'. This progress took time: everybody wanted to greet us, touch us, *namaste*. Children were thrust forward as if to be blessed. We touched as many as possible. During the offertory many people brought gifts individually to the altar where the team of ministers received them, touching each donor's head with a blessing. Mothers wanted their children blessed. They brought offerings in cash and kind, including a lamb, hens, and coconuts which were a favourite gift from Muslims.

Many then came over to where we were sitting, leaned over to touch us, shake hands or just humbly *namaste*. One elderly lady climbed into the pew and bent down to kiss our feet. When I later spoke to the Bishop of our embarrassment he explained that CWP was seen as a saint whose stature tended to grow with the passage of time: as his son and daughter-in-law we merited veneration which would bring blessing upon them. This was the Indian way and no occasion for us to be embarrassed.

By the time the service ended we had been in, sometimes out of, our seats for more than four hours. But despite hard seats and an overlong sermon by the Moderator (which had to be translated into Telugu because he came from Kerala) we felt no strain. As the procession formed to leave the cathedral we speculated with Eric Lott whether we would ever find our shoes. He smiled.

'Yours have probably been taken as holy relics,' he said.

However our shoes lay there by the entrance. The only person who lost his sandals was the Bishop of Dornekal who said he hoped they were now in heaven.

At the afternoon ceremony the Governor of Andhra Pradesh arrived with his wife and addressed an immense crowd on the football field.

'Aim high,' he said. 'Build for the future as Charles Posnett did.'

Before departing, the Governor invited us to call on him in Secunderabad when we were there. This was to have a surprising sequel.

The next day, our last in Medak, I found time to visit Medak township and to climb to the old fort on the hill behind it. Huge blocks of granite, rampart upon rampart, defences in depth with battlements and firing positions, all commanded superb views over the surrounding plain and down to the roofs of the town below. The fort covers most of the hill and near the top there is a water tank about 30 feet deep and the size of a swimming pool.

Back in the township we were pressed to enter the house of a Muslim family. On spotless floors, chairs were arranged for us and tea and biscuits served with smiles and bows. The old father, aged about 70, appeared and told us how, as a young teacher, he had been helped by Posnett *Doragaru*. Now he wanted to offer his respects to a member of the family.

With Victor and Daisy we set off next day on a three day tour of their widespread diocese with Nanti at the wheel of the Ambassador. After opening a girls hall with the usual speeches and garlanding, we pressed on to Dichpalli and the renowned leper hospital that has led the world in leprosy therapy techniques and is now supported by the

WHO. The latest treatment by three drugs together, eliminates contagion within 24 hours, so that patients can now be sent home at an earlier stage and thenceforward treated as outpatients. Giving the pills different colours has given them a new mystique and boosted patient confidence.

Founded in 1914 by Dr Isobel Kerr, a Methodist medical missionary who lies buried there, the hospital's administration was now in the capable hands of Lieut. Col. Ponnaiya, a former officer in the Gurkhas, who showed me round and pointed out his carefully tended cricket pitch. The hospital team which includes several leprosy patients, now plays matches at home and away and is entertained quite normally.

Touring the diocese with Victor was like a non-stop seminar on wheels. Having studied and taught in Asia, Europe and America, he turned down an offer of a senior appointment in the World Council of Churches because of his perceived responsibility to the poor people of his diocese. As we drove along he explained the relationships between the different languages of the subcontinent and tried to teach me the scripts of Telugu and Urdu. His travel tales kept us fascinated, whether about the lack of hygiene in remote villages in Yugoslavia, conditions in Korea, or his sermon in Secunderabad during the Queen's visit when the British High Commissioner tactlessly attempted to interfere in an Indian occasion. He is equally at home with Hindus, Buddhists and Muslims, and manages to extract financial support from businessmen of whatever persuasion — like my father I thought.

Despite the lapse of 60 years, I found that I still recognized words and phrases of Telugu. When I managed to bring out the occasional sentence it caused merriment and surprise. That this had been stored away in my memory bank and carried around with me unknown for all those years, I found astonishing.

The next day took us north to the great Godaveri River which rises in the Western Ghats barely 100 miles from the west coast and flows right across the peninsula to the Bay of Bengal. I had old photographs of us crossing the river in a *putti* during a tour with my parents 60 years before. Now the river is spanned by a dam of prodigious proportions containing a huge new lake, the far bank out of sight. Irrigation for hundreds of miles and electricity for the villages, this more than anything has contributed to the rise in living standards over the past half century. But can the water and food supplies keep pace with the exploding population?

It was a long drive to our next appointment to open a new church. There, we were greeted by a raucous band with dancers raising a cloud of dust through which we followed. After the mandatory three circuits (perhaps to drive away devils) I cut a tape across the verandah and Shirley cut a second tape across the door — the usual double act. Inside, during the service everyone wanted to come up for a blessing. Then, after communion, 12 mothers asked for their children to be baptized. Finally Victor was called upon to bless a bullock. He smiled at me and went out to perform the ceremony. The bullock had been ill and I told Victor that it had better not die after being blessed.

Next day we parted from Victor and Daisy and, after a visit to Karim Nagar, returned to Medak. Bishop Devasahayan came with us part of the way, having organized, improbably, some bread and jam to eat as we rattled along. First he said grace and I stole a nervous glance at Nanti, relieved that he did not take his hands off the wheel during the prayer.

Our departure from Medak the next morning started with a walk down an avenue of humans, shaking a hundred hands as we moved the quarter mile from the church to the compound gate. Waving banners carried all manner of good luck greetings: one, fixed over the back of the waiting car, read FAREWELL TO POSNETT. So we went out on a high note without time for regrets.

In Secunderabad a busy day of visits preceded an afternoon call on the Governor. His residence was very grand, reflecting the style of the former British Residents. Uniformed servants ushered us into a large room where the Governor, dressed all in white, soon joined us. As his wife chatted with Shirley on a long settee, the Governor and I discussed constitutional law on another. He spoke of Cambridge, where he had taken his LLB, and I mentioned Islamic law. Suddenly, we looked at each other and both realized that it was he who had coached me for the Bar exams all those years ago. We exploded with astonishment and burst into laughter to the alarm of the servants and the surprise of our wives, until we explained the situation. An extraordinary coincidence in an improbable setting.

Dr Sharma went on to become President of India. He died at the end of 1999 after a notable career in his country's service.

Kotagiri

An hour's flight from Hyderabad took us south to Bangalore, the capital of Karnataka whose parliament building is a stunning example of neo-Dravidian architecture. This beautiful city is notable for the Lalbagh Botanic Gardens founded in the eighteenth century by Hyder Ali and developed by his son Tipu Sultan. There we wandered happily among the many beautiful and exotic trees including giants more than 200 years old — a superb example of how such a collection should be laid out, tended and labelled.

From there by train to Mysore, the diesel locomotive pelted down the slopes to get up speed for the following climb. We halted at Seringapatam, a fortified town with massive ramparts overlooking the Cauvery river. This was the historic citadel from which Hyder Ali and Tipu ruled most of south India and, with French help, fought off the British in no fewer than four Mysore wars. It was here that Tipu was finally defeated in 1799 and killed by a British bayonet, a sad end for a remarkable man. The booty the British found is said to have amounted to more than £2 million, an indication of the wealth and power of the old Muslim dynasty.

The British later installed a line of Hindu rulers whose main claim to fame seems to have been ostentation. The Maharajah's new twentieth century palace is hideously garish, worse inside than out. By contrast, 30 miles away at Somnathpur we found a fabulous temple dating from the thirteenth century and the earliest of the Hoysala kings. Quite remarkably beautiful, it is intricately carved in soapstone which has the fortunate property of being easy to work but hardening on exposure to the atmosphere so that it resists erosion. Nearby stands one of Ashoka's fabulous pillars, a slender cylinder over twenty feet high, inscribed with the edicts of the Emperor which it has borne for all to see since about 250 BC.

The Nilgiri hills rise from the plains south of Mysore to an altitude of more than 8000 feet. Hidden in the mountain forests, the Todas, the original inhabitants, were secluded from the dwellers in the plains, whose wars, migrations, culture and history had passed them by. But the cool climate attracted European settlers who found fertile soil on which to grow coffee, tea and vegetables which now help to feed the large cities in the plains.

The British army established a post at Wellington, not far from Oota-camund, known as Ooty, and the surrounding hills became a popular resort for families or for British personnel on leave. My father acquired a house at Kotagiri, 30 miles from Ooty, where my mother could stay with her children during the hot weather. It was there in a house called 'Woodlands' that I was born. It was my ambition to find the house.

As our taxi from Ooty drew near to Kotagiri, the landscape and tree-covered hills seemed faintly familiar. In the town we sought contact with the CSI and were passed from one person to another, ending up with David Thrower, a 75-year-old former Baptist mission-ary who had spent ten years writing a Tamil concordance. He was delighted to have visitors and we discovered we had a friend in common in our home town of Godalming, but he did not know of Woodlands. We had given up hope and returned to the bazaar when I had the sudden notion of turning back up the hill to make a last enquiry at the mission guest house. It seemed to be deserted until a little white haired English lady appeared and introduced herself as Miss Rose. After thinking about my question she finally nodded, remembering the name of the house.

'Yes. I think it belonged to Mr O'Brien and has now been taken over by the Pandyaraj School.'

My hopes rose and I thanked her. On the road out of the village, we saw some modern school buildings and a board proclaiming the Pandyaraj Memorial School. A dusty lane led off to the left and we followed it uphill. Coming to a fork in the road we chose the right and soon came to a building. It was not Woodlands, yet the setting was reminiscent. Going back to the fork we tried the other way. This led up through wattle and eucalyptus woods, swung up past some bushes and there it was — Woodlands — with gables at each end, round openings above bay windows, a shady central porch and unfor-gettable diamond-shaped panes in all the windows.

Two young Indian women appeared. When we explained the reason for our visit, they welcomed us warmly. The house was now a hostel for orphans and we were shown round the spacious rooms, several large bedrooms, and the kitchen, down some steps at one end. Round the fireplace in the drawing room were the original green tiles. Some pieces of old and heavy furniture looked as though they had been there since the house was built. The pervading scent of the blue gums was just as I remembered it. The wheel had come full circle.

Mother India

India's chequered and layered history confronts one at every turn, the ancient, the more newly old and the modern jostling happily together like passengers on one of India's overcrowded trains.

Before leaving Ooty I paid a visit to the celebrated Ooty Club which still maintains its British traditions although the members are now Indian. It has one curious claim to fame as the place where, in 1875, a certain young British subaltern by the name of Neville Chamberlain added a coloured ball to the game of billiards and so invented the game of snooker whose original rules still hang there on a board. I was courteously received by the Secretary and shown some of the old boards on which the names of each year's officers were inscribed, including the Master of Hounds. Over a cup of tea I heard one elderly member compliment the Secretary on some newly arrived English magazines. 'Glad to see you've got *Horse and Hound*. Well done! What!' An amiable cariacature.

The Indian railways carry more passengers than any other system in the world, from the thundering overnight expresses crossing the sub-continent to the narrow gauge mountain railways such as that linking Ooty with the mainline down on the plains. This descends 7000 feet in 25 miles to Mettupalayam, with a rack rail on the steepest sections. At Ooty station we found the two first class compartments already full but a porter pushed and pulled our luggage into some small spaces and we squeezed in, five a side in a compartment designed for eight. At the first stop three more got in. But we were surrounded by smiling faces. 'This is India. This is how we make friends on trains.' Cheerful chatter offered us all manner of nuggets of Indian lore. In the tunnels we got nearly choked by smoke from the steam engine, built in Switzerland in 1899. But it was a piece of romance to travel again in the same train as I had done as a child, and seen more recently in the film of *A Passage to India*.

Sharing our compartment in the overnight express to Madras a Hindu couple were returning from their honeymoon to his place of business in Lagos, Nigeria. A Tamil engineer was going back after leave to his job in Washington DC. An English couple were returning to their home in Canada after a visit, like ours, to his birthplace in the Nilgiris. Trains in India are places to meet, to talk, to learn, to make new friends. They have helped to create a nation. One should perhaps say recreate a nation which Ashoka ruled more than two thousand years ago and whose pillars bearing immemorial edicts for human conduct stand lonely sentinels to testify and guard a people's soul.

In Madras the superb museum enshrines the relatively recent history of Clive, Cornwallis, Wellesley and the British raj, while only a few miles away stands Kanchipuram, one of India's seven sacred cities. There, among towering gopurams, an old guide showed us a mango tree reputed to be 3500 years old. A third of that would have been impressive — and more believable. The earliest temple dates from the AD seventh century, built by the Pallava king Rayasunha, and in the alcoves one can still make out the colours of the paintings more than a thousand years old. At the hard to pronounce Mahabalipuram near the sea the wonderful Pallava sculptors created a huge tableau carved upon the living rock, 60 feet long and 30 from top to bottom, depicting not gods but people going about their daily business with life size animals including two elephants.

We could not leave India without visiting the north. A different world, the January climate was cool and bracing. The boldness of the architecture — for example the Qutab Minar with its tower 190 feet high started in AD 1193 when the Pathans overthrew the last Hindu monarchy in Delhi — was in striking contrast to the figured intricacy of the temples in the south.

No less memorable than the Taj Mahal were the exquisite palaces at Fatehpur Sikri, started by Akbar in 1571 as his new capital but abandoned later for lack of water. The white marble mosque was a tribute to Shaikh Salim Shisti, a holy man who was credited with enabling three of Akbar's wifes to produce heirs in fulfilment of his own prophecy. To this day prayers are offered at this mosque not only by Muslims but also by Hindus, Jains and others seeking fertility in their marriages. This would have been approved by Akbar who, during his reign as Moghul, consulted with religious leaders of all faiths including Portuguese Catholic priests from Goa, seeking to devise a new religion which he called Din-I-Ilahi (religion of God) and which he hoped to see adopted by all in his kingdom. How fitting that it should have been in India that the ecumenical breakthrough was made that led to the establishment of the Church of South India, later followed in the north and in other countries.

India's immensely old and eclectic civilization has absorbed visitors, settlers and conquerors, assimilated religions and cultures of which the Mongols and the British were only the most recent. I was glad to have been able at last to pay my respects to this remarkable country which has nurtured me.

Bibliography

Anderson, Professor J. N. D., *Islamic Law in Africa* (London: HMSO, 1954)

Armstrong, Karen, *Islam* (London: Weidenfeld & Nicholson, 2000)

Baker, Samuel, *The Albert Nyanza: Great Basin of the Nile*, 2 vols (London: Macmillan, 1966)

Bere, Rennie, *The Way to the Mountains of the Moon* (London: A. Barker, 1966)

Birch, John P., *The Merchant Venturers' Servant* (London: Cadogan, 1993)

Bullock, Alan, *Hitler: A Study in Tyranny* (London: Odhams Press, 1952)

Busk, Sir Douglas L., *The Fountain of the Sun: Unfinished Journey in Ethiopia and the Ruwenzori* (London: M. Parrish, 1957)

Chenevix Trench, C., *Men Who Ruled Kenya: The Kenya Administration, 1892–1963* (London: Radcliffe Press, 1992)

Cohen, Sir Andrew, *British Policy in Changing Africa* (London: Routledge & Kegan Paul, 1959)

Cowen, D. V., *Flowering Trees and Shrubs in India* (Bombay: Thacker, 1950)

Cradock, Sir Percy, *Experiences of China* (London: John Murray, 1994)

Dobson, Narda, *A History of Belize* (Port of Spain: Longman Caribbean, 1973)

Drower, George M. F., *Britain's Dependent Territories: A Fistful of Islands* (Aldershot: Dartmouth, 1992)

Dunne, J. W., *An Experiment with Time* (London: A. and C. Black, 1927)

Eddington, Sir Arthur, *The Nature of the Physical World* (London: Dent, 1928)

Filippi, Filippo de, *Ruwenzori: An Account of the Expedition of HRH Prince Luigi Amedeo of Savoy, Duke of the Abruzzi* (London: A Constable & Company, 1909)

Finch, George, *The Making of a Mountaineer* (London: Arrowsmith, 1924)

Foot, Hugh, *A Start in Freedom* (London: Stoughton, 1964)

Frazer, Sir J. G., *The Golden Bough: A Study in Magic and Religion* (London: Macmillan, 1922)

Gaddis, Professor J. L., *We Now Know: Rethinking Cold War History* (Oxford: Clarendon, 1997)

Gascoigne, Bamber, *The Great Moghuls* (London: Jonathan Cape, 1971)

Grant, Professor C. H., *The Making of Modern Belize: Politics, Society and British Colonialism in Central America* (Cambridge: Cambridge University Press, 1976)

Grimble, Arthur, *A Pattern of Islands* (London: J. Murray, 1952)

Gwynn, Stephen, *The Life of Mary Kingsley* (London: Macmillan, 1933)

Humphreys, R. A., *The Diplomatic History of British Honduras: 1638–1901* (London: Oxford University Press, 1961)

Hunt, Sir David, *On the Spot: An Ambassador Remembers* (London: P. Davies, 1975)

Huxley, Elspeth, *Red Strangers* (London: Chatto & Windus, 1939)

Ingham, Kenneth, *The Making of Modern Uganda* (London: Allen & Unwin, 1958)

Jabavu, Noni, *Drawn in Colour: African Contrasts* (London: Murray, 1960)

James, Lawrence, *Raj: The Making and Unmaking of British India* (London: Little, Brown, 1997)

Junker, Wilhelm, *Travels in Africa during the Years 1875–1878* (London: Chapman & Hall, 1890)

Kavuma, Paulo, *Crisis in Buganda: 1955* (London: Rex Collins, 1979)

Keay, John, *India: A History* (London: HarperCollins, 2000)

Kenyatta, Jomo, *Facing Mount Kenya: The Tribal Life of Gikuyu* (London: Secker & Warburgh, 1938)

Kirk-Greene, Anthony, *On Crown Service: A History of HM Colonial and Overseas Civil Services, 1837–1997* (I.B.Tauris, London, 1999)

Klucker, Christian, *Adventures of an Alpine Guide* (London: J. Murray, 1932)

Leathart, Scott, *Trees of the World* (London: Hamlyn, 1977)

Low, D. A. and R. Cranford Pratt, *Buganda and British Overrule: 1900–55* (Oxford: Oxford University Press, 1960)

Mboya, Tom, *Freedom and After* (London: A. Deutsch, 1963)

Molony, J. C., *A Book of South India* (London: Methuen, 1926)

Morris, James, *Pax Britannica* (London: Faber & Faber, 1978)

Mummery, A. F., *My Climbs in the Alps and Caucasus* (Oxford: B. Blackwell, 1936)

Murphy, Philip, *Alan Lennox-Boyd: A Biography* (London: I.B.Tauris, 1999)

Mutesa II, Kabaka, *Desecration of My Kingdom* (London: Constable, 1967)

O'Brien, Conor Cruise, *To Katanga and Back: A UN Case History* (New York: Grosset and Dunlap, 1962)

Reed, Nelson, *The Caste Wars of the Yucatan* (Stanford: Stanford University Press, 1964)

Sackett, F. C., *Posnett of Medak* (London: Cargate Press, 1951)

Schweitzer, Dr Albert, *On the Edge of the Primeval Forest: Experiences and Observations of a Doctor in Equatorial Africa* (London: A. & C. Black, 1922)

Seligman, C. G., *Races of Africa* (London: Butterworth, 1930)

Stanley, H. M., *In Darkest Africa* (London: Sampson Low, Marston, Searle & Rivington, 1890)

Stigand, C. H., *Equatoria: The Lado Enclave* (London: Constable, 1923)

Sundkler, Bengt, *Church of South India: The Movement Towards Union* (London: Lutterworth Press, 1937)

Thomas, H. B. *Uganda* (Oxford: Oxford University Press, 1935)

Tilman, H. W., *Snow on the Equator* (London: G. Bell & Sons Limited, 1937)

Ward, Clive, *Snowcaps on the Equator* (London: Bodley Head, 1989)

Warner, Rex, *Imperial Caesar* (London: Collins, 1960)

Yeoman, Guy Henry, *Africa's Mountains of the Moon: Journey to the Snowy Sources of the Nile* (London: Elm Tree, 1989)

Index